Japan
Remodeled

A volume in the series

CORNELL STUDIES IN POLITICAL ECONOMY

edited by Peter J. Katzenstein

A full list of titles in the series appears at the end of the book.

Japan Remodeled

HOW GOVERNMENT AND

INDUSTRY ARE REFORMING

JAPANESE CAPITALISM

STEVEN K. VOGEL

Cornell University Press   ITHACA AND LONDON

First published 2006 by Cornell University Press
First printing, Cornell paperbacks, 2007
Printed in the United States of America

Library of Congress Cataloging-in-Publication Data
Vogel, Steven Kent.
    Japan remodeled : how government and industry are reforming Japanese capitalism / Steven Vogel.
        p. cm.—(Cornell studies in political economy)
    Includes bibliographical references and index.
    ISBN-13: 978-0-8014-4449-4 (cloth : alk. paper)
    ISBN-10: 0-8014-4449-7 (cloth : alk. paper)
    ISBN-13: 978-0-8014-7371-5 (pbk. : alk. paper)
    ISBN-10: 0-8014-7371-3 (pbk. : alk. paper)
    1. Japan—Economic policy—1989– 2. Capitalism—Japan.
    3. Industrial policy—Japan. 4. Corporate reorganizations—
    Japan. I. Title. II. Series.
    HC462.95.V64 2006
    338.952—dc22
    2005032190

Cornell University Press strives to use environmentally responsible suppliers and materials to the fullest extent possible in the publishing of its books. Such materials include vegetable-based, low-VOC inks and acid-free papers that are recycled, totally chlorine-free, or partly composed of nonwood fibers. For further information, visit our website at www.cornellpress.cornell.edu.

Cloth printing   10 9 8 7 6 5 4 3 2
Paperback printing   10 9 8 7 6 5 4 3

To my mother

CONTENTS

TABLES AND FIGURES

ACKNOWLEDGMENTS

I am grateful first and foremost to the many Japanese politicians, bureaucrats, business people, and others who agreed to be interviewed for this research project. They were extremely generous with their time and patient with my inquiries, and many graciously assisted with fact checking and updates. Many individuals facilitated the research in a myriad of ways, such as locating data resources, making introductions, and offering advice. Among these, Christina Ahmadjian, Geoffrey Bennett, Didier Guillot, Kōji Hirao, Takeo Hoshi, Keiko Hjersman, Yuki Ishimatsu, Gregory Jackson, Richard Katz, Jun Kayano, Nami Matsuko, Yoshio Nakamura, Toshiyuki Ōkubo, Naoko Sakaue, Yoshihiro Tajima, Kazufumi Tanaka, and Jirō Yoshida deserve special thanks. Christina Ahmadjian, Jennifer Brass, Clair Brown, John Cioffi, Christina Davis, Richard Deeg, Ronald Dore, Robert Fannion, William Grimes, Kenneth Haig, Roselyn Hsueh, Gregory Jackson, Peter Katzenstein, Kenji Kushida, James Lincoln, Gregory Linden, Robert Madsen, Jonathan Marshall, Yasuyuki Motoyama, Seio Nakajima, Keith Nitta, Gene Park, Hugh Patrick, T. J. Pempel, Ezra Vogel, Charles Weathers, John Zysman, and two anonymous reviewers offered helpful comments on earlier drafts. Many others read small excerpts to check for errors or misinterpretations. Kenneth Haig, Michiko Ishisone, Kenji Kushida, Keith Nitta, Jennifer Oh, Gene Park, Naoko Sakaue, Tetsuji Sugayoshi, and Masaya Ura provided superb research assistance. Robert Fannion collaborated on the German field research and gave useful feedback throughout the project. Yasuyuki Motoyama was a tireless partner for much of the research, and he and Iris Hui conducted the data analysis. James Lincoln has been an incredibly patient and generous mentor.

The Smith Richardson Foundation provided financial support, and Allan Song was instrumental in helping me to sharpen my proposal. I also benefited from financial support from the Center for Japanese Studies and the Committee on Research at the University of California, Berkeley. The Clausen Center for International Business and Policy at the Haas School of Business contributed to the purchase of data from the Development Bank of Japan. Roger Haydon of Cornell University Press guided the manuscript from submission through production; Ange Romeo-Hall oversaw the editing; and Kimberley Vivier edited it. Most of all, I thank Susan, Justin, and Ellie for their love, patience, and support. I dedicate this book to my mother, Suzanne Hall Vogel, who taught me—among many other things—that to understand Japan, you have to start by talking with some Japanese people.

Berkeley, California   S. V.

Japan
Remodeled

1

THE
JAPANESE
MODEL
AND
INSTITUTIONAL
CHANGE

Once upon a time, would-be reformers from around the world looked to Japan for lessons. Japan had somehow discovered how to balance competition and coordination in a modern economy. It fostered cooperative relations between government and industry, between financial institutions and manufacturers, and between labor and management. The Japanese model delivered tangible signs of success: rapid economic growth, a rising standard of living, booming exports, technological leadership, and financial power. Japan performed well across a broad range of social indicators, with high educational achievement, excellent health standards, low crime rates, and little income inequality. By the 1980s, even the modest Japanese had developed a certain confidence and pride in their economic system.

Japan's economic miracle did not fizzle out quietly but erupted in a moment of market euphoria in the late 1980s—now referred to simply as "the Bubble"—in which investors poured money into real estate and stock markets. When the Bubble finally burst in 1991, Japan descended into a prolonged economic slump. As the Nikkei stock index plunged, economic growth faltered, and recovery failed to materialize, experts and amateurs alike rushed forward with a daunting array of theories to explain Japan's plight and to offer prescriptions for revival (see Chapter 2).

Many government officials, business executives, and opinion leaders simply concluded that the Japanese economic model had gone terribly wrong. They questioned the very institutions that had been credited with Japan's past success: a powerful bureaucracy guiding the economy, close government-industry ties, "lifetime" employment, the main bank system, and dense inter-firm networks. Reform advocates declared that Japanese government and industry would have to fundamentally alter their ways. The government should liberate the economy, and companies should sever long-term ties with workers, banks, suppliers, and other firms.

Despite popular perceptions to the contrary, Japanese government and industry translated this collective reform frenzy into action. The government lowered interest rates, increased and decreased public spending, lowered and raised taxes, coddled and cracked down on ailing banks, liberalized financial

FIGURE I. *GDP Growth in the United States and Japan, 1980–2004*

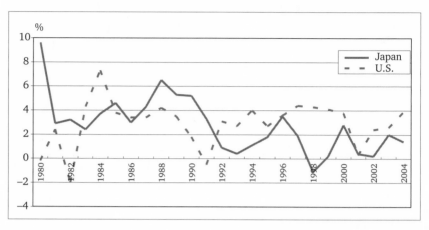

Source: International Monetary Fund, World Economic Outlook Database.

flows, eased labor standards, revised corporate law, lifted the ban on holding companies, privatized special public corporations, and revised the pension system. Just for good measure, the government also reorganized itself. Meanwhile, Japanese companies sold off subsidiaries, spun off divisions, switched supply sources, moved production overseas, renegotiated loan repayment schedules, introduced merit-based wage systems, reorganized their boards of directors, and experimented with stock options and share buybacks.

As the United States and Japan traded places—with the Japanese economy languishing and the U.S. economy resurging—U.S. government and business leaders looked less to Japan as a model, and Japanese leaders looked more to the United States as a model (Figures 1 and 2).[1] Japanese government officials grew more reticent about touting the merits of their economic model in bilateral talks and multilateral forums, and their American counterparts grew more confident in insisting on the superiority of the U.S. model.[2] Japanese corporate executives became less assertive in transferring their practices to their U.S. business partners, and U.S. executives became more aggressive in imposing their standards on their Japanese business partners.[3] The Japanese

1. See Grimes 2002.

2. By the mid-1990s, for example, the Japanese government became less active in promoting Japan's own experience as a model for developing countries, and the U.S. government grew bolder in promoting liberalization on a global scale through multilateral initiatives on telecommunications and financial reforms.

3. See Chapter 6 for detailed case studies of U.S. companies transferring practices to their Japanese partners.

FIGURE 2. *Major Stock Indexes in the United States and Japan, 1980–2004 (1980 = 100)*

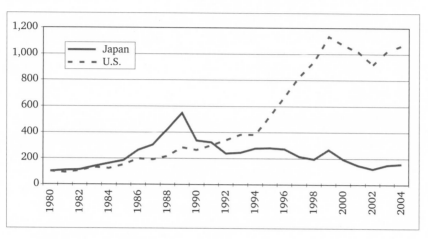

Sources: *Nihon Keizai Shimbun*; Dow Jones.

government embraced the U.S. government's rhetoric of privatization, deregulation, and globalization, and the private sector hailed American industry's focus on flexibility, core competence, and shareholder value.

Yet a funny thing happened on Japan's way to the U.S. model: it never got there. As government officials and industry leaders scrutinized their options, they selected reforms to modify or reinforce existing institutions rather than to abandon them.[4] This in itself should come as no surprise. After all, Japan preserved considerable institutional continuity through more dramatic upheavals after the Meiji Restoration and World War II.[5] Japan could not preserve its old system in the new environment, but it could not replicate the American one either.

The tricky part is to specify *how* Japan is changing. This book seeks to do so by carefully analyzing government and private-sector reforms. Political scientists tend to focus on the "macro" level of politics and policy whereas business experts address the "micro" level of corporations and strategy. Yet we cannot understand government reforms without investigating how private-sector institutions and corporate strategies drive support for and opposition against reform proposals, and we cannot understand corporate restructuring

4. See Zeitlin and Herrigel 2000, especially 1–50, for a theoretical discussion of "Americanization" that stresses selective adaptation and creative modification rather than the wholesale adoption of the U.S. model.
5. Westney 1987, Noguchi 1995.

without examining how policy reforms generate new options and foreclose others. This book describes and explains patterns of institutional change in Japan through the extended use of the comparative case method: systematically comparing across countries (Japan versus the United States and Germany), across policy issues (labor market reform versus financial reform, for example), across industrial sectors (automobiles versus retail), across companies (Toyota versus Nissan), and across time (Seiyu before and after allying with Wal-Mart).[6]

How the Japanese Model Shapes Its Own Transformation

To understand how the Japanese economic model is changing, we must first recognize that the existing institutions of Japanese capitalism are shaping their own transformation. Market systems are embedded in a complex web of laws, practices, and norms. The process of liberalizing markets—just as much as the process of constraining markets—involves the transformation of these laws, practices, and norms. Liberal reformers sometimes contend that if only the government would pull back, then markets would flourish. Yet governments must create and foster the institutions that sustain market competition. Some authors imply that the Japanese model is more embedded in societal institutions than the U.S. model.[7] Yet an American-style external labor market is not less embedded than a Japanese-style internal labor market; an American equity-based financial system is not less embedded than a Japanese credit-based system; and an American antitrust regime is not less embedded than a Japanese corporate network (keiretsu). Scholars have stressed that the historical transition to market society in western Europe, the creation of market institutions in developing countries, and the transition to a market system in post-Communist countries all entail a complex process of building market institutions.[8] Yet few have extended this logic to the more modest transition from one type of market system to another. For Japan to shift toward the U.S. model, it would not simply have to dismantle existing institutions but also create new ones, and a full conversion would involve changes at all levels of the system: laws, practices, and norms. So long as Japan does not make a full conversion, therefore, the legacy of earlier institutions powerfully influences the trajectory of change.

6. On the comparative case method, see Lijphart 1971 and 1975, George 1979.

7. Crouch and Streeck 1997. Hall and Soskice (2001, 64) also suggest that it should be easier for coordinated market economies to become more like liberal market economies than vice versa.

8. Polanyi 1944, North 1981, Chaudhry 1993, Cohen and Schwartz 1998, Fligstein 2001, World Bank 2002.

To illustrate this point, let us engage in a brief thought experiment: What would it take for Japan to shift to a U.S.-style liberal market system, with active external labor markets, a market for corporate control, and the free market entry and exit of firms? Table 1 presents selected examples of the types of changes that would be required. In the employment system, for example, Japan lacks an external labor market for "permanent" employees (*shain*) at large corporations in the sense that companies do not buy and sell these employees' labor on the free market. Employers do not ordinarily poach workers from other firms, and employees do not move from one company to a competitor. The government cannot simply legislate a change in these practices. To cultivate such a market, the Japanese government would have to reduce legal restrictions on dismissal, disseminate more information to employers and workers, cultivate organizations to match employers with workers, promote portable pension plans, and expand unemployment insurance. It would have to revise financial regulations, accounting standards, and corporate law to encourage firms to be more responsive to shareholders and less beholden to their workers. Companies would have to renegotiate their compacts with their workers and redesign their systems of employee representation. Employers would have to become less loyal to their workers, and workers would have to become less loyal to their employers. And sufficient numbers of employers would need to be looking for workers, and workers for new employers, to provide adequate liquidity in the market.

We can think of institutional change as occurring when an exogenous shock pushes actors to reassess the balance between the costs and benefits of the status quo. But institutional change is a function of the level of this shock plus the incentives and constraints built in to the existing system. For our purposes, the forces for change outlined below comprise the exogenous shock, and the Japanese model itself constitutes the incentives and constraints that shape the response to this shock. This means that even when the shock is big enough to impose change, existing institutions still shape the substance of change. In the Japanese case, these institutions leave an especially heavy imprint owing to the stability of the actors. In politics, the same economic ministries collaborate with the same ruling party to dominate the policy process, so the primary arena of decision making is unlikely to shift, for example, from the bureaucracy to the judiciary or from the national government to local authorities. In business, few large firms exit the market and few new firms rise to challenge them, so change comes via the incremental reform of existing firms rather than their replacement by new firms with radically different practices. Therefore, outside forces—such as foreign governments demanding policy reforms or foreign companies bringing new business

TABLE I. *What Would It Take to Turn Japan into a Liberal Market Economy? Selected Examples*

LABOR

GOVERNMENT POLICY	CORPORATE BEHAVIOR
Laws	**Practices**
• Labor market reform	• Lay off workers when necessary
• Changes in case law doctrine	• Do not favor new graduates over
• Corporate governance reform	midcareer hires
• Pension reform	• Shift from seniority to merit-based pay
• Lift holding company ban	• Introduce stock options
Norms	**Norms**
• The government should not use regulation to preserve employment.	• Companies should not preserve employment at the expense of profits.

Net Result: An Active External Labor Market

FINANCE

GOVERNMENT POLICY	CORPORATE BEHAVIOR
Laws	**Practices**
• Financial reform	• Sell off cross-held shares
• Banking crisis resolution	• Banks make lending decisions and price
• Corporate governance reform	loans on the basis of risk
• Pension reform	• Corporations choose banks on the basis
• Lift holding company ban	of price
	• Banks stop lending to insolvent firms
Norms	**Norms**
• The government should not protect banks or manipulate financial markets.	• Companies should maximize shareholder value.

Net Result: A Market for Corporate Control

COMPETITION

GOVERNMENT POLICY	CORPORATE BEHAVIOR
Laws	**Practices**
• Strengthen antitrust policy	• Choose business partners on the basis of
• Regulatory reform	price and not relationships
• Bankruptcy law reform	• Do not cooperate or collude with competitors
• Strengthen social safety net	• Banks refuse to bail out failing firms
Norms	**Norms**
• The government should not try to protect companies from failure.	• Companies should not favor long-term business partners.

Net Result: Free Market Entry and Exit

practices—play an especially important role in institutional change. Having lost confidence in their own institutions since the 1990s, Japanese government and business leaders are especially susceptible to this outside influence.

In addition, the complementarity (interaction) among the different components of the economic system conditions the trajectory of institutional change.[9] Masahiko Aoki stresses that national systems of economic governance incorporate complementary labor, financial, and political systems. The Japanese financial system, with patient capital channeled to firms by banks, for example, complements the Japanese labor system, with long-term employment stability and strong labor-management collaboration at the firm level. Japanese firms can uphold their employment guarantee to workers in a downturn because they are not subject to shareholder pressures for short-term returns.[10] This means that the evolution of the Japanese labor relations system is shaped not only by the existing institutions of the labor market but by the distinctive institutions of the financial market as well. Moreover, actors are likely to be cautious in tampering with one element of the system for fear that it will negatively affect other parts. For example, firms might be reluctant to embrace new financial strategies—such as courting international investors or listing on a foreign stock exchange—that could undermine their labor relations systems.

The existing institutions of Japanese capitalism do not simply act as friction, impeding fuller liberalization or convergence on the U.S. model. These institutions shape the trajectory of change in a much more active way: they enable other types of institutional innovation. The Japanese government and industry can build on their existing ties, for example, to forge new public-private partnerships to facilitate adjustment to changing market conditions (Chapter 4). Or company managers and labor union leaders can use existing channels of communication to design new pacts to preserve employment and enhance productivity (Chapter 6). One could view Japan as doubly constrained: it cannot maintain its existing economic system owing to the forces for change, and it cannot converge on the liberal market model owing to the logic of its existing institutions. Yet these dual constraints are themselves major drivers of institutional innovation.

---

9. Paul Pierson (2000) describes this dynamic in terms of increasing returns: the probability of further steps along a given path increases with each move down the path because the relative benefits of these steps over other options increase over time. So once a critical institution, such as a collective bargaining system or a main bank system, takes hold, it is reinforced over time by complementary laws, regulations, norms, and procedures, as well as by the entrenchment of supporting political interests.

10. Aoki 1988.

The Japanese Model

Before shifting to the model of institutional change, let us briefly review the core features of the postwar economic system before 1990 and outline the forces driving change. For present purposes, we can define the Japanese model as a constellation of institutions (including political institutions, intermediate associations, financial systems, labor relations systems, and interfirm networks) linked together into a distinct national system of economic governance. Japan was similar to other coordinated market economies (CMEs) such as Germany and different from liberal market economies (LMEs) such as the United States in that it fostered long-term cooperative relationships between firms and labor, between firms and banks, and between different firms.[11] These relationships combined to produce relatively stable networks of business relationships (*keiretsu*), including horizontal industrial groups and supply and distribution networks.[12] The bureaucracy played a critical role in protecting industry from international competition, promoting industry through an active industrial policy, managing competition in sectoral markets, and establishing and maintaining the framework for private-sector coordination. Industry associations served as important intermediaries between the government and industry, especially in industrial sectors with a large number of firms.[13] Here we focus particularly on the core "micro" institutions of the Japanese model: the "lifetime" employment system, the main bank system, the corporate governance system, and supplier networks.

The labor relations system combined a grand bargain of wage moderation and few strikes in exchange for employment security with firm-level pacts that promoted labor-management cooperation. Labor unions were organized primarily at the enterprise level, rather than at the sectoral level, facilitating cooperative agreements between management and labor. Large Japanese firms developed channels to incorporate labor into the management process and to enhance communication between managers and workers. They cultivated the loyalty of their core workers by offering long-term employment, by tying wage increases primarily to seniority, and by offering firm-specific benefit programs such as nonportable pension plans. They fostered internal labor markets by encouraging personnel transfers within the firm or the corporate group while impeding external labor markets by restricting most hiring to recent graduates. With lower turnover, Japanese firms had a greater

---

11. Hall and Soskice 2001.

12. Gerlach 1992, Lincoln and Gerlach 2004. The Japanese originally differentiated the horizontal industrial groups (referring to them as *kigyō shūdan*) from other corporate networks, but they now employ the term *keiretsu* for the horizontal groups as well.

13. Representative works on government-industry relations include Johnson 1982, Samuels 1987, Okimoto 1989, Hiwatari 1991, and Schaede 2000.

incentive to invest in training their workers. At the same time, they retained considerable flexibility with a starkly tiered system of permanent employees, who enjoyed job security and full benefits, and nonregular workers, who might work full time but did not enjoy the same level of wages, benefits, or security.[14]

The financial system centered on bank lending rather than capital market finance. The government actively directed the allocation of credit through public financial institutions and private banks. The government insulated the market from international capital flows, segmented financial institutions into distinct niches (securities houses, insurance firms, and various types of banks), and heavily regulated the financial sector to prevent both market entry and exit. Meanwhile, firms maintained long-term relationships with their "main" banks. The main banks would provide their clients with a stable line of credit at favorable rates, monitor the clients' performance, and aid the clients in the case of financial distress. The firms, in turn, would conduct a large and consistent share of their borrowing and transaction business with the main bank.[15] Firms and their main banks often shared ties to a common industrial group—also known as a horizontal *keiretsu*—such as the Mitsubishi, Mitsui, Sumitomo, Daiichi Kangyo, Sanwa, and Fuyo groups. Companies within these groups tended to engage in preferential business relationships and to cross-hold each other's shares. In this way, they kept a large proportion of their shares in stable hands, insulating them from outside shareholders and all but eliminating the risk of hostile takeover. Japanese managers practiced "stakeholder" governance in the sense that they viewed workers, banks, suppliers, and distributors as members of a corporate community, and they considered the interests of this broader community in making management decisions. Corporate boards were typically composed of a large number of career executives, with little or no input from outsiders.[16]

Japanese manufacturers cultivated extensive supply networks, also known as vertical *keiretsu*. Assemblers remained loyal to their suppliers in exchange for supplier efforts to control costs, maintain quality, develop products to specification, deliver supplies in a timely fashion, and provide superior after-delivery service. Assemblers collaborated closely with their core suppliers on research and design, and they often cemented these relationships with cross-shareholdings. Toyota incorporated this approach to supply-chain management into its "just-in-time" lean production system, which emerged as the

---

14. Koike 1988, Aoki 1988, Ariga et al. 2000.
15. Aoki 1988, Aoki and Patrick 1994, Aoki and Dore 1994.
16. Teramoto 1997, 32–36; Itami 2000; Inagami 2000; Dore 2000, 23–48; Itō 2002; Jackson 2003, 263–67.

dominant production paradigm in the world in the auto sector.[17] Japanese firms in other manufacturing sectors, such as electronics, adopted similar practices. These supply networks offered firms an attractive alternative to a stark buy-or-make decision. They could hold down labor costs and shift some of the burden of adjustment onto suppliers by outsourcing yet also leverage long-term relationships to collaborate on reducing costs, raising quality, and fostering innovation.[18]

The Forces for Change

More than any other factor, the prolonged economic slump that began in 1991 has driven institutional change in Japan. We review the economic crisis in more detail in the following chapter, but for present purposes we can simply note that it generated enormous economic and political pressures for change. It strained core institutions of the Japanese model such as the lifetime employment system, the main bank system, and supplier networks by forcing firms to cut costs. It forced the ruling Liberal Democratic Party (LDP) and the opposition parties to propose major reform programs. And it undermined the legitimacy of the postwar model, leading opinion leaders to question the merits of their own economic system and to view the U.S. model more favorably.[19]

Japan also confronted the accumulated legacy of its own postwar success.[20] As the economy matured, the natural growth rate slowed, exacerbating distributional conflicts. The government had to adjust industrial policies as Japan moved from catch-up to technological leadership, to redesign fiscal and social policies as population growth slowed, and to reorient programs as public priorities shifted from recovery and growth to quality of life. Meanwhile, corporations moved from competing for scarce capital to leveraging the benefits of abundant capital, and from capitalizing on low-cost labor to investing in high-skill labor.

Furthermore, Japan faced the challenge of integration into the global economy. The growing mobility of capital and corporate activity broke down the relative insulation of the Japanese market: it not only undermined the government's ability to control corporate behavior but also encouraged the government to reform policies to prevent capital or corporate flight. Firms had a greater ability to move production abroad, to switch to foreign suppliers, or

---

17. Womack et al. 1990.
18. Aoki 1988, 208–23; Gerlach 1992; Lincoln and Gerlach 2004.
19. The economic crisis is not a purely exogenous shock, for the institutions of Japanese capitalism have played a role in the crisis. We survey this debate in detail in the next chapter.
20. Lincoln 1988.

to shift from domestic borrowing to global capital market financing. Japanese companies were exposed to new patterns of behavior as they moved abroad, and domestic markets were increasingly infiltrated by foreign companies that did not behave according to local norms. Japan also experienced a sharp appreciation of the yen in the late 1980s and early 1990s, which increased pressure on corporations to cut costs to compete in international markets.

Meanwhile, scholars, journalists, financial analysts, and other opinion leaders argued that Japan should conform to "global standards," which they equated with U.S. standards. The U.S. government, other national governments, and international organizations such as the World Trade Organization (WTO) pressed Japan to lower trade restrictions, to promote competition in domestic markets, and to adopt international regulatory standards. In the chapters that follow we examine how the distinct mechanisms of globalization—including market pressures, the diffusion of norms, and direct political pressures—shape reform outcomes across issue areas and across companies within Japan. Specifically, we assess whether the government enacts more substantial policy reforms in issue areas subject to strong foreign pressure and whether corporations with greater exposure to foreign influence—such as firms with high levels of foreign ownership, exports, or investments abroad—restructure more aggressively.

A Model of Institutional Change

Here I build on insights from the New Institutional Economics, the Varieties of Capitalism school, and economic sociology to outline a simple model of institutional change and apply it to Japan today.[21] The New Institutional Economics suggests that actors create and reform institutions in order to reduce "transaction costs," such as the cost of obtaining information about a firm or a product (information costs) and the cost of monitoring and enforcing contracts (enforcement costs). Sometimes these elements simply make the transaction more costly, as the term implies, but often they are sufficiently high to prevent the transaction from taking place at all. Institutions such as labor relations systems, financial systems, and interfirm networks can reduce transaction costs. Ronald Coase, in his seminal article, argues that businesses create firms (corporate organizations) to reduce transaction costs.[22] Oliver Williamson refines this approach to explore how firms choose among different institutional arrangements. He uses it to explain, for example, how firms choose when to incorporate parts production within the hierarchy of the firm,

21. Coase 1952, Williamson 1985, Aoki 1988, North 1990, Hall and Soskice 2001, Fligstein 2001.
22. Coase 1952.

when to negotiate long-term contracts with suppliers, and when to procure parts on the open market.[23]

Douglass North applies the transaction costs approach explicitly to the question of institutional change, arguing that actors reform institutions when exogenous shocks alter relative prices. He takes a more functionalist line in his earlier work, implying that economic actors respond to altered incentives by developing better institutional solutions over time.[24] In later work, however, he depicts institutional change as a more open-ended process in which politics and ideology weigh heavily and changes may or may not constitute improvements.[25] Masahiko Aoki applies institutional economics to Japan, demonstrating how actors use institutions such as lifetime employment, the main bank system, and supplier networks to reduce transaction costs.[26] He depicts institutional change as an evolving equilibrium. Building on a game-theoretic model, he suggests that actors revise institutions in response to exogenous shocks but do so within the context of an existing matrix of institutions. So they are more likely to adopt revisions that are compatible with existing institutions than to opt for ones that undermine the prevailing equilibrium.[27]

The Varieties of Capitalism literature adopts the basic logic of institutional economics but embraces a wider range of political and sociological factors. Although it builds on earlier traditions in comparative political economy, it gives greater attention to the "micro" level of the firm. Peter Hall and David Soskice focus especially on the dichotomy between liberal market economies and coordinated market economies, arguing that these constitute alternative models with distinctive logics. Like Aoki, they emphasize the interconnections between the components of national models and suggest that partial deviations from these equilibria are likely to be less stable and less successful than more internally consistent versions of the models. They contend that governments and firms are likely to adjust to changing circumstances by trying to preserve their comparative institutional advantages and that this process is more likely to reinforce national differences than to erode them.[28]

Hall and Soskice emphasize how these national models have comparative advantages in some sectors and not others but do not explore the sectoral variations within the national models themselves. German and Japanese

23. Williamson 1985.
24. North 1981.
25. North 1990.
26. Aoki 1988.
27. Aoki 2001.
28. Hall and Soskice 2001, especially 62–66.

firms have an advantage in sectors that rely on incremental innovation, such as machine tools and factory equipment, consumer durables, engines, and specialized transport equipment. U.S. firms have the edge in sectors that require radical innovation, such as biotechnology, semiconductors, and software development.[29] Hall and Soskice generalize from core sectors, such as machine tools for Germany and automobiles for Japan, producing characterizations of national models that are more valid for these sectors than for others, such as finance or retail. The Varieties of Capitalism framework does not preclude a more fine-grained analysis of sectoral variations, however. In fact, the logic of the argument should lead us to expect substantial variation across sectors within a given country precisely because the foundation of comparative institutional advantage varies across sectors. The value of a long-term employment system, for example, depends on the level of training required and the nature of the work, and that in turn varies considerably by industrial sector. So we should expect countries not to develop one-size-fits-all employment systems but rather to create differentiated variations on the national model that reflect the different requirements of these sectors. Hence in this study I propose to examine the *sectoral varieties of capitalism* as well as national varieties. In later chapters I explore the broader variation between manufacturing and services as well as the more subtle variation between manufacturing sectors characterized by more integrated production systems, such as autos, and those geared toward more modular production, such as electronics.

Sociological institutionalists generally depart from the rationalism of institutional economics and stress a logic of appropriateness over a logic of calculation. Mark Granovetter accepts the assumption of rationality but argues that it should be broadened to focus more on social structure.[30] Walter Powell and Paul Dimaggio reject the rationality assumption outright, emphasizing that actors are more likely to satisfice than to maximize, to search for meaning than to pursue utility, and to conform to norms than to calculate interests.[31] Neil Fligstein combines a sociological perspective with a more political one, showing, for example, how dominant firms exert control over sectoral markets.[32] Sociologists tend to view institutional change as a diffusion process: the diffusion of new norms or beliefs across countries, firms, or arenas of social interaction.

I begin with a simple model based on a New Institutional Economics/ Varieties of Capitalism logic and then explore ways to expand it to incorporate

29. Hall and Soskice 2001, 39.
30. Granovetter 1985, 505–6.
31. Powell and Dimaggio 1991.
32. Fligstein 2001.

a broader range of political and social factors. Let us first view Japanese capitalism as a system of incentives and constraints. That is, actors within the system (firms, banks, unions) use institutions such as lifetime employment, main bank relations, and interfirm networks to reduce transaction costs. They then incorporate these institutions into their cost-benefit calculus as they adapt to new circumstances. Corporations will abandon their stable partners—such as labor unions, banks, and other corporations—only when the efficiency gains from doing so outweigh the cost of forgoing future benefits from cooperation with these partners. And in most cases, the marginal increase in efficiency does not justify the large fixed cost of undermining these relationships. This perspective helps to explain not only why the Japanese model has been slow to change but also *how* it has been changing. Corporations will adjust in ways that preserve the benefits of these long-term relationships, or even build on these benefits if possible.

In many cases, we can account for the resilience of these relationships equally well in economic terms, with reference to rationality and interests, or in sociological terms, with reference to legitimacy and norms. If a Japanese firm is reluctant to lay off workers, for example, it may be calculating the cost savings against the potential damage to its cooperative relationship with remaining workers, or it may be simply adhering to prevailing norms of acceptable firm behavior. The concept of reciprocity offers some clues as to how a rational calculus and an adherence to norms might blend in practice, for relationships of reciprocity have both a rational and a normative element. Japanese managers feel that they benefit from long-term relationships of reciprocity with workers, banks, and other firms, but they also have normative commitments to these relationships.

We can attempt to incorporate norms and social ties into a cost-benefit framework by thinking in terms of broadening circles of rationality. In the first circle, for example, a manager would simply calculate the estimated costs of financing with the firm's main bank versus the costs with a U.S. investment bank. If the competitor were less costly, he would abandon the main bank. In the second circle, however, he would consider the implications for the firm's comparative institutional advantage: he would weigh the cost savings against the potential damage to the long-term cooperative relationship with the main bank. And in the third circle, he would broaden the calculus further to include possible costs beyond the main bank relationship, such as damage to the firm's reputation or strains in relationships with workers, other business partners, intermediary associations, or the government. The first circle represents a simple economic calculus, the second adds institutional factors along the lines of the Varieties of Capitalism approach, and the third incorporates broader social factors.

Three Circles of Rationality
1. Simple cost-benefit analysis (market calculus)
2. Add institutional costs and benefits (Varieties of Capitalism perspective)
3. Add social/reputational costs and benefits (broader sociological perspective)

In practice, of course, the three circles of rationality overlap to a considerable degree. The case studies and other evidence presented in Chapters 3–6 cannot prove that one logic of rationality trumps another, but they can help us to specify how these different logics combine to shape outcomes.

The task of analyzing institutional change is made all the more difficult because it operates simultaneously at many different levels of the political-economic system. Japanese firms are renegotiating agreements with their workers, banks, and business partners; industry associations and union federations are reorganizing and redefining their missions; and the government is revising regulatory procedures and passing reform legislation—all at the same time. To make the situation even more complex, adjustments at one level have ramifications for adjustments at other levels. In order to make sense of this analytically, I simplify the picture and focus on adjustments at two levels, those of the firm (micro level) and the government (macro level).

1. *The Micro Level.* At the firm level, the forces for change outlined above translate most tangibly into increased pressure to cut costs. As Japanese firms strive to cut costs, however, they are constrained from laying off workers, abandoning their main banks, and cutting off stable suppliers by the logic of the Japanese model itself. Their options for adjustment are limited by legal and regulatory constraints, such as laws governing the dismissal of workers, and their preferred strategies for adjustment within these legal constraints are shaped by their existing relations with workers, banks, and other firms (Figure 3).

We can view a company's options in terms of Albert Hirschman's categories of "exit" and "voice."[33] The Japanese system differs from the liberal market model in that it imposes greater constraints on exit (withdrawal) from business relationships but has more fully developed channels for voice (negotiation) within these relationships. This is no accident, of course, because actors who are constrained from exit have a greater incentive to cultivate mechanisms for voice. So when Japanese firms confront tougher competition or a weaker economy, they are more likely to exercise voice than exit.

This simple model already provides us with substantial hints about the substance of corporate adjustment. As much as possible, Japanese companies

33. Hirschman 1970.

FIGURE 3. *Micro Level: Factors Shaping Patterns of Corporate Adjustment*

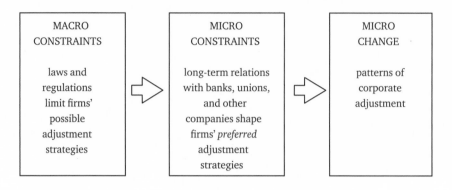

will not abandon their workers, their banks, and their suppliers, but they will renegotiate the terms of their relationships with these partners. They will not lay off workers but will demand wage restraint or greater flexibility in deploying workers. They will not abandon their main banks but will press the banks to hold down lending rates or to offer more sophisticated financial instruments. And they will not cut off their loyal suppliers but will ask the suppliers to cut prices or to improve delivery and after-sales service. In short, as we shall see in detail in Chapters 5 and 6, companies will strive to adjust without undermining these relationships, and they will leverage the benefits of these relationships to ride out their problems.

We can fill out this pattern further by building on more specific knowledge of the Japanese model. For example, the proposition that Japanese firms will leverage the benefits of long-term relationships does not mean much until we specify what these benefits are. In labor relations, we know that large Japanese companies offer employment security to their permanent employees in exchange for wage moderation and cooperation in raising productivity. So in an economic downturn, we would expect them to press for further wage restraint or to redouble efforts at labor-management coordination. Likewise, in bank relations, we know that companies remain loyal to their main banks in exchange for an enhanced level of service plus insurance that the bank will extend credit or otherwise bail out the company if necessary. In hard times, then, we would expect stronger companies to demand enhanced services and weaker companies to cash in on this insurance. And in supplier relations, we know that companies remain loyal to suppliers in exchange for flexibility on price and service, investment in research and development, and co-development of higher-quality or lower-cost products. So in a recession, we would expect them to reinforce their collaboration with their most

FIGURE 4. *Macro Level: Factors Shaping Patterns of Policy Reform*

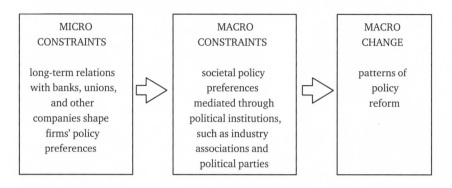

MICRO CONSTRAINTS	MACRO CONSTRAINTS	MACRO CHANGE
long-term relations with banks, unions, and other companies shape firms' policy preferences	societal policy preferences mediated through political institutions, such as industry associations and political parties	patterns of policy reform

important suppliers to cut production costs. "We do not ask our suppliers to cut *prices*," explains one Toyota executive, "but we work with them to reduce real *costs*. In this way, we both benefit."[34]

2. *The Macro Level.* Just as firms' preferred business strategies reflect the incentives and constraints of the Japanese model, so do their positions on policy reform. There is a *micro* logic to *macro* preferences: industry policy positions reflect the institutions of Japanese capitalism, such as labor relations, financial systems, and corporate networks. Firms derive comparative advantage from these institutions, so they have to weigh the expected efficiency gains from policy reforms against the possible costs of undermining these institutions (Figure 4).

Political economy models typically deduce industry policy preferences from their (macro) position within the economy.[35] That is, they deduce these preferences from economic models of how various policies affect different economic groups, such as employers versus workers, or producers versus consumers, or firms in competitive sectors versus firms in protected sectors. Employer interests, for example, are expected to differ from worker interests in fairly predictable ways across different national contexts: employers will want policies that lower wages and benefits, and workers will want policies that raise them. In contrast, the Varieties of Capitalism approach pushes us to look at the microlevel determinants of policy preferences. In this view, employer interests reflect the specific market institutions of a given country. Employers in liberal market economies will support labor deregulation because they rely on competitive labor markets to minimize production costs

34. Interview with Hidehiko Tajima, General Manager, Global Purchasing Division, Global Purchasing Center, Toyota Motor Corporation, Toyota City, January 18, 2002.
35. Frieden and Rogowski 1996, Frieden 1999.

FIGURE 5. *Micro-Macro Interaction*

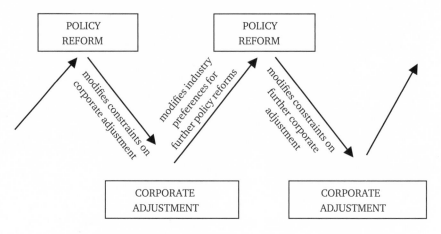

whereas employers in coordinated market economies may oppose it because they rely on close labor-management collaboration to maximize product quality.[36] In Japan, market institutions tend to modify industry preferences for liberal market reforms: fewer firms advocate these reforms than one would otherwise expect, and those firms that do so are more ambivalent than one would otherwise expect.[37] As a result, Japanese government leaders move cautiously on reforms, package delicate compromises, and design reform to preserve the core institutions of the Japanese model and to leverage the strengths of the model as much as possible (Chapters 3 and 4).

3. *Micro-Macro Interaction.* Thus the Japanese model generates relatively predictable patterns of corporate adjustment and policy reform. But the actual trajectory of change over the longer term is complicated by the fact that the two levels interact. As the government enacts policy reforms, these reforms create new opportunities and constraints for further corporate adjustment; and as firms adjust to new challenges, these adjustments modify firms' policy preferences and thereby affect future policy reforms (Figure 5).

We can see the interaction between these two levels of adjustment in examples from postwar Japanese history. When the Japanese government relaxed capital controls in the 1960s, it prompted Japanese firms to increase their cross-holding of shares, producing what came to be considered a primary feature of the Japanese model. In doing so, the firms helped to preserve fea-

36. Thelen 1999, Hall and Soskice 2001 (especially chapters by Soskice, and King and Wood).

37. Moreover, these preferences are aggregated in the political arena in a manner that further moderates demands for liberal reform (Chapter 3).

tures of the Japanese system—such as industrial policy, administrative guid-ance, and interfirm collaboration—that function best in a market protected from foreign capital. And they were able to accomplish this only in the context of close government-industry collaboration, relatively weak antitrust regula-tion, and well-organized interfirm networks. In the 1970s, when the Japanese government moved forward with trade liberalization, some industries replaced tariffs and quotas with private-sector substitutes, including prefer-ential procurement practices, exclusive dealerships, and cartels. Kodak argued this point in its WTO case against Fuji Film, contending that the Min-istry of International Trade and Industry (MITI) worked with Fuji to establish exclusive dealer networks that effectively shut out foreign suppliers.[38] Then, in 1985, the G-5 governments launched a substantial appreciation of the yen with the Plaza Accord. Many Japanese firms responded by shifting manufac-turing activity to Southeast Asia to reduce production costs. But rather than abandon their favored suppliers, large manufacturers moved abroad in tandem with their suppliers, extending national supply networks into the Asian region.[39] In each of these cases, the Japanese model transformed yet did not converge on the liberal market model. In fact, government and indus-try interacted to produce a transformation of the model conditioned by the incentives and constraints of the model itself. I contend that this is precisely what has been happening since the 1990s. We shall review more recent exam-ples in the case study chapters and speculate about possibilities for the future in the conclusion.

Refining the Model

This simple model allows us to describe and explain Japan's distinctive trajectory of institutional change, yet it excludes some important factors. Here I present two ways to flesh out the model, albeit at the expense of parsi-mony. The case study chapters do just that: they build on the simple model but incorporate a broad range of social and political factors to portray Japan's ongoing transformation in its full complexity.

A MORE SOCIOLOGICAL PERSPECTIVE

One could argue that the simple model is still too rationalistic. It incorpo-rates social factors via the third circle of rationality, but it cannot fully resolve the tension between the logics of the three circles. Efficiency concerns and normative commitments can complement each other, but they may also con-flict. For example, firm managers sometimes have to make a stark choice

38. Johnson 1982, Dewey Ballantine 1995, Tilton 1996.
39. Hatch and Yamamura 1996.

among maximizing profits (first circle), enhancing their comparative institutional advantage (second circle), and honoring social obligations (third circle). Furthermore, there are limits to how effectively one can incorporate normative commitments, social networks, or cognitive maps into a cost-benefit framework. Sociological perspectives suggest that actors facing new circumstances do not rationally calculate costs and benefits so much as fall back on existing norms, beliefs, and routines.[40]

Focusing on beliefs and identity would turn our attention more to decision makers' own qualities. This poses a challenge for a model that centers on the profitability, comparative advantage, or reputation of the firm rather than the beliefs or social ties of the individual decision makers. To illustrate this point, let us look at two examples of how the simple model might not capture the decision process. First, the model implies that firm managers might be reluctant to damage a long-term cooperative relationship by cutting off a stable supplier but that they would act once they determined that the efficiency benefits outweighed the long-term costs. In reality, however, managers may not adhere to their own cost-benefit analysis. One Japanese manager recalls precisely such a debate in which board members agreed that they would save money without compromising quality by switching from a stable domestic supplier to a foreign rival. The board member with the closest personal relationship to the domestic supplier's managers nonetheless successfully fought off the proposal because he personally felt that he could not betray these partners.[41] Second, we find in the case studies that foreign managers sometimes shift a Japanese company in a dramatically new direction. A cost-benefit model cannot account for such a shift because the company's objective circumstances have not changed. The new manager has greater freedom because he is less encumbered by the values and/or social ties of his Japanese predecessors. For precisely this reason, we go beyond the simple model in the case study chapters (especially Chapter 6) to examine how the identity of the managers influences a company's behavior. At the same time, however, our third circle of rationality may help us to understand how foreign opinion leaders or foreign firms might accelerate institutional change by disseminating new ideas or practices widely enough to alter the prevailing discourse about policy reform or corporate adjustment, thereby shifting actors' judgments about what constitutes an appropriate response. We shall explore this international diffusion of policies and practices throughout the book.

40. Powell and Dimaggio 1991, Herrigel 1996.
41. Interview, February 1997.

A MORE POLITICAL PERSPECTIVE

The model is inherently political because it suggests that corporate adjustments are subject to legal and regulatory constraints and that changes in these constraints must survive the political process. It emphasizes how institutions shape societal preferences about policy reforms and how these preferences in turn affect the substance of reforms. Nonetheless, this leaves open the question of how these preferences are aggregated in the political arena. We shall fill out the politics of reform by addressing how the overall structure of the political system facilitates or impedes reform (Chapter 2), how bureaucratic ideology constrains policy outcomes (Chapter 2), and how political parties, government ministries, and industry associations mediate preferences in ways that tend to produce incremental reforms with substantial compensation for the potential losers from reform (Chapter 3). Nonetheless, I would argue that the micro institutions that shape industry preferences are even more critical in shaping the *substance* of reform than the macro institutions that mediate these preferences. Political institutions may determine how the government weighs the demands of business versus labor, for example, but market institutions shape the specific content of the demands that business makes.

2   THE CRISIS OF JAPANESE CAPITALISM

Japan astounded the world with its economic performance not once, but twice. Japan performed its economic "miracle" from the 1950s through the 1980s, and then it produced an equally stunning descent into crisis in the 1990s. In the former period Japan had the strongest economic performance in the industrialized world; in the latter it had the worst.[1] Japan's transition from hyper-success to hyper-failure presents a compelling puzzle for analysts: What went wrong? This book's primary purpose is not to unravel this puzzle but to assess what new Japanese economic system is emerging. Nevertheless, we must grasp the nature of Japan's economic problems in order to analyze the reforms the government and corporations designed to address these problems.

The Policy Failures

Economists have engaged in an extraordinary debate about the causes of and cures for Japan's prolonged economic stagnation. Many Western commentators have implied that the solutions were all too obvious, and only politics stood in the way. In reality, however, the experts themselves disagreed about how the government should respond to the crisis, and the lack of consensus on remedies constituted a major impediment to decisive action. Meanwhile, popular commentators spun out an even wider array of theories about how to reform Japan, from the psychological to the geo-strategic, and their views have shaped the public debate as well.[2] We begin by making a crude distinction between the "policy failure" and the "structural crisis" schools of thought and then review the considerable variations within each category. As we shall see, most serious analysts acknowledge that Japan has suffered from both macroeconomic policy failures and structural inefficiencies, but they

1. The Institute for the German Economy calculates that Japan led the field of twenty industrialized countries by a substantial margin in economic performance over the course of the twentieth century with 1,660 percent growth (*Asahi Shimbun*, November 26, 1999, 12). But Japan came in dead last among OECD countries in the 1990s (Katz 2003, 25–26).

2. Uchihashi 1995, Kikkawa 1998, Sakakibara 2002. See Gao 2000 on competing views within Japan.

differ in the relative weight they ascribe to the two and in the prescriptions they propose.[3]

Those in the policy failure school emphasize that the Japanese government made policy errors that are crucial to understanding Japan's dismal economic performance after 1990. The government fueled the bubble economy of the late 1980s, responded inappropriately to the downturn in the early 1990s, addressed the banking crisis slowly and ineffectively, and made mistakes in macroeconomic management in the late 1990s. Those within this broad camp vary substantially, for example, in how they judge the relative importance of fiscal policy, monetary policy, and banking regulation. They generally differ from those in the structural crisis school, however, in that they interpret Japan's dilemma primarily as one of insufficient demand rather than excess supply, and they view the bubble economy as a major cause of the prolonged stagnation rather than simply as a symptom of underlying structural problems.

THE BUBBLE ECONOMY

On May 31, 1989, the Bank of Japan (BOJ) raised the official discount rate from 2.5 to 3.25 percent, setting in motion a process that eventually led to a drastic plunge in stock and real estate values, a full-fledged crisis of the financial system, and more than a decade of near-zero economic growth. The Bank's primary error was not in bursting the asset bubble, however, but in allowing it to inflate so much in the first place by waiting too long to raise interest rates. The bank then overshot in response by hiking rates too much.

From mid-1985 to mid-1989, the total valuation of stocks on the first tier of the Tokyo Stock Exchange soared from ¥169 trillion to ¥527 trillion.[4] By 1987, Bank of Japan officials realized that the economy was overheating, and Deputy Governor Yasushi Mieno and others recommended raising interest rates. Although consumer prices were stable, asset prices were booming and the money supply was expanding. So why didn't the Bank act? Some bank officials suggest that financial liberalization had increased the volatility of monetary indicators by the 1980s, making it more difficult to control the money supply. Therefore, they were justified in ignoring signs of asset

---

3. Posen 1998, Krugman 1999, Svensson 1999, and Harada 1999 stress policy failures, for example, whereas Nakatani 1996, Yoshitomi 1998, Katz (1998 and 2003), Kobayashi 2000, Porter et al. 2000, McKinsey Global Institute 2000, and Madsen 2004 emphasize structural factors. Muramatsu and Okuno 2002 and Ito and Patrick 2005 provide useful overviews of the debate.

4. Grimes 2001, 138.

inflation, which is inherently difficult to judge, because Japan did not have price inflation.[5]

Moreover, Bank officials insist that they had an obligation to stimulate aggregate demand under the September 1985 Plaza Accord among the G-5 countries, and raising interest rates would have violated this agreement.[6] Yet Japanese officials had already complied with the accord by intervening in exchange markets and lowering interest rates since 1985, so they probably could have raised rates by 1988—when their German counterparts did—without alienating their G-5 partners. In any case, the Japanese authorities are somewhat disingenuous to blame external pressures, for they have not always caved in to such pressures. U.S. negotiators maintain that they pressed the Japanese government to stimulate the economy in the early 1990s, and the Japanese refused to comply.[7] Thus one could argue that the Japanese government cooperated with the United States in the late 1980s when it should not have, and did not cooperate in the early 1990s when it should have.

Richard Werner adds an interesting twist to this tale, contending that the Bank guided monetary policy more through "window guidance"—nonbinding directives to banks about how much to lend—than through standard mechanisms such as interest rates. He suggests that during the bubble period the window guidance figures became targets that banks strived to reach rather than limits that they sought not to exceed. Left to their own devices, in other words, the banks would have lent less, not more. The banks were reluctant to undershoot the targets, fearing a permanent reduction in their lending quota. Over time, Werner contends, this dynamic fueled the asset bubble.[8]

The Ministry of Finance (MOF) could also have tightened fiscal policy. MOF officials resisted U.S. pressure for substantial expansion via construction spending, but they did not shift toward fiscal consolidation either.[9] The MOF also may have contributed to the bubble by intervening in the stock market. In October 1987, for example, the MOF responded to the "Black Monday" plunge in U.S. markets by calling in the major securities houses and asking them not to sell off shares. Not surprisingly, ministry officials specifically directed the securities firms to purchase shares in Nippon Telegraph and Telephone (NTT), which was still mostly owned by the government itself.[10]

---

5. Grimes 2001, 2–3.

6. McKinnon and Ohno (1997) take this argument a step further, arguing that the U.S. government generated a perpetual expectation that the yen would rise after 1985, setting the stage for Japan's economic difficulties since the 1990s.

7. Interview, October 2000.

8. Werner 1998, 2003.

9. Grimes 2001, 143–45.

10. Schaede 1990.

Although ministry officials may have forestalled a major drop in the stock market, we might question in retrospect whether they actually prevented a much-needed correction and thereby made the market crash more severe when it finally came.

MACROECONOMIC POLICY AFTER THE BUBBLE

The Bank of Japan had to raise interest rates to burst the bubble, but it raised rates too quickly and too far and then moved too slowly when it finally reversed course.[11] The Bank's defenders contend that although analysts may be able to discern that the Bank overshot in retrospect, it is extremely difficult for a central bank to determine the point at which it has raised rates enough. The Bank eventually lost the interest-rate mechanism as a tool of policy as it lowered rates close to zero. John Makin argues that the Bank relied too much on nominal interest rates instead of focusing on stable monetary growth. The Bank allowed money base growth to rise too far in the late 1980s—from a 6 percent annual rate in 1987 to 12 percent in 1989—and then allowed it to drop too far in the early 1990s: to 2 percent during most of 1991, 1992, and 1993.[12]

The Japanese government adopted several fiscal stimulus packages in the early 1990s, but they were too small to have the necessary impact. The government's pronouncements consistently overstated the size of these packages because they included previously planned projects and allocations from the "second" budget funded from postal savings (the Fiscal Investment and Loan Program). Moreover, the packages were less effective than they could have been because they focused spending on stagnant sectors such as construction rather than growing sectors such as information technology. The government's fiscal stimulus efforts were also undermined by their stop-and-go quality, with periods of fiscal expansion interspersed with contraction.[13]

BANKING REGULATION

Economists come closest to a consensus on the issue of banking regulation, arguing that Japanese financial authorities failed to monitor the banks effectively during the bubble period (and after) and then moved too slowly to press the banks to write off or sell off nonperforming loans.[14] The ministry was oriented more toward regulating prices (interest rates) and market entry and exit than performing detailed prudential regulation, and it did not have the staff to support a more intensive supervisory regime. Ministry officials became

11. Grimes 2001, 157–59.
12. Makin 2001.
13. Posen 1998, 29–54.
14. Posen 1998, Mikitani and Posen 2000, Fukao 2002, Katz 2003.

concerned about the banks' exposure to real estate loans by the late 1980s, but the banks could get around ministry regulations by making loans through nonbank subsidiaries. Meanwhile, the ministry's tacit guarantee to bail out failing financial institutions encouraged risky lending behavior. As in the case of the U.S. savings and loan debacle, the government fueled the crisis through poorly planned deregulation. Financial liberalization not only intensified competition between financial institutions but also gave financial institutions greater freedom to invest in risky assets. The banks were losing their best corporate clients to international capital markets, so they turned to making riskier loans to small businesses and speculating in real estate. The government failed to combine liberalization with stricter prudential regulation, thus setting the stage for a crisis.[15]

The banking crisis also reflects the macroeconomic policy failures discussed above: the bursting of the asset bubble generated the financial crisis in the first place, and more effective macroeconomic management after the bubble would have provided a better growth environment for writing off bad loans.[16] The bubble's collapse devastated the financial sector because the banks counted stockholdings toward Bank of International Settlements reserve requirements, so the drop in share prices directly reduced their reserves.[17] The banks had engaged heavily in real estate speculation, so they were hit by falling real estate prices as well. To make matters worse, most borrowers used real estate as collateral for their loans, so when the borrowers got into trouble, the banks were left unprotected. The nonperforming loans then only grew as economic stagnation lingered and the government failed to crack down on the banks. Moreover, deflation increased the debt burden in real terms.

Once the banking crisis developed, the ministry could have resolved the nonperforming loan problem more effectively at a lower cost if it had moved more quickly and decisively, as the U.S. government did during the savings and loan crisis of the 1980s.[18] The authorities could have pressed the banks to write off or sell off bad loans, created a mechanism for the government to purchase bad loans and then sell them off, allowed the weakest banks to fail, and recapitalized other banks while attaching stringent conditions for restructuring. As the financial crisis deepened in the late 1990s and early 2000s, the

15. Friedman 2000, 44–47; Posen 2002.

16. Weinstein 2001, 35; Lincoln 2003.

17. In 1998, the MOF revised accounting rules to allow banks to value their shareholdings at historical rather than market prices, thereby easing the burden of meeting reserve requirements (Amyx 2004, 184).

18. The U.S. government was slow to respond to the savings and loan crisis as well, but not as slow as the Japanese government in the 1990s (Amyx 2004, 2).

government eventually adopted many of these measures, but it was reluctant to crack down too harshly for fear of causing widespread bankruptcies and unemployment.

POLICY DILEMMAS

Fiscal packages appeared to be pushing the Japanese economy out of recession by 1997, when the Japanese government stopped the nascent recovery in its tracks by raising taxes. The economy's downturn played a role in the LDP's dismal showing in the 1998 Upper House elections, which prompted Prime Minister Ryūtarō Hashimoto's replacement by Keizō Obuchi. Obuchi finally pressed forward with a bolder fiscal stimulus plan loaded with pork-barrel spending. By the late 1990s, the Japanese government found itself with much less room to maneuver because of a ballooning budget deficit. Although the government still needed to sustain prudent fiscal expansion to promote recovery, many worried that the budget deficit could lead to a crisis in the government bond market.[19] Meanwhile, the government faced an emergency in the financial sector with the failure of Hokkaido Takushoku Bank and Yamaichi Securities in the fall of 1997. The government was reluctant to use public funds to bail out financial institutions because it was unpopular politically and would exacerbate the fiscal deficit. Ultimately, the government devised a package in 1998 to recapitalize the banks, but it did not tie the package to strict conditions for restructuring. The Financial Services Agency (FSA) publicly declared that this would be the last government infusion of capital, and this pledge hampered its ability to cope with the growing nonperforming loan crisis in subsequent years. Nobel laureate Joseph Stiglitz, among others, argued that the Japanese economy was so fragile at that point that the government would have to focus on macroeconomic policies designed to ensure recovery and refrain from any attempt to resolve the banking crisis or to engage in other structural reforms that could be destabilizing in the short term.[20]

BATTLING DEFLATION

Japan's unprecedented experience with a prolonged period of deflation has generated a lively debate among professional economists. The BOJ had already lowered interest rates virtually to zero by the early 1990s, so conventional monetary policy tools could not go any further. However, many econo-

19. Broda and Weinstein (2005) argue that the Japanese fiscal situation is not as grave as it is widely perceived to be, for modest increases in tax revenues could make the burden sustainable.

20. *Nikkei Weekly* (April 21, 2003), 5.

mists argued that the Bank's monetary policy was still too tight because even a near-zero interest rate implies a positive real interest rate in a deflationary environment. Paul Krugman, Lars Svensson, Mitsuhiro Fukao, and Kenneth Kuttner and Adam Posen, among others, contended that the Bank of Japan should use nontraditional mechanisms to expand the money supply. Specifically, the Bank should "print" money by purchasing government bonds and other assets, combining this measure with an explicit inflation target of 2 to 3 percent. This would convince market actors that the Bank was committed to expanding the money supply until it achieved its target and would prompt households to consume and corporations to invest—thus breaking the deflationary cycle.[21] Ben Bernanke took this a step further, recommending that the Bank not only promise to produce modest inflation but compensate for some of the past monetary tightness by initially setting the inflation target that much higher.[22] Some experts stressed that monetary expansion would be most effective if it were properly coordinated with fiscal stimulus. Bernanke, for example, proposed that the Bank finance tax cuts directly.[23] Central bank independence may be valuable in an inflationary environment, but it can become a liability in a deflationary economy because it impedes policy coordination. Further monetary expansion would have the additional benefit of bringing down the yen, thereby helping Japanese exporters to compete on international markets. Some analysts have focused more on the exchange rate side of this equation, suggesting that Japan needed a weaker yen and a larger current account surplus to adjust to its chronic savings-investment gap.[24] The skeptics, including most Bank of Japan officials, argued that monetary expansion would not work. The Bank had effectively run out of mechanisms to expand the monetary supply, they asserted, so a failed attempt to produce inflation would only undermine the Bank's credibility. Attempts to generate more liquidity would not have their intended effect because the banks were too weak to act as a proper conduit for monetary policy. The banks would absorb the increased liquidity to balance their own books rather than lend it out and thereby increase the active money supply.[25] To make matters worse, the Bank raised interest rates in August 2000, when the economy once again appeared on the road to recovery. The Bank adjusted rates by only a tiny margin, but its action sent a strong negative signal to the markets.

21. Krugman 1999, Svensson 1999, Fukao 2000, Kuttner and Posen 2001. See Yoshikawa 2000 for a more skeptical view.
22. Bernanke 2003.
23. Bernanke 2003.
24. *Economist* (January 20, 2001), 74.
25. Grimes 2001, 212–13. Bernanke 2003 argues that the Bank could resolve this problem by increasing the money supply through mechanisms that would not require transmission via the banks.

Japan's recovery after 2003 did little to resolve the debates over the nation's economic problems. The policy failure school could point to some modest improvements in government policy.[26] Under Heizō Takenaka, a professional economist who became an influential adviser to Prime Minister Junichirō Koizumi, the FSA gradually took a tougher line with the banks, pressing them to get bad loans off their books. This shift, along with an upturn in the stock market, produced real progress in reducing the overall volume of nonperforming loans, and the large banks' nonperforming loan ratio dropped from 8.4 percent in March 2002 to 2.9 percent in March 2005.[27] This improvement in turn fostered greater confidence in the marketplace. The Bank of Japan became more assertive in pumping liquidity into the markets after Toshihiko Fukui took over as governor in 2003, and deflationary pressures appeared to ease. Unlike in earlier periods of tentative recovery, the authorities did not make the mistake of raising taxes or tightening monetary policy.[28] Those in the structural crisis school gave more credit to the private sector for finally getting serious about restructuring, thereby reducing capacity and raising profits.[29] Meanwhile, the economy was buoyed by strong demand from China and the United States. Although the recovery did not definitively prove either school right, it undermined the contention that the government would have to undertake drastic reforms before the economy could recover, or that Japan would have to suffer a large-scale crisis before the government would begin effective reforms.[30]

The Structural Crisis

Those in the structural crisis school span an even wider range of perspectives, but they differ from the policy failure group in that they maintain that deeper structural problems underlie Japan's economic stagnation. Macroeconomic policies alone would be insufficient to generate a sustainable economic recovery, and attempts at quick fixes could risk weakening the pressure for more fundamental structural reforms. These analysts tend to emphasize deregulation and other "structural" reforms, such as antitrust and corporate governance reforms, that would press firms to reduce capacity and raise profits.

Many analysts contend that the very institutions that fostered Japan's economic success later contributed to its failure.[31] At the level of popular

26. Posen 2004.
27. FSA data.
28. Bergsten 2004.
29. Madsen 2004.
30. Katz 2003.
31. Sakakibara 2002.

discourse, Japanese commentators have engaged in an almost endless barrage of self-criticism, blaming the crisis on any and all of the institutions of Japanese capitalism. They contend, for example, that the labor relations system impedes companies from adjusting efficiently to changing market circumstances. Supplier networks prevent companies from shifting to lower-cost suppliers. Industrial groups foster discriminatory trading practices that stifle competition. The main bank system encourages companies to rely too heavily on loans and not enough on direct finance, to borrow too much, and to select financial intermediaries on the basis of relationships rather than price or service. The corporate governance system prevents shareholders from holding managers accountable for performance. The cross-holding of shares among companies forestalls the efficient reallocation of capital via mergers and acquisitions. Politicians do not exercise leadership, bureaucrats intervene too much in markets, and the education system does not foster creativity.

The more sophisticated versions of this argument focus on low productivity in the protected sectors of the economy. David Weinstein, for example, demonstrates that Japan has a huge productivity gap between manufacturing sectors, which have converged on U.S. levels, and less competitive sectors such as agriculture, construction, utilities, transport, and communications, which have lost ground to their U.S. counterparts and in some cases experienced real losses in productivity. He argues that government regulation accounts for this gap and that market liberalization would greatly enhance productivity in the lagging sectors.[32]

If the Japanese economic system is so inefficient, however, why did Japan perform so well before the 1990s? Posen notes that the Japanese system has always had inefficiencies, so they cannot explain the enormous gap between Japan's potential growth rate in the 1990s and its actual performance.[33] Katz believes he can account for this gap: the Japanese government masked the structural flaws through the 1980s by artificially stimulating demand through a large trade surplus, budget deficits, and low interest rates—but this strategy ran out of steam by 1990.[34]

Many analysts credibly claim to have an answer to one of Japan's two great economic puzzles: explaining the miracle or explaining the crisis. But they have much greater difficulty finding a model that can account for both. The policy failure school has an advantage here, for it can simply posit that policy mistakes explain the shift from success to failure. The structural school,

32. Weinstein 2001.
33. Posen 1998.
34. Katz 2003, 18, 30.

however, must explain why institutional features that were functional during one period became dysfunctional over time.

FROM PROMOTING WINNERS TO PROTECTING LOSERS

Most of the arguments about a structural crisis in the Japanese economy center on Japan's inability to make a successful transition from catch-up to maturity, but they formulate the argument in different ways. Katz argues that the Japanese government promoted industrial winners during the high-growth era but then shifted to protecting losers. Japan's postwar system rested on a grand settlement in which the government pursued a high-growth economic strategy of low interest rates, tight fiscal policy, the transfer of personal savings into industrial investment, and active industrial policy; and it matched this with a political strategy in which it compensated specific constituent groups, notably farmers and small businesses, through protection, subsidies, and public works spending.[35] Katz suggests that the government shifted its emphasis from the competitive to the protected sector over time, so the benefits from promotion dwindled, the costs of compensation soared, and the efficient sectors could no longer bankroll the system without losing their competitive edge.[36] The government was less able to reach viable bargains among the two sectors as economic growth slowed. In this view, the government was eventually forced to promote regulatory reform and to scale back public works spending to reduce the burden of politically motivated policies on the economy as a whole.[37]

FROM HIGH SAVINGS AND INVESTMENT TO EXCESS SAVINGS AND INVESTMENT

Others stress a different type of structural problem: a chronic excess of savings rather than microeconomic inefficiencies.[38] This perspective has the advantage of integrating the macro- and microeconomic pictures and providing an explanation for the shift from high to low performance. It differs from the focus on structural inefficiencies in that it does not necessarily imply that

35. Calder 1988; Vogel 1999b, 9; Bullock 2000.
36. Naoki Tanaka (1997), an adviser to Prime Minister Koizumi, makes a similar argument. Masahiko Aoki (2000, 130) puts it slightly differently, contending that Japan's fundamental dilemma was that competitive sectors naturally drifted away from the government's industrial policy framework while the less competitive sectors relied more and more heavily on government support.
37. See Pempel 1998, Bullock 2000, Mulgan 2002, and Katz 2003 on these distributional tensions.
38. Madsen (2004) highlights this as the core of Japan's problem, although many others (Ito and Patrick 2005, for example) emphasize excess savings as well.

the microinstitutions of Japanese capitalism are outmoded. Japan's high levels of savings and investment were critical in driving the postwar miracle, yet they became a liability over the long run as the economy matured, growth slowed, and returns on investment declined.[39] The debate over Japanese industrial policy has focused primarily on the government's policy of allocating credit to favored sectors, but the heart of the policy was to raise levels of savings and investment even more than to direct this investment. The authorities understood that Japan needed high levels of savings and investment to propel growth but that the private sector would be likely to underinvest unless the government shared some of the risk.[40] The government deployed a wide array of tools to promote savings, including government promotional campaigns and tax incentives. Savers subsidized investment by depositing money into savings accounts that earned lower-than-market rates of interest, thus raising the demand for credit and giving the government the leverage to allocate credit to priority sectors. The banks were willing to go along because they could lend to firms at below-market rates and still maintain reasonable spreads (margins between deposit rates and lending rates).[41]

This policy worked well as long as the government was right that higher levels of investment could find productive use given the country's high natural growth rate. As the economy matured, however, high investment fueling growth gradually turned into overinvestment driving overcapacity. Firms continued to invest, but they had more difficulty finding productive uses for the investment, so the returns on investment inevitably declined over time. A blue-ribbon commission led by former Bank of Japan governor Haruo Maekawa proposed a fundamental shift toward a more demand-driven economy in 1986, but the commission's recommendations were largely ignored. The problem was exacerbated during the bubble period when corporations took advantage of low interest rates and new financial techniques to invest even more.

High savings rates fueled high investment, but they also implied suppressed consumption.[42] As the economy matured, Japanese households continued to save at high rates, so the Japanese economy was left with a stubborn savings-investment gap and could not shift from investment-driven to

39. Gao (2001) offers another view, through the lens of competition policy. Government efforts to manage competition supported industrial growth in the early postwar period but fostered overinvestment and overcapacity later on.

40. See Dosi et al. 1989 for a cogent review of economic rationales for a Japanese-style industrial policy.

41. Zysman 1983, 234–51.

42. Katz (2003, 59–80) argues that Japan's insufficient demand is due to supply-side factors that keep prices high rather than to failed macroeconomic policies.

consumption-driven growth. Japanese savings rates only began to drop substantially in the early 2000s, as the population aged and households began to draw on their savings as slow growth persisted.[43]

Robert Madsen argues that Japan's economic problems really began in the mid-1980s and not in 1990, and the bubble simply masked the more fundamental problem of the savings-investment gap for a few years. He argues that demographic factors explain why savings rates did not drop by the mid-1980s: Japan's baby boomers were reaching middle age, just the point in the life cycle when they are most inclined to save, because of the combination of rising income and approaching retirement.[44] This line of argument identifies a central piece of the story, yet it discounts the independent impact of the bubble, and the agency of government officials in fostering it, by viewing it as a symptom of the savings-investment gap.

FROM INSULATED MARKETS TO OPEN MARKETS

Japan's postwar economic system presupposed a relatively closed market, as noted in Chapter 1, so liberalization challenged elements of this system. Financial liberalization, for example, undermined the government's ability to allocate credit to preferred sectors. Trade liberalization and capital liberalization allowed foreign competitors to challenge the close ties between Japanese firms and their banks, suppliers, and distributors in the marketplace by offering lower prices or better products. Growing ties between Japanese and foreign firms made it more difficult for the government to design policies to favor domestic firms. Meanwhile, as the Japanese economy grew and matured, Japan's trading partners pressed it to further lower trade barriers, relax capital controls, reduce anticompetitive regulation, and strengthen antitrust enforcement. They also requested that Japan take measures to strengthen the yen. Over time, Japan adopted some U.S. and international regulatory standards as the economic system became more integrated into the global economy. Some Japanese commentators viewed this pressure as an American conspiracy to deprive them of their comparative advantage by forcing them to play by rules that favored U.S. firms.[45]

FROM LEAN PRODUCTION TO THE IT ERA

Many analysts have argued that Japanese policies and institutions were better suited to catching up with Western technology than fostering innova-

---

43. The household savings rate dropped from 17.3 percent in 1980 to 13.9 percent in 1990, 9.6 percent in 2000, and 7.5 percent in 2003 (Annual Report on National Accounts, Cabinet Office).

44. Madsen 2004.

45. Kikkawa 1998.

tion.[46] To make matters worse, the technological paradigm shifted from lean production, which favored the Japanese model, to the information technology era, which favors the U.S. model. Japanese institutions—including close-knit supplier networks, stable employment relations, and patient finance—were especially well adapted to an era in which incremental improvements in production processes were critical to comparative advantage in leading sectors such as automobiles and electronics. This was no accident, of course, for Japanese producers drove the evolution of the lean production paradigm. These institutions were less well matched to the emerging information technology paradigm, in which users rather than producers drive key innovations, software makers and components suppliers share control over technology with assemblers, and radical innovation is more important than production processes. This was no accident, either, for U.S. firms drove the evolution toward a new technological paradigm that played to their advantage. Japan's heavy regulation of the telecommunications and finance sectors forestalled the development of large dynamic users of telecommunications services that could drive innovation in information technology. Japan's low labor mobility, lack of entrepreneurs, and lack of venture capital financing became liabilities in an era in which innovation and applications are more important than manufacturing systems.[47]

Kozo Yamamura analyzes this slightly differently, arguing that the U.S. model performs better during periods when technology is changing fundamentally and rapidly whereas the Japanese model performs better during periods when technology is evolving more gradually. This interpretation would explain why the U.S. model has performed better during the period of the information technology revolution since the 1990s, but it would also imply that the Japanese economy could rebound as the pace of technological change slows.[48]

CAUGHT BETWEEN TWO PARADIGMS

Alternatively, Japan's error may not have been sticking with a model that was outmoded but abandoning a model that worked without converting to a new one. This perspective is consistent with the previous chapter's assertion that it would be very difficult for Japan to shift to a liberal market model. Japan found itself stuck in a no-man's land between two viable alternatives. In this view, Japan's reforms to date are more of a problem than a solution. Bai Gao, for example, argues that financial reforms undermined the stability

46. Callon 1995.
47. Cohen et al. 2000, Vogel and Zysman 2002, Cole forthcoming.
48. Yamamura 2003.

of the economic system, exacerbating the tendency of banks to reduce lending in an economic downturn just when corporations needed credit the most. He also notes that labor market reforms sapped consumer confidence, reinforcing the problem of low aggregate demand.[49]

Many popular commentators blame Japan's elite bureaucrats for the prolonged economic crisis, contending that these bureaucrats were too powerful and too inclined to meddle in markets. Yet the opposite may be closer to the truth. Analysts have debated long and hard about the lack of political leadership in Japan, but the most profound change since 1990 has been the loss of bureaucratic leadership. Japan's bureaucrats have forfeited their legitimacy in the eyes of the public, owing to the mismanagement of the economy and corruption scandals at the most elite ministries.[50] The bureaucrats have lost confidence in a more interventionist model of industrial policy, but they do not have the capacity to adopt a more liberal model in its place. As a result, they have opted for ambivalent packages combining elements of old-style industrial policy with halfhearted liberal reforms (see Chapter 4). For example, Japan could deal with excess industrial capacity in one of two basic ways: it could adopt the traditional Japanese approach of government-industry-coordinated reductions in capacity (recession cartels), or it could opt for the market approach of allowing firms to fail.[51] The Japanese government did neither, however, leaving the problem of excess capacity to fester. In telecommunications, likewise, one could argue that Japan is stuck between two paradigms: a government-led model, in which the government guides investment in infrastructure, unifies technical standards, and coordinates private-sector activity; and a market-based model, in which it aggressively promotes competition and allows free entry and exit in the market. Government officials have lost confidence in the former approach, yet they lack the conviction to make a full shift to the latter.

Implications

Japan suffers from both policy failures and structural inefficiencies, so adjudicating this debate depends largely on how one frames the central question. Short-term recovery requires macroeconomic solutions, for example, whereas raising productivity over the long term favors microeconomic remedies. If we ask why Japan's potential growth rate has slowed since the 1980s, then we must look to the changing structure of the Japanese economy. If we

49. Gao 2001, 271–74. Likewise, Katz (2003, 278–83) argues that certain reforms—such as regressive tax reforms—only exacerbated Japanese economic woes because they reduced households' capacity to consume.

50. Amyx (2004, 290–91) provides a partial list of these scandals.

51. Dore 1986, Tilton 1996, Uriu 1996.

ask why Japan performed so far below its growth potential after 1990, however, then the policy failure school has the edge. We cannot explain the timing of the shift from boom to bust, or the scale of the gap between potential and actual performance, without reference to policy failures. The Japanese economic system has always had structural strengths and weaknesses, and the relative balance did not abruptly shift around 1990.

Although there are reasons to believe that some aspects of the Japanese model have become less functional over time, as outlined above, other elements have not. Many of the core institutions studied in this book—including a long-term employment system, stable supplier networks, an elite bureaucracy, and close government-industry ties—still bestow benefits as well as costs. For example, stable employment relations impede rapid adjustments to changing market conditions, but they also encourage firms to invest more in training their workers. Long-term supplier relations make it harder for manufacturers to lower procurement costs rapidly but also foster collaboration between manufacturers and suppliers on research and design. Close coordination between government and industry makes government agencies more vulnerable to industry lobbying and companies more vulnerable to government interference, but it also facilitates setting common technical standards and coordinating research across firms.

Of course, this debate is intractable precisely because Japan's policy failures and its structural inefficiencies are interrelated.[52] Those on the policy failure side stress that policy mistakes generated some of the worst structural problems, including overinvestment and overcapacity as well the banking crisis, and that better policies would ameliorate the structural inefficiencies.[53] These analysts also stress that structural reforms could aggravate macroeconomic problems by dampening demand and fueling deflation. Those on the structural reform side contend that the Japanese government's policy failures were themselves products of structural weaknesses and that only structural reforms such as deregulation can resolve macroeconomic problems such as chronically low aggregate demand.

The debate between the two perspectives hinges in part on estimates of the potential benefits from structural reforms. Posen cites a relatively modest impact on growth rates whereas Weinstein and Katz offer higher estimates.[54]

---

52. Many economic analysts explicitly link macroeconomic and microeconomic factors, combining elements from both of the broad schools presented here (Lincoln 2001 and 2003, for example). Kobayashi and Katō (2001) explicitly reject analyses that focus on one side or the other, arguing that the microeconomic problem of debt forbearance created a macroeconomic problem of insufficient demand.

53. As Posen (1998, 154) puts it, structural inefficiencies are not "procyclical": they are not exacerbated by growth and eased by recession.

Both sides concede that these are essentially educated guesses, yet I would argue that the structural reform advocates tend to overestimate the positive impact of reform on productivity and growth: they assess the benefits of structural reforms but not the costs, they ignore problems of implementation, and they overrate the ability of government measures to alter private-sector behavior. Japan would certainly benefit from productivity improvements in its most inefficient sectors, but the proposed policy reforms are not likely to deliver the anticipated level of efficiency gains.

The Varieties of Capitalism perspective helps to clarify what gets missed in a narrower economic analysis. Let us imagine, for example, that the Japanese government could enact reforms that would make it easier for companies to hire and fire workers at will. This would facilitate more rapid adjustments to changing market conditions and promote more competitive labor markets, but it would also weaken the labor-management cooperation that helps Japanese companies sustain productivity increases. Reforms might enhance efficiency in the short term while undermining the comparative institutional advantage of Japanese firms over the long term. Therefore, the impact of labor deregulation on productivity and growth would be much more ambiguous than the proponents of reform assert. As we shall see in later chapters, the real-life Japanese actors in reform debates view their options in precisely this way: as a complex trade-off between the potential benefits from increased efficiency versus the costs from undermining valued institutions.

Even if we leave aside Japan-specific institutional effects, the economic benefits from pro-competitive reform still vary considerably across sectors, and the balance between benefits and costs depends critically on the specifics of implementation. In a sector in which government regulations were simply impediments to perfect competition, then removing regulations might have benefits and no costs. In the real world, however, many sectors require regulation because of externalities such as information asymmetries or network effects. Hence the government's goal is not to eliminate regulation but to recalibrate it to maximize the benefits and minimize the costs. In some sectors, such as telecommunications, the benefits from pro-competitive regulation clearly outweigh the costs.[55] In other sectors, such as energy or finance, however, the balance of costs and benefits is more ambiguous and depends critically on regulatory design.[56] The lesson from the U.S. savings and loan

54. Posen 1998, Weinstein 2001, Katz 2003.

55. Cohen et al. (2000) argue that the deregulation of telecommunications had the dynamic benefit of generating a new tier of aggressive telecom firms that drove innovation, fueling the information technology revolution. Kushida (forthcoming) demonstrates that telecommunications reform has bestowed substantial benefits in Japan as well.

56. O'Neill 2005.

debacle and the California energy crisis is not that deregulation failed—or that deregulation did not go far enough—but rather that governments must pursue regulatory reforms in a particular manner and sequence in order to maximize benefits and minimize risks.[57] We have no reason to expect that Japanese authorities would be especially skillful at getting deregulation right.

Weinstein and Katz point to government intervention as a major impediment to efficiency, referring to data that show a correlation between less government protection and regulation and greater productivity across sectors in Japan. They assume that the causality runs in the direction of less protection fueling higher productivity, however, without considering that the causality may run the other way, with higher productivity prompting less protection. If we look at Japan's postwar history, of course, we find a consistent pattern in which the government liberalizes sectors that become competitive and protects those that do not.[58]

Furthermore, even well-designed government reforms might not be sufficient to get Japan's least productive sectors to converge on U.S. productivity levels. The impact of reforms could be muted by private-sector substitutes for government regulation, resilient market practices, or distinctive features of certain sectors in Japan. In fact, government deregulation in Japan has typically spurred greater private-sector coordination or outright collusion.[59]

Japan's prolonged stagnation bears some important lessons for those interested in the link between institutions and economic performance, including scholars in the Varieties of Capitalism school and the field of comparative political economy more broadly. Comparative institutional advantages matter, but they affect economic performance only in combination with basic macroeconomic management. Institutions are more likely to shape long-term performance whereas macroeconomic policy determines short-term performance. This leads to the very real possibility that analysts could mistakenly jump to conclusions about shifts in comparative institutional advantage on the basis of short-term fluctuations in economic performance. I contend that this is precisely what has occurred in Japan's case since 1990.

This is an important point for our purposes, for the Japanese economic crisis is more the cause of Japan's structural problems than the result of them. The bubble economy, for example, fueled overinvestment and undermined

---

57. Friedman 2000, 44–47; O'Neill 2005.

58. Weinstein 2001, Katz 2003. Moreover, one might question Katz's judgments regarding which sectors have been liberalized, for he appears to conclude that there has been meaningful liberalization in those sectors where he finds substantial increases in productivity.

59. Schaede 2000.

structural adjustment. Firms took advantage of the economic conditions at the time to finance investments at virtually no cost, but this practice also made them prone to invest without due attention to potential returns.[60] Moreover, in the mid-1980s many firms had developed plans for restructuring, which they then shelved because of the bubble economy. We shall see in Chapter 6 how Long-Term Credit Bank (LTCB) executives discarded a detailed plan for strategic transformation because they were making too much money in the domestic loan business. The loan boom of the bubble period became the nonperforming loan crisis of the 1990s, setting the stage for LTCB's failure less than a decade later.

The Japanese labor and financial systems naturally function better during periods of economic growth, so the economic slump severely strained these institutions. The long-term employment system, for example, works better when labor is relatively scarce and close labor-management collaboration fuels productivity gains, and functions less well when labor is relatively abundant and stable employment slows adjustment.[61] So although commentators blame the employment system for bringing down the economy, the opposite is closer to the truth: the weak economy undermined the employment system. Likewise, the Japanese government's tacit guarantee to bail out banks and the main banks' commitment to support their most valued corporate clients worked smoothly so long as there were not too many troubled banks or too many troubled borrowers at one time. The financial crisis of the 1990s overwhelmed these arrangements.

If Japan truly confronts a structural crisis, then it would follow that the institutions of Japanese capitalism should be transformed. Those who advocate this view recommend a shift toward a liberal market model in the sense of more competitive markets for products, labor, and capital. As noted in the previous chapter, such a shift would imply a massive change in laws, practices, and norms. If Japan's primary problem is one of policy failure, however, then such a fundamental transformation would not be required. Japanese policymakers and corporate executives should be more selective in their reforms, carefully assessing the strengths and weaknesses of current institutions and reinforcing the strengths while jettisoning the weaknesses. My own view, to be developed further in the conclusion, is that the evidence is highly ambiguous on the relative strengths and weaknesses of the distinctive institutions of Japanese capitalism. Therefore, the effort to reform these institutions is most accurately viewed as a social and political movement rather than a rational response to Japan's actual problems.

60. Zielinski and Holloway 1991.
61. Boyer and Juillard 2000, Ariga et al. 2000.

Why Can't Japan Reform?

The economic puzzle of why Japan went from boom to crisis begets an equally compelling political puzzle. Why did Japan fail to extract itself from this crisis? After all, many other countries have experienced severe recessions and banking crises, but only Japan has been unable to resolve these challenges for so long. In this section we review three possible answers to this puzzle and assess their respective strengths and weaknesses.

1. *Japanese political institutions impede reform.* Many analysts place the blame squarely on the political system.[62] Japan obviously required bold economic reform, they proclaim, yet the government could not deliver. Ichirō Ozawa—who bolted from the LDP in 1993, formed three different new parties, and then joined the Democratic Party of Japan (DPJ) in 2003—grew frustrated with the constraints embedded in the Japanese political system and proposed reforms to overcome them. As a rising star within the LDP in 1991–92, Ozawa had been the party's point man in coordinating Japan's participation in the Gulf War. He secured a major financial contribution but failed to push through a more active Japanese role in the conflict. He subsequently developed a program to reform the Japanese political system, which has reshaped Japanese politics ever since. He proposed strengthening the prime minister's office and the cabinet, increasing the number of politicians with ministerial portfolios, and changing the electoral system.[63] He had been a central player in the LDP's own debate over how to shape a political reform package that could mollify public outrage over a series of corruption scandals. He focused especially on electoral reform, arguing that Japan's multimember district electoral system fostered pork-barrel politics and corruption and impeded more issue-oriented political competition. The system forced LDP members to compete with each other for seats in order to secure a majority in the Lower House, yet they could not differentiate themselves from one another on policy grounds because they rarely differed on policies—and in any case, they would vote as a bloc on the Diet floor. So, the argument goes, LDP candidates would try to outdo one another by delivering public works projects and other favors to targeted groups of constituents, giving political competition a material bias that easily slipped into corruption. Ozawa was particularly keen on a single-member district (first-past-the-post) system because he felt that it would encourage a two-party system that would produce

---

62. Mulgan 2002, Pempel forthcoming.

63. Ozawa 1993, especially 65–80. Many of Ozawa's proposals have been implemented in one form or another. See Mulgan 2002, 177–212, and Pempel forthcoming for further discussion of these reforms, and Schlesinger 1997, 252–78; Gaunder 2001, 128–56; and Samuels 2003, 326–33, for more detailed profiles of Ozawa.

more majoritarian (versus consensual) politics and more effective governance.

We can evaluate this thesis by comparing across countries, across issue areas, and over time. The Japanese political system resembles the British parliamentary system in that the government enjoys a majority in the legislature by definition, and therefore it should be able to pass reform legislation with relative ease. In practice, however, it differs from a classic Westminster system in that the prime minister and the cabinet do not exercise real control over their own party or the bureaucracy.[64] They must constantly negotiate with ruling party bosses and frequently coordinate with opposition leaders as well. The British system is much closer to a winner-take-all political system in which the two major parties represent clearly defined sets of constituents, and the prime minister and the cabinet can implement a program without deference to the opposition or dissenters within their own party. Meanwhile, the Japanese bureaucracy plays a distinctly political role in packaging bargains between societal groups. This biases policy toward slow and elaborate compromises and gives ministry officials the leeway to insert their own agenda into policy outcomes.[65] In practice, the ministries and the LDP negotiate closely with each other, leaving political scientists to debate endlessly over which one really dominates the policy process.

On balance, therefore, the British parliamentary system makes it easier to formulate and implement bold reforms than the Japanese version. This comparison can be misleading, however, for Britain is more the exception than Japan. We can appreciate this point by shifting our comparison to the United States and Germany, two countries where commentators are equally convinced that their political systems prevent much-needed reforms. The United States has a presidential system, so the president does not necessarily enjoy a majority in Congress. Even a president with a majority in Congress must struggle to line up votes because party discipline is weaker than in Britain or Japan, so he cannot count on his own party's support. The U.S. system has an unusually even division of power among the three branches of government—in contrast to the dominance of the executive branch in most other countries—with elaborate checks and balances. And the United States has a strong federal system. Thus the president may initiate a policy change only to find it challenged in court, reversed by Congress, or undermined by state governments.[66] In the paradigmatic case of reform gridlock, President Bill Clinton

64. Mulgan 2002.
65. Vogel 1994, Schwartz 1998.
66. In the language of political science, the U.S. political system has multiple "veto points."

came to power in 1993 with a powerful mandate to enact health care reform yet failed to pass it despite having a Democratic majority in Congress during his first two years in office. Many commentators lamented that this case demonstrated how the U.S. political system impedes big reforms, but others approvingly noted that this is precisely what the founders of the constitution had in mind.[67]

In Germany, the mixed electoral system has fostered coalition governments, making it impossible for any one party to impose change. The federal structure of government also gives the states (*Länder*) considerable power, especially since they are represented directly in the upper house of parliament (the Bundesrat). Business and labor are represented through peak associations at many different levels of government, ensuring that both sides have a virtual veto on policy change. The party system and the federal structure combine with powerful parapublic institutions such as the Bundesbank and the Federal Employment Office to form dense policy networks with multiple veto points and a marked bias toward incremental policy change.[68] As in Japan, there is a common perception that the postwar economic model has failed and that the government must enact major economic reforms, yet the government has been unable to forge a consensus on the substance of reform. In Germany's most blatant instance of gridlock, all parties agreed on the need for a major tax reform in the mid-1990s, yet the government could not push it through because of a split over the terms of the reform in the Bundesrat. Hans-Olaf Henkel, the outspoken leader of the German business federation (BDI), proposed reducing the power of the Bundesrat and revising the electoral system to break the reform logjam (*Reformstau*).[69]

The U.S., German, and Japanese political systems may be roughly equal in terms of the difficulty of enacting broad policy change, but the conditions for change differ considerably. In the United States, a powerful president can overcome institutional obstacles by mobilizing public support directly. In Germany, a skillful chancellor can forge bargains with coalition parties and social partners (business and labor) to push through reform. In Japan, leaders often try more subtle tactics to end-run the standard policy process. For example, they deploy foreign pressure (*gaiatsu*) or manipulate deliberative councils to increase the chances for reform or undermine resistance. Prime ministers can appoint policy councils that report directly to the cabinet rather than to a government ministry, or ministry officials can select council members favorable to reform. In fact, struggles over the arena of debate and the com-

67. Wilson 1994.
68. Webber 1992, Katzenstein 2005.
69. *Frankfurter Allgemeine Zeitung* (January 2, 1998), 43.

position of policy councils have been at the heart of the politics of reform in post-bubble Japan (Chapter 4).

The Japanese government could enact political and administrative reforms to empower top leaders and produce more majoritarian decision-making procedures, and it has taken some substantial steps in that direction. For example, it created a powerful new Cabinet Office, strengthened the Cabinet Secretariat, increased the number of politicians with ministerial portfolios, and established a Council on Economic and Fiscal Policy, which reports directly to the prime minister. T. J. Pempel argues that these reforms give the prime minister considerably more leverage to push forward his own agenda and to break through older patterns of painstaking bargaining in sectoral networks linking ministries with LDP policy specialists (*zoku*).[70] It does not follow, however, that a more powerful political leadership would be more likely to enact bold liberal economic reforms. Those who advocate reforms to the political system, such as Ozawa and Henkel, tend to assume that the newly empowered leaders would pursue the reforms they themselves endorse. In the Japanese case, strong leaders might just as easily push through misguided reforms or block reform altogether. If the Japanese people are highly ambivalent about liberal reforms, then a strong leader would be as likely to forestall reforms as to embrace them. In that case, however, the government's failure to reform would represent not a defeat of Japanese democracy but its vindication.

The argument that the Japanese political system blocks reform breaks down further when we turn to comparisons over time and across issue areas. If the Japanese political system really prevents reform, then how can we account for the government's record of substantial policy changes at important junctures throughout the postwar era? The Japanese government performed a complete turnabout in environmental policy and a major expansion of welfare policy in the early 1970s, responded decisively to the oil shock in the mid-1970s, and enacted substantial fiscal reforms and privatization in the 1980s. Gerald Curtis offers a possible answer to this puzzle, pointing to four factors that have made reform more difficult since the 1990s: the loss of a public consensus on goals, the weakening of large integrative interest groups, the decline of bureaucratic authority, and the end of LDP hegemony.[71]

That brings us to the cross-issue comparisons, for these four factors still cannot explain why the Japanese government has enacted major reforms since the 1990s in some areas but not others. After all, the Japanese government revised the electoral system in 1994 and completely reorganized the bureaucracy in 2000. It drafted a series of legal reforms with the potential to

70. Pempel forthcoming. Mulgan (2002, 177–212) is more skeptical of the impact of these reforms.
71. Curtis 1999, 25–64.

redefine the relationship between state and society, including the Administrative Procedures Act of 1994, the Information Disclosure Law of 1997, and the Non-Profit Organization Law of 1998. It enacted a wide range of policies that affect the nature of the Japanese economic model, including labor, finance, accounting, and corporate governance reforms (Chapter 4). So Japan has not failed to reform. The real puzzle concerns the substance of reform, not its scale. Why has the Japanese government enacted so much reform and yet failed to deliver on those reforms that were most critical to reviving the economy?

2. *The Japanese political system favors the concentrated interests of the few, who oppose reform, over the diffuse interests of the many, who support it.* Collective action theory might help us to move beyond the argument that the Japanese political system as a whole is incapable of reform to one that could account for the particular pattern of reform and nonreform. George Stigler, for example, has argued that a small group with high stakes in a given policy, such as producers, will press its views more effectively than a much larger group with a smaller stake, such as consumers. He builds on this logic to predict that producer interests are likely to "capture" regulatory policy.[72] We might apply this logic to Japan's dilemma by suggesting that although reform would benefit Japan as whole, it would hurt certain interest groups, and the political system favors precisely those groups most likely to oppose reform. The ruling LDP favors farmers and small businesses, which benefit from trade protection, and the ministries favor their own client industries, which benefit from anticompetitive regulation.[73]

It is true that the LDP and the ministries favor some groups over others, but this line of analysis still misses the heart of the story because it assumes that the wider public supports reforms and that narrow interests oppose them. In Japan, however, the public is highly ambivalent about many of the reforms most commonly recommended by economic experts. Those groups most likely to benefit from reforms—including competitive exporters and household consumers—oppose many of these reforms, waver on others, and cautiously support others.

3. *Japan does not want many of the proposed reforms.* This leads us to the simplest answer of all, yet one that is surprisingly absent from much of the literature on Japan's efforts to reform. Maybe Japanese politicians and bureaucrats and the Japanese people just do not want reforms that would make Japan society more competitive yet less stable or that would attack structural

---

72. Stigler 1971.
73. Much of the literature on Japanese politics stresses how the political system favors these groups. See, for example, Calder 1988, Woodall 1996.

problems at the expense of massive unemployment or other social dislocation. So there really is no puzzle here after all: why should we expect the Japanese political system to deliver reforms that the Japanese people do not want? The recognition that Japan is ambivalent about reform marks the starting point, however, not the end point for our analysis of the politics of reform. To move beyond this recognition, we must uncover the logic driving policy preferences, specify these preferences, analyze how they are aggregated by political institutions, and demonstrate how preferences and institutions combine to shape reform outcomes. The remainder of this chapter and the subsequent two chapters seek to do just that.

We must first sort out the variations in political dynamics across issue areas. Kent Calder demonstrates how Japanese politics differs between more developmental policy sectors, such as industrial policy, and more clientelistic policy sectors, such as agricultural policy.[74] More recent works offer even more fine-grained analyses about how dynamics differ across policy domains.[75] For present purposes, we can distinguish two broad categories of reform, paralleling the review of the economic debate above: measures that address specific policy failures, including adjustments in fiscal policy, monetary policy, and banking regulation; and measures that address structural inefficiencies, including labor, financial, and regulatory reforms. The former are more critical for economic recovery, yet the latter are more central to the primary theme of this book: the transformation of the Japanese economic model. The political dynamics differ as well. Macroeconomic policy and financial regulation are characterized by a more technocratic policy pattern, in which the bureaucrats' own predispositions leave an especially strong imprint on policy outcomes, while the structural reforms are characterized by more of a bargaining pattern, in which industry preferences are more critical in shaping the substance of reforms. In the following section, we review the politics behind the policy failures described earlier in this chapter, focusing on how bureaucratic ideology affected the government's initial response to the economic crisis in the early 1990s and how the relative autonomy of the bureaucracy delayed a fundamental change in course until the late 1990s and early 2000s. Then, in Chapters 3 and 4, we turn to the politics of microeconomic, or "structural," reforms.

Explaining Policy Failures

FISCAL POLICY

Why did the Japanese government fail to respond to the bursting of the bubble with the appropriate fiscal stimulus? The Japanese economy would

74. Calder 1988.
75. Muramatsu 1990, Kato 1994, Woodall 1996, Vogel 1996, Grimes 2001.

have performed better if the government had stimulated the economy sooner, more decisively, and more consistently and had targeted spending increases in those sectors with the highest potential for growth. Not only would the economy have expanded at a rate closer to its potential growth rate, but the government would have ended up with a smaller fiscal deficit. To unravel this puzzle, we must turn to the MOF itself and its ideological commitment to fiscal balance, and to the interaction between the ministry and party politicians. MOF officials have maintained a strong preference for balanced budgets throughout the postwar era.[76] They achieved this goal until the 1970s, when they confronted two challenges: slower economic growth in the wake of the oil crisis and the political entrepreneurship of Kakuei Tanaka and his LDP colleagues. Political scientists identify the 1970s as a turning point in Japanese politics when LDP policy specialists (*zoku*) began to assert greater power over the bureaucracy, often managing to exceed the ministry's budget ceilings.[77] Revenue increases slowed because of the economy while spending increases continued owing to LDP efforts, and the result was a massive fiscal deficit by the late 1970s.

The relationship between the MOF and the LDP was not a simple zero-sum contest, however, and the two managed to achieve a cooperative outcome in the 1980s. The ministry's desire to reassert fiscal balance meshed nicely with the business community's interest in limiting tax increases, and this led to an ingenious political bargain under the rubric of the Second Provisional Council on Administrative Reform (Rinchō). The Rinchō addressed a broad agenda that included fiscal rehabilitation, the privatization of public corporations, bureaucratic reorganization, and deregulation. It was most successful, however, in those areas directly related to fiscal reform: limiting government spending and privatizing public corporations. The MOF gave its support for the program in exchange for an emphasis on fiscal rehabilitation and the exclusion of finance from the deregulation agenda. The LDP, meanwhile, shifted the blame for spending limits to the Rinchō so the party would not have to pay the political price.

When MOF officials confronted the economic downturn in the early 1990s, they were naturally reluctant to use large fiscal stimulus packages because they were concerned about increasing the budget deficit, especially in light of Japan's rapidly aging population. Moreover, they were skeptical of whether these packages would deliver the intended results. As a result, the government failed to adopt an aggressive and consistent fiscal stimulus policy in the early 1990s when it would have been most effective and least costly. LDP

76. See Grimes 2001, 74–80; Amyx 2004, 124–26.
77. Satō and Matsuzaki 1986, Inoguchi and Iwai 1987.

leaders were less concerned about budgetary balance so they were more favorable toward stimulus packages, and they preferred spending increases over tax cuts because they could use public works spending to reward key constituent groups such as construction companies. MOF officials adopted a more expansive fiscal policy only in the late 1990s after milder measures had failed to bring a sustained recovery, and their success in convincing Prime Minister Ryūtarō Hashimoto to raise taxes in 1997 had turned a fragile recovery into a major recession. By the early 2000s, as noted above, the economy was weaker, the banking crisis was worse, and the budget deficit was higher, so the government faced a much trickier policy dilemma. Prime Minister Koizumi agreed with the MOF's priority for fiscal balance over stimulus and set a cap of ¥30 trillion for deficit bonds per year. With the economy weakening, however, he abandoned this target and allowed modest tax cuts beginning in 2002. Then, as the economy began to recover in 2003, the government launched extended deliberations over scaling back tax cuts and phasing in tax increases (see Chapter 4).

MONETARY POLICY

Why did the Japanese government move too slowly to lower interest rates in the early 1990s and too timidly to expand the money supply in the late 1990s? Here again, the experts disagree on how much these measures would have helped, but the evidence suggests that the Japanese economy would have performed better if the government had acted more decisively. To address this puzzle, we must turn first to the Bank of Japan itself. BOJ officials have maintained a devotion to price stability in the postwar period that rivals the MOF's commitment to fiscal balance. The Bank was generally successful in achieving this goal, and this helped to sustain sound economic growth. However, the Bank lacked independence, for the MOF oversaw it through its supervisory bureau and MOF officials alternated with BOJ officials as the Bank's governor. As a result, MOF priorities superseded Bank goals when the two conflicted, and for practical purposes this meant that the Japanese government had a bias toward monetary easing over fiscal expansion as a means of economic stimulus. William Grimes argues that Bank officials acted against their own better judgment and clear economic signals from mid-1987 through May 1989 because MOF officials pressured them to stick with easy money policy.[78]

When the bubble burst, therefore, Bank officials moved too slowly and too gradually to lower interest rates. Then, when they did lower rates to near zero,

78. Grimes 2001, 2–5.

they still remained bound by their postwar fixation with combating inflation, so they had a tendency to overestimate the risk that further monetary expansion (quantitative easing) could set off inflation—even though by that point deflation was the greater threat to Japan's prosperity. In 1997 the Bank of Japan won greater independence from the MOF. Yet this only compounded Japan's problems because the Bank used its newfound independence to fight off pressures for more aggressive monetary expansion. Although the Bank maintained low interest rates and engaged in some quantitative easing after gaining independence, Bank officials felt that they did not have the means to go further and stressed that monetary expansion would have limited impact in the absence of more fundamental banking reform. Then they raised interest rates slightly in 2000, sending a strong negative signal to the marketplace, in turn forcing them to reverse course in 2001. Meanwhile, the Bank under Governor Masaru Hayami engaged in a costly policy stalemate with the FSA, insisting that it would not engage in greater monetary expansion unless the FSA tackled the nonperforming loan problem more aggressively. Governor Toshihiko Fukui was more effective than his predecessor in communicating expectations to the market and in cooperating with the MOF and the FSA, and he pursued more aggressive quantitative easing, with positive results.

BANKING REGULATION

Why did the Japanese government take so long to respond effectively to the banking crisis? The political dynamics behind Japan's distinctive response to the banking crisis are even more complex than its macroeconomic policies, in some ways falling between the more technocratic policy process in fiscal and monetary policy and the more political bargaining process characteristic of other structural reforms. Jennifer Amyx takes up this particular puzzle and concludes that ministry-centered networks that had performed well during much of the postwar era became dysfunctional by the 1990s. She points to two factors in explaining this shift: the information requirements for effective financial regulation grew as the finance business became more complex, so the MOF's traditional approach of informal relations-based regulation became outmoded, and the networks themselves became unstable with party realignment and coalition government in the 1990s, so the ministry was forced to focus more on defending itself from political attack than managing the banking crisis.[79] She is certainly right that financial regulation became more complicated, but this does not explain either the emergence of the finance crisis (which was more a result of macroeconomic policy failure and the bubble economy, as discussed above) or the government's response to it (see

79. Amyx 2004.

below). She is likewise correct that party politics shifted after 1993 and that this played a role in the debates over reorganizing the ministry. If the ministry had not been challenged, however, it might have proceeded with its initial approach to managing the financial crisis even longer and delayed the shift to a more effective policy even further.

I propose a simpler explanation for our puzzle: MOF officials were committed to a particular mode of banking regulation that had served them well in the past, so they were naturally slow to change their ways in the face of new challenges. Moreover, the ministry's relative insulation from political pressures allowed it to stay the course longer, until the crisis finally grew out of hand and politicians intervened. Under the postwar regulatory regime, controlled deposit interest rates (described above) allowed the ministry to allocate credit to favored sectors and permitted banks to earn stable profits from the steady margins between deposit interest rates and lending rates. The ministry had enormous leverage over the banks because it licensed new branches and regulated banks' activities, and the banks' fortunes hinged on their ability to expand their deposit base by building up their branch networks. Ministry officials regulated with a heavy hand to minimize the chances of banking failure. When they discovered that a bank was in trouble, they would downplay or even hide the problem for fear that public disclosure might lead to a run on the bank. They would work closely with the bank to alleviate the problem, helping the bank to conceal the problem and offering regulatory breaks as necessary. And if this was not sufficient, they would mobilize affiliated financial institutions to bail out the bank. In this way, the ministry was able to maintain financial system stability without relying on a large deposit insurance fund or resorting to the use of public funds to bail out banks. Under this model, not a single bank failed from World War II through the mid-1990s.

When confronted with the banking crisis in the 1990s, MOF officials naturally turned first to the regulatory model that had worked so well in the past. They were slow to recognize how circumstances had changed and to adjust their approach accordingly. To make matters worse, they misjudged the economic situation, assuming that an imminent recovery would boost the stock market and strengthen the financial institutions.[80] They helped financial institutions to conceal their problems, offered regulatory breaks, and supported the low-interest-rate policy in part because it allowed financial institutions to increase lending margins and thereby bolster profits.[81] They actively sought to organize mergers to achieve the orderly consolidation of

---

80. Also see Fukao 2002 and Muramatsu and Yanagikawa 2002.
81. See Amyx 2004, 150–52, for details.

the industry they had been trying to impose for decades. Ironically, of course, in striving so hard to protect the financial sector, the ministry nearly destroyed it.

As the economy weakened, however, the banking crisis grew beyond the ability of the authorities to manage with their traditional approach. They could not orchestrate private-sector bailouts because the stronger banks were no longer able to bail out the weak ones. Their efforts to downplay the problem backfired because market players already recognized the gravity of the situation. Their record of never using public funds to rescue banks came to haunt them, as the public opposed any form of taxpayer-funded bailout. And the postwar regime had relied so heavily on the ministry's own prestige and authority that when the ministry itself failed, market players lost confidence in the entire financial system. Given the scale of the crisis, the financial authorities should have adopted the approach that had succeeded elsewhere, one that cuts against the very grain of MOF tradition. This would have meant publicly disclosing the full scale of the problem, using public funds to recapitalize the banks, creating a new debt-collection agency to buy up the bad loans from the banks and then sell them off in the market, and pressing the banks to write off or sell off their bad loans in an efficient manner. The situation reached a crisis with the failure of Hokkaido Takushoku and Yamaichi Securities in 1997, and at that point the politicians finally became more involved and the ministry began to change its stance. Under the "Financial Diet" of 1998, the government reorganized the MOF itself, creating the Financial Services Agency; shifted to a more rules-based regulatory regime; and injected public funds into the banking system. The FSA under Takenaka pressed the banks harder, as noted above, and the government finally brought the crisis under control by 2005.

To understand the politics of reform, therefore, we must break down the question into two parts, along the lines outlined above. If we want to know why the Japanese government made critical errors in fiscal policy, monetary policy, and banking regulation, then we must begin with the bureaucrats who oversee these policies and whose ideologies inform the substance of these policies. If we want to understand the politics shaping those reforms with the greatest potential to alter Japan's economic model—including labor market reforms, financial market reforms, and other regulatory reforms—then we must look to industry preferences about the substance of these reforms and how these preferences are aggregated by industry associations, political parties, and government ministries.

3 POLICY
REFORM
JAPANESE
STYLE

Japanese opinion leaders have called for drastic liberal reforms since the economy faltered in the 1990s, and yet Japan has not embraced the liberal market model.[1] Why not? To address this puzzle, let us begin with the popular image of "two Japans": one made up of highly competitive export firms, primarily in manufacturing, and the other populated by inefficient protected domestic firms, primarily in services.[2] The former comprise the potential winners from liberalization while the latter comprise the potential losers. Thus the political battle pits the winners, who favor reform, against the losers, who oppose it.

The two-Japans thesis misses the actual political dynamics in two ways: it misjudges the policy preferences of societal actors, and it misinterprets how these preferences are aggregated in the political arena. In Japan, even the winners do not fully advocate liberal market reforms. Those groups with the greatest apparent stake in liberalization, such as large manufacturing exporters, are reluctant to embrace reforms that might undermine long-term relations with workers, financial institutions, other business partners, and the government. By analyzing the dynamics underlying these partnerships, we not only grasp why the winners are ambivalent about many reforms but understand their positions on specific reform issues. We can explain why they favor some reform measures and oppose others and why they seek to impose particular conditions on reform. In this way, we can begin to explain the substance of reform. Furthermore, those actors who favor liberal reforms cannot forge a strong political coalition because the major industry associations and political parties incorporate both the potential winners and the potential losers from reform. The associations and the parties must work out internal compromises between constituent groups before proposing reforms. As a result, Japan winds up with a distinctive pattern of reform. Japanese government officials proceed with reforms slowly and cautiously; they

---

1. This chapter builds on Vogel 1999b.
2. *Business Week* cover story on "Two Japans," January 27, 1997; Tanaka 1997; Katz 1998.

package delicate compromises, including considerable compensation for those who might be disadvantaged by the reforms; they design reforms to preserve the core institutions of the model as much as possible; and they seek novel ways to build on the strengths of these models.

Industry Preferences

We return here to the model introduced in Chapter 1 (Figure 4): Japan's competitive firms derive comparative institutional advantage from the micro-institutions of Japanese capitalism, such as the labor relations and financial systems, so they must weigh the expected efficiency gains from liberal reforms against the potential costs of undermining these institutions. Therefore, they are much less favorable toward these reforms than they would be in the absence of such institutions and are more favorable toward reforms designed to preserve or reinforce these institutions.

All else being equal, for example, competitive firms should favor reforms to make labor markets operate more efficiently because this would give them access to better workers at a lower cost. They should advocate financial and corporate governance reforms designed to make equity markets operate more efficiently because this would reduce financing costs and stimulate financial innovation. And they should favor deregulation because they would benefit from lower costs for communications, transport, energy, and distribution. In the specific context of Japan, however, all else is not equal.

If Japan's competitive exporters are not staunch supporters of liberal reform, we cannot be sure whether this is because they do not favor these reforms or because they simply refrain from publicly advocating them. In the language of the model from Chapter 1, we cannot be sure whether these firms are operating within the second circle of rationality, judging that these reforms might undermine their comparative institutional advantage, or the third, fearing that advocating these reforms might strain social or political relationships. We can identify industry associations' declared policy positions, but these "revealed" preferences may or may not reflect underlying industry preferences.[3] However, the evidence suggests that both mechanisms are in place. That is, Japan's competitive firms are ambivalent about liberal reform *and* they are reluctant to articulate any preference for liberal reform in the political arena. In any case, both mechanisms are consistent with the argument presented here, for they modify pressures for liberal reform.

3. Political scientists generally deal with the problem of revealed versus actual preferences in one of two ways: they side-step the problem by deducing preferences from theory, or they use empirical research to specify preferences as accurately as possible. See Frieden 1999 for the case for the former approach and Vogel 1999a for the case for the latter.

Even when Japanese firms favor certain liberal reforms, that is, they may be reluctant to take a public stand for fear of undermining close long-term relationships with workers, financial institutions, other firms, and the government. They will not advocate liberalization when they judge that such a view could invite retaliation or otherwise jeopardize beneficial economic or political relationships. A Nippon Life executive recalls how his firm refrained from demanding the liberalization of brokerage commissions despite the fact that it was losing huge sums by paying exorbitant commission fees. Company executives feared that if they took a stand, then others might retaliate by advocating the liberalization of insurance commissions.[4] Likewise, Mark Elder argues that Japanese exporters have tolerated trade protection for intermediate-goods industries, even though this substantially increased their costs, because they themselves benefited from government protection and/or promotion, and they were linked to intermediate-goods producers directly through business relationships and indirectly through common links to banks, trading companies, and MITI.[5]

Corporations also mute their demands for reform to preserve good working relations with government ministries. When the government was working on legislation to liberalize the market for value-added network (VAN) services, for example, many of the would-be VAN service providers sided with the more modest approach of the Ministry of Posts and Telecommunications (MPT) instead of MITI's more liberal proposal. They realized that they would soon come under MPT's jurisdiction, and they did not want to alienate their future regulator.[6]

Consumers

We have focused thus far on industry preferences, but one would expect consumers to advocate liberal market reforms as well. After all, many economists argue that consumers are the ultimate beneficiaries of liberalization.[7] Yet Japanese consumers and consumer groups do not hold the expected preferences for liberalization. They value social stability, product safety, and/or environmental protection over economic efficiency, and they sympathize with producer groups such as farmers and retailers.[8]

Japan's postwar economic system fundamentally favored producers over consumers. The financial system shifted resources from consumers to producers by maintaining deposit interest rates below market levels. Trade barriers

4. Interview, August 1991.
5. Elder 1998.
6. Vogel 1996, 146–50.
7. Itō 1992.
8. This section builds on Vogel 1999a.

allowed domestic producers to maintain higher prices and prevented consumers from purchasing cheaper and/or better products from abroad. Weak
enforcement of and bountiful exemptions to antitrust laws permitted price
cartels and other forms of collusion between producers. A wide range of
economic regulations impeded competition, bolstered corporate profits, and
increased price levels in sectors as diverse as retail and construction. According to standard economic theory, each of these features implies a substantial
welfare loss for consumers. Yet Japanese consumers and consumer groups
have not advocated liberalization; indeed, they have often strongly opposed
it.

Japanese consumer groups have vocally opposed agricultural liberalization, for example, one policy change that could substantially improve their
economic welfare. They cite three primary concerns: liberalization would
undermine food self-sufficiency, increase the risk of contamination or disease,
and threaten the livelihood of farmers.[9] It is tempting to conclude that the
consumer groups must have been misrepresenting consumers at large, yet
public opinion polls throughout the 1980s and 1990s show that consumers
supported this position.[10] Consumer groups have also reinforced trade protection by demanding tough regulatory standards that effectively discriminate
against imports.[11] Japanese consumer groups have been more ambivalent on
regulatory reform, but they certainly have not rallied to the cause.[12] Consumer groups have even resisted retail deregulation, arguing that price is not
everything and that deregulation would not only hurt small retailers but
perhaps wipe out entire neighborhood shopping districts.[13] Although consumers themselves have not embraced deregulation, other groups have
increasingly stepped in to articulate what consumers *should* want. Economic
journalists, economists (especially U.S.-trained economists), discount retailers, and U.S. negotiators have all heralded deregulation in the name of

9. Shōhisha Dantai Rengōkai 1987, 132–35; *Kokumin Seikatsu Kenkyū* (March 1996),
55–56.

10. For example, Prime Minister's Office surveys in 1978, 1981, 1987, 1993, 1997, and 2000
revealed strong support for food self-sufficiency even if it meant higher prices (Prime
Minister's Office 1988; *Nikkei Weekly*, March 31, 1997, 7; Prime Minister's Office 2000). In
the 2000 survey, 84.2 percent of respondents favored self-sufficiency—for all foods (43.6
percent), or at least for staple foods such as rice (40.6 percent)—even if it meant higher
prices, and only 10.5 percent favored importing if that were cheaper.

11. D. Vogel 1992.

12. Administrative Reform Committee (1996, 300–364) records consumer positions on
specific regulatory issues. Uchihashi (1995) articulates many consumer concerns, and
Takeuchi (1990) presents one prominent consumer activist's perspective.

13. In one survey, for example, 40.9 percent of respondents disagreed with U.S. government claims that retail deregulation would help consumers while only 35.5 percent agreed
(*Yomiuri Shimbun*, May 4, 1990).

Japanese consumers.[14] Consumer groups have gradually softened their opposition to deregulation since the mid-1990s, as they witnessed how some liberalization measures brought real benefits to consumers. They now stress that they welcome some relaxation of economic regulation, such as price and entry controls, as long as it does not undermine social regulation such as health, safety, and environmental codes. Even so, the consumers themselves remain indifferent. "The people are not going around shouting 'banzai' because taxi fares have gone down by ¥100," laments Yoshihiko Miyauchi, who served as chair of the Deregulation Subcommittee (see Chapter 4), "so there is no voice in favor of deregulation."[15]

Japanese consumer groups' distinctive policy preferences are rooted in their history. Through mobilization, war, and recovery, consumer groups sacrificed their own self-interest for the cause of national economic strength. They actively collaborated with the government in national campaigns to *suppress* consumption (to generate savings for industrial investment) and to buy Japanese products.[16] Most consumer groups allied in one way or another with farm groups, trade unions, the traditional leftist opposition parties, and/ or environmental groups. Many of the local chapters of consumer organizations still work directly with farm groups today, especially the farmers' cooperatives, and thus feel bound by mutual ties of obligation. In fact, a substantial proportion of consumer groups are actually producer groups at the same time.[17] Ultimately, the consumer groups' allegiance with farmers and workers is not simply a matter of reciprocal alliances but also one of identity. Japanese are less likely than Americans to distinguish their identity as consumers from their identity as producers. Many of the consumer groups themselves have embraced the concept of *seikatsusha*, literally "lifestyle person," which fuses the notion of consumer with that of worker and citizen.[18] In addition, consumers see "weak" groups such as farmers and workers as their allies, and "strong" groups such as big businesses and foreign governments as their adversaries. In fact, they often use the very language of weak versus strong to justify their policy positions. They contend that trade liberalization and deregulation, for example, merely serve to promote the interests of the strong at the expense of the weak. And if that is the case, then they would prefer to side with the weak. In contrast, U.S. consumer groups such as Nader's Raiders were

14. Itō 1992, Nakatani and Ōta 1994.
    15. Interview with Yoshihiko Miyauchi, Chairman and CEO, ORIX Corporation, June 18, 2003.
    16. Garon 1997.
    17. Cabinet Office, Quality-of-Life Policy Bureau, 2002.
    18. Maclachlan 2002, 78–83.

instrumental in launching the deregulation movement in the 1970s, and other U.S. groups have actively supported trade liberalization.[19]

Industry Associations

Some Japanese firms advocate liberal reform, but the institutional context of Japanese capitalism means that fewer firms advocate it than one would otherwise expect and those firms that do advocate it are more ambivalent. Moreover, these preferences are aggregated in a manner that *further* moderates demands for liberal reform. The major industry associations and political parties represent both the advocates and opponents of reform, so they do not push for the all-out victory of one side but rather arrange careful compromises between the two. If anything, they tend to favor the potential losers from liberal reform.

On the surface, the most powerful industry federation in Japan, the Japan Business Federation (Nippon Keidanren) appears to represent competitive rather than protected sectors and to advocate bold liberal reform. Nippon Keidanren is the product of the 2002 merger between the Federation of Economic Organizations (Keidanren) and the Japan Federation of Employers' Associations (Nikkeiren). Even before the merger, however, Keidanren was stymied by internal dissension, preventing it from putting forth a unified voice. Keidanren was more effective in pursuing positions with uniform support from the entire business community, such as lowering corporate taxes, than in brokering disputes among its own ranks on more contentious issues, such as regulatory reform. It was unable to speak with a single voice on energy deregulation, for example, because it relied so strongly on the energy sector for its own finances. The petroleum industry association, which not coincidentally is located in the Keidanren headquarters building, forced Keidanren to drop oil from its widely publicized deregulation proposal of November 1994. Financial institutions pushed Keidanren to qualify its support for financial reforms, and Nippon Telegraph and Telephone (NTT) constrained Keidanren from pressing for the reduction of interconnection charges in the telecommunications sector.[20]

Before the merger, Nikkeiren took the lead on employment and social issues. Because Nikkeiren worked closely with the unions, it went to great lengths to frame reform proposals in a manner acceptable to workers. In the

---

19. Derthick and Quirk 1985, 40–45.

20. Yoshimatsu (2000, especially 160–200) contends that Keidanren has taken a fairly clear and consistent stance in favor of deregulation, although he notes some exceptions (176). I would argue, however, that he exaggerates Keidanren's support for deregulation, which has been more reluctant than proactive, more formalistic than substantive, and more selective than comprehensive.

late 1990s, Nikkeiren chairman and Toyota Motors president Hiroshi Okuda launched a personal campaign to defend the Japanese model of labor relations from its detractors, extolling the virtue of employers' long-term commitment to their workers. "The first thing American companies do when they restructure is to lay off workers, but Japanese companies avoid this if at all possible," he insists. "This may compromise efficiency in the short term, but it benefits companies over the long run."[21]

Keidanren and Nikkeiren merged to streamline their activities and lower operating costs, with Okuda taking over as the inaugural chairman. The new organization represents an even broader segment of industry than the original Keidanren, since Keidanren's membership was limited to large companies whereas Nikkeiren included smaller company members as well. Hence Nippon Keidanren has found it even more difficult to overcome internal cleavages on reform issues, such as Prime Minister Koizumi's proposal for reforming Japan's special public corporations (Chapter 4).

One might expect sectoral associations representing competitive exporters to be freer to articulate positions favoring reform. Yet even at this level, most major industry associations in Japan incorporate groups both favoring and opposing reform. For example, the Electronic Industry Association of Japan has difficulty resolving differences among its members. "Our industry is not that heavily regulated, but we do have some regulated areas, such as radio, medical instruments, and cable television and broadcasting," reports association official Kazuaki Ogasawara. "So we leave deregulation up to Keidanren."[22]

The Chambers of Commerce (both local chambers and the national federation) are the primary advocates for small businesses. Their members include large companies, yet they almost always aggregate preferences in favor of the smaller businesses. "On retail deregulation, we represent both sides: big stores and small ones," explains Japanese Chamber president Shōichi Tanimura. "But we do not have any major disagreements because the strong ones accept that they must consider the situation of the weak."[23] The chambers are extremely powerful, especially at the local level, with strong ties to the LDP. Thus, to the extent that Nippon Keidanren advocates liberal reform, albeit moderate reform, it is offset by a politically privileged small business lobby.

Frieden and Rogowski suggest that there also may be a divergence of interest between unions in the competitive sector, which favor liberalization, and those in the protected sector, which oppose it. That is, there might be greater harmony of interests between employers and unions within the competitive

21. Interview, June 18, 2003.
22. Interview, February 27, 1997.
23. Interview, June 10, 1998.

sector (a cross-class alliance) than between unions in the two sectors.[24] In Japan, however, there are cross-class alliances to *defend* the labor relations or welfare systems but not to advocate liberalization, because unions in the competitive sector are reluctant to advocate liberalization at the expense of their brethren in the protected sector. The automobile, electronics, and steel unions recognize that they stand to benefit from more competition in service industries, yet they hesitate to take a strong stand politically because they are bound to unions in protected sectors. "We favor deregulation," reports Rikio Kōzu of the Federation of Nippon Steel Workers' Unions, "but we still have to get along with our friends in the electricity industry unions."[25] Rengō and other large union federations incorporate both the competitive and protected sectors, so they must resolve this conflict in-house. "When there is a conflict," stresses Tsuyoshi Takagi, president of the textile union federation (Zensen), "we try to determine which group has a more reasonable argument and which group has a more difficult situation. And we give preference to the group with the tougher situation."[26]

Political Parties

During its period of hegemony (1955–93), the LDP enjoyed unusually broad support from a coalition spanning both the competitive and protected sectors, so it tried to avoid policies that would blatantly sacrifice one part of the coalition in favor of another. As noted in Chapter 2, the party satisfied big business with a high-growth economic strategy while compensating specific constituent groups, notably farmers and small businesses. The LDP is not a "liberal" party in the classical sense of the word: it is considerably less likely than its U.S. or British counterparts to embrace liberal economic policies.[27] In part, this reflects the party's recognition of the industry preferences and industry association positions outlined above. In addition, the protected sector of the Japanese economy is larger than that of the United States or Britain and is especially powerful politically.[28] So the LDP represents both advocates and opponents of liberal reform.

Prime Minister Ryūtarō Hashimoto promoted broad-based reform from 1996 through 1998, but in practice he made the most progress on a limited

24. Frieden and Rogowski 1996. Kume (1998) makes this case for Japan, arguing that competitive and protected-sector unions differ considerably.

25. Interview, February 26, 1997.

26. Interview, June 16, 1998.

27. Kitschelt 2003.

28. The groups that oppose liberal reform—farmers, workers, and protected businesses—offer more reliable financial and electoral support than those that advocate it. They are more likely to vote than other groups and less likely to change party affiliation (Bullock 2000).

agenda that focused on financial and administrative reform (Chapter 4). His successors, Keizō Obuchi and Yoshirō Mori, considerably slowed the pace. Obuchi primarily used fiscal stimuli to prop up the economy, and Mori stressed reforms to promote the information technology sector. Meanwhile, Kabun Mutō, who had previously overseen the deregulation program as director-general of the Management and Coordination Agency (MCA), forged a group of 150 LDP Diet members to block deregulation in politically sensitive sectors such as retail. "In principle I believe in reducing economic regulation," asserts Mutō, "but we must protect health and safety. We have a dual structure in our economy, with smaller businesses playing an important role, so we need to keep them strong. Complete liberalization would put them out of business, and I do not want to go that far."[29]

Junichirō Koizumi took over as prime minister in 2001, pledging to enact bold economic reform without protecting any sacred cows. Koizumi rose to power in an unusual way, building on his popularity among rank-and-file party members to force the party to nominate him. He turned the public's frustration with the LDP into an asset, publicly criticizing his own party's political machine and vowing fundamental reforms. Ironically, he was so successful with this political strategy that he saved the party from certain defeat in the 2001 Upper House elections. Koizumi made "structural reforms," including postal reform and privatization of special public corporations, a priority during his administration, yet he was forced to compromise with his LDP colleagues on the substance of these reforms (see Chapter 4). The opposition Democratic Party was stunned, meanwhile, because Koizumi had adopted many of their reform proposals as his own. The LDP has a long history of preempting opposition policy proposals to maintain power.[30]

Koizumi took the strategy of saving the LDP by attacking it to new heights in the September 2005 Lower House elections when he banished members of the party's old guard who had voted against his postal privatization bill. Many of these "rebels" proceeded to run in the election as independents or members of new parties, but Koizumi selected his own candidates—the so-called assassins—to run against them. The assassins prevailed in fourteen of the thirty-three head-to-head contests in single-member districts. Koizumi successfully framed the postal bill as a litmus test for reform and portrayed the opposition Democratic Party of Japan (Minshutō) as being opposed to reform. This was particularly audacious given that the population remained ambivalent about the merits of postal privatization, the privatization bill had already been watered down through compromises with LDP opponents, Koizumi's own

29. Interview, April 4, 2002.
30. Curtis 1988.

record of economic reform was mixed at best, and the DPJ actually had bolder and more specific proposals for reforms in other areas. The strategy worked brilliantly, nonetheless, as the LDP won an outright majority of 296 seats and a two-thirds majority of 327 seats with its partner, the Kōmeitō. The LDP emerged from this victory more unified because it had purged some of the prime minister's most ardent opponents, and the newly elected representatives owed their success to the prime minister and the party more than to longstanding personal support organizations. The election did not substantially improve the prospects for liberal economic reform beyond postal privatization, however, because the Japanese public remained ambivalent about these reforms and the LDP still incorporated a broad spectrum of views, from true liberal reformers to opponents who simply voted for the postal bill to follow the party line.

The LDP also remained constrained from pursuing liberal reforms by its coalition partner. The Kōmeitō, which is associated with the Sōka Gakkai, a popular Buddhist sect, stresses "humanitarian" economic policies, including expanding the social safety net, strengthening support for small businesses, and increasing social regulation.

During the period of LDP hegemony, the opposition parties distinguished themselves from the LDP by pressing for more protection and more regulation, not less. Since 1993, new opposition parties have emerged that could represent those groups, such as consumers and exporters, whose interests in liberalization were not represented by the LDP and the traditional opposition parties. Furthermore, the Diet changed the Lower House electoral system in 1994 to one purported to give parties greater incentive to differentiate themselves along policy lines. It replaced the old multimember district (or single nontransferable vote) system with a combination of three hundred single-member districts and two hundred proportional representation seats in eleven regional blocs.[31] Some of the new parties have indeed tried to portray themselves as proponents of small government, yet none of them has been able to break free from reliance on support from protected sectors of society.

The DJP represents an awkward union of politicians of diverse origins, ranging from economic liberals (including Ozawa) to former socialists. Naoto Kan, who was party president in 1998–99 and 2002–4, stresses that Japan needs to spend more on social services, not less. "We want to help people feel better about the future, especially old people," he declares. "This means pensions, health care, and nursing care."[32] Yukio Hatoyama, party leader from 1999 to 2002, notes that the party distinguishes itself from the

31. The number of proportional representation seats was later reduced to 180.
32. Interview, August 8, 2000.

LDP not by pushing for bolder liberalization but by advocating government intervention to ease economic adjustment. "The LDP advocates deregulation as well, so people ask us how we are different," explains Hatoyama, "and we say that we stress employment adjustment and creating new jobs."[33] "Politics should not intervene in the market, because a strong economy depends on free competition," remarks Katsuya Okada, who succeeded Kan as party president in 2004. "The role of politics is to moderate the economic inequality that arises from this competition. We do not advocate a U.S.-style bipolarized society."[34] Even Tetsundo Iwakuni, a former Merrill Lynch executive who represents the wealthy residential area of Setagaya in Tokyo, sees little merit in touting the liberal cause: "The people do not want to move from a world of low risk and low return to a world of high risk and high return. So I do not get any votes by walking around championing deregulation."[35] In practice, the party struggled to differentiate itself from the LDP after Koizumi endorsed his structural reform program. The party issued campaign manifestos for the November 2003 Lower House and July 2004 Upper House elections which outlined specific policy proposals, but it was not able to position itself clearly as either a more economically liberal or a more progressive alternative to the LDP. Even so, the party made impressive gains in both elections, largely at the expense of the smaller opposition parties. After the party's humiliating defeat in the 2005 Lower House elections, however, DPJ members began to rethink their political strategy. Party president Seiji Maehara appointed a younger shadow cabinet, distanced the party further from labor unions, and vowed to assert stronger leadership in devising the party's policy platform.

The Bureaucracy

Like the political parties, government ministries are simultaneously proponents and opponents of liberal reforms. In general, they favor deregulation in areas outside their own jurisdiction. Even within their jurisdiction, they are more zealous in trying to shape the substance of reform than in trying to stop it altogether. The Cabinet Office and the Ministry of Internal Affairs and Communications (MIC) serve as the coordinators for regulatory reforms, but they must constantly negotiate with the individual ministries.[36] The Fair Trade Commission (FTC) has attempted to take advantage of the reformist mood of the 1990s to strengthen antitrust policy and has made influential proposals on issues such as breaking up Nippon Telegraph and Telephone and

33. Interview, June 17, 1998; Hatoyama 1996.
34. Interview, April 1, 2002.
35. Interview, June 12, 1998.
36. The Management and Coordination Agency played this role until 2000, when it was folded into the MIC.

lifting the ban on holding companies. It is notoriously weak politically, however, and its jurisdiction is limited to matters of competition policy. The Foreign Ministry supports trade liberalization and deregulation to ease Japan's relations with the United States and other trading partners but defers to the Ministry of Economy, Trade, and Industry (METI, formerly MITI) and the other regulatory ministries on specific issues. Among the regulatory ministries, METI has taken the strongest stand in favor of selective liberal reforms. METI lacks credibility as a lead reformer, however, because it represents constituencies on both sides: competitive sectors, such as autos and electronics, and protected sectors, such as energy and retail.[37] And METI's own organization—with a combination of functional and industry bureaus and a coordinating secretariat—facilitates the internal balancing of these interests and the structuring of bargains across industries.[38]

The regulatory ministries have overseen their own bargains between the industry players within their jurisdictions. The Ministry of Finance, for example, presided over a complex regulatory regime under which it assigned specific rights and duties to different types of financial institutions, such as securities houses, insurance companies, and various kinds of banks. Long-term credit banks provided long-term financing for industry, enjoyed the exclusive privilege of issuing bank debentures, and endured a prohibition on accepting retail deposits and strict limits on building new branches. The city banks could not issue bank debentures but could accept retail deposits and set up more branches. This pact between the ministry, the long-term credit banks, and the city banks was embedded in a larger bargain between banks and securities houses, and that sectoral bargain was in turn embedded in a broader political settlement between big business, small business, and farmers.

Given the embedded nature of these sectoral bargains, liberalization requires a complex process of renegotiation. The government ministries often take the lead in this process. They can serve as effective brokers between industry actors because jurisdiction over a given sector rarely shifts to another ministry or branch of government. Ministry officials manipulate the balance of power in this process by determining the representation of societal groups in policy councils (shingikai).[39] They structure policy change in a way that respects the norms of fairness and balance between societal players, incorporating the potential losers from policy change into the process of reform itself. Although the potential losers cannot always block reform, they can strongly influence its substance. Typically, they gain compensation in the form of

37. *Nikkei Business* (October 24, 1994), 14–18.
38. Elder 1998.
39. See Schwartz 1998.

strategic delays plus government support to help them prepare for greater competition.

In renegotiating sectoral bargains, the ministries do not simply allocate resources according to the relative political power of the constituent industries but pursue their own agendas at the same time. They try to promote their views of the national interest, facilitate their own functional responsibilities, and preserve their own power. They tend to see the national interest in terms of long-term growth over short-term efficiency, and social stability over competition as a goal in and of itself. Ministry officials have even been known to ask industry associations to withdraw their support for deregulation when it might undermine other goals. One auto industry lobbyist reports, "Ministry officials will say things like: 'Now, would you really like the union to know that you are asking us to reduce worker safety regulation?'"[40] Ministry officials are especially concerned with how policy change in one area might affect other policies within their jurisdiction. MOF officials, for example, carefully considered how financial reform proposals would affect the ministry's ability to service the national debt.[41] Japanese bureaucrats have resisted the devolution of authority to independent regulatory agencies, have guarded their discretion in implementing policy, and have designed reforms to maintain some leverage over industry.[42]

Reform American Style

We can better understand what is distinctive about the Japanese pattern of reform by placing it in a comparative context: contrasting it with the U.S. approach and comparing it with the German one.[43] The U.S. experience differs with respect to both process and outcome. In the United States, corporations have aggressively pursued liberalization through challenges in the marketplace, in the courts, and through political channels; industry associations generally have not forged compromises with reform opponents; the Republican Party has promoted a bold liberal reform agenda; and the Democratic Party has supported liberal reforms in selected areas. As a result, the U.S. government has moved much further than Japan with liberal reforms. Here we briefly review the U.S. experience with policy reforms, highlighting the same features examined in the Japanese case: industry preferences; the aggregation of those interests via industry associations, political parties, and the bureaucracy; and the pattern of reform outcomes. We survey reforms in

40. Interview with Mamoru Hoshino, Coordinator-in-Chief, Japan Automobile Manufacturers Association (JAMA), March 27, 2002.
41. See Mabuchi 1994.
42. Vogel 1996, 207–11.
43. This section builds in part on Vogel 1996, 217–30.

several of the issue areas—economic regulation, finance, corporate governance, labor, and welfare—that we cover in more detail in the next chapter with reference to Japan.

The Frieden-Rogowski model (see Chapter 1) works better for liberal market economies such as the United States and Britain because firms in these countries rely less on long-term relationships with workers, banks, and other businesses for their competitive advantage and more on flexible labor markets and sophisticated capital markets. As Desmond King and Stewart Wood demonstrate, the micrologic of industry preferences in the liberal market economies differs from that of the coordinated market economies. Because firms compete more on the basis of cost and less on quality, they advocate market liberalization and other policies designed to lower costs. And because firms rely less on coordination with other firms or the government, they do not tend to support policies to cultivate, preserve, or strengthen institutions that foster such coordination.[44]

Moreover, the U.S. political system is not characterized by the corporatist bargaining patterns of Japan. The United States has powerful industry lobby groups, but they are much more fragmented than their Japanese counterparts, and they are not systematically incorporated into the policy process through regularized channels. U.S. corporations are more likely to lobby on their own, to form new lobby groups and disband others, and to put together ad hoc coalitions to promote specific reforms.[45] So industry groups favoring liberal reforms are better able to promote reform without having to make concessions to dissenters within their midst.

The Republican Party has a stronger commitment to liberal economic policies than the LDP and less commitment to protecting societal actors from market competition. Republican president Ronald Reagan launched a neoliberal offensive in the 1980s, and his successors have continued in the same direction. The U.S. Democratic Party also differs from its Japanese namesake in that it has supported deregulation and trade liberalization. Senator Edward Kennedy and President Jimmy Carter were early proponents of the deregulation movement, and President Bill Clinton actively promoted trade liberalization. Unlike their Japanese counterparts, U.S. cabinet departments are not linked into tight networks of coordination with industry so they have not tried to protect such relationships from liberal reform.[46] In addition, the fragmented nature of the U.S. political system makes the reform process more uneven and less coherent. Decisions are more likely to proceed in fits and

44. King and Wood 1999.
45. D. Vogel 1989; Lehne 2001, 115–33.
46. The Department of Defense represents a partial exception.

starts, with the primary decision-making arena shifting among the regulatory agencies, Congress, and the courts and between the federal and state levels. This political structure has facilitated some pro-competitive reforms because firms wishing to challenge the status quo have multiple avenues for appeal whereas opponents cannot easily reverse decisions to allow more competition in a given market.

Japan has not converged on the U.S. model in part because the U.S. model itself has been a moving target. While Japan has been cautiously experimenting with some liberal reforms, the United States has been surging forward more boldly.[47] Statistical indices of economic liberalization are certainly not perfect indicators of liberal reform, but the available studies suggest that the gap between Japan and the United States has been widening, not narrowing. The Fraser Institute finds that "economic freedom" actually declined in Japan from 1990 to 2002 while it rose slightly in Germany and more substantially in the United States (and from a higher base than Germany).[48] The Heritage Foundation reports that economic freedom dropped substantially in Japan from 1995 to 2005 while it increased in the United States and Germany.[49]

With respect to regulatory reform, for example, the U.S. government launched the global deregulation movement in the mid-1970s, when Senator Kennedy and others began to herald the cause in congressional hearings. Kennedy began with the airlines, but the movement quickly spread to other areas including trucking and energy. Ronald Reagan made deregulation a pillar of his supply-side economic program and extended reform beyond economic regulation to social regulation as well. President George H. W. Bush was accused by die-hard Reaganites of permitting creeping reregulation, but his Council on Competitiveness pushed for regulatory relief and he declared a three-month moratorium on new regulations in early 1992—just in time for the reelection campaign. Bill Clinton, who defeated Bush, asked Vice President Albert Gore to run a program to "Reinvent Government" by streamlining regulatory procedures and cutting red tape. Then, in February 1995, the new Republican majority in the House raised the ante, declaring a moratorium on new regulations for the rest of the year and passing a bill to subject new regulations to strict risk-assessment and cost-benefit tests and to give regulated firms the right to sue if these tests were not properly conducted. The George W. Bush administration has focused on easing the burden on businesses from

47. King and Wood 1999; Schmidt 2000. For data demonstrating the nonconvergence of Germany and Japan with the United States and Britain, see Golden et al. 1999 on labor and Jackson 2003 on corporate governance/finance.

48. Gwartney and Lawson 2004.

49. Miles et al. 2005.

health, safety, and environmental regulations, bypassing Congress via regulatory notices and new federal regulations where possible.[50]

Private-sector actors were especially aggressive in challenging the regulatory regime in telecommunications. The Hush-a-Phone Company contested AT&T's equipment monopoly by developing a device to attach to telephones to make it easier to communicate in noisy places; the Carter Communications Company followed with a phone to translate voice signals into radio signals for mobile communications systems; and MCI challenged the transmission monopoly by proposing a microwave link between St. Louis and Chicago. Each of these steps generated court cases, and the Federal Communications Commission (FCC) responded by reviewing the regulatory regime more broadly. The Department of Justice brought an antitrust suit against AT&T in 1974, finally reaching a settlement in 1982 whereby AT&T would divest the Bell operating companies. The U.S. Congress made several attempts to pass comprehensive reform legislation in the late 1980s and early 1990s but achieved a resolution only in 1996 after the telecommunications industry had engaged in an extraordinarily protracted and expensive lobbying battle. The bill allowed regional Bell operating companies, long-distance carriers, and cable television companies to enter one another's lines of business, but it also subjected them to complex entry tests. In essence, the Bell companies would have to permit competition in their own markets before they would be allowed to expand into new markets. The bill left much of the detailed implementation to the FCC, yet the FCC's first two attempts to set rules for "unbundling" local markets (setting interconnection charges) were struck down in court. In short, the telecommunications bill has only made the regulatory process more contentious and more complex than ever.[51]

Likewise, U.S. financial institutions have driven regulatory changes through marketplace innovations and political appeals. A few investment banks challenged the New York Stock Exchange's system of fixed brokerage commissions in the 1960s by offering discount service on some listed stocks, and institutional investors began to protest the commission rates for subsidizing individual investors at the expense of institutions. The Securities and Exchange Commission ultimately decided to force the stock exchange to liberalize commissions in 1975. Meanwhile, investment banks challenged the regulatory divide between commercial and investment banking by creating money market funds. The banks responded by developing interest-bearing checking accounts known as negotiable order of withdrawal (NOW) accounts. Congress moved to allow "super" NOW accounts and money market deposit

50. *New York Times* (August 14, 2004), A1.
51. Rich 2005.

accounts in 1982 and removed deposit interest-rate ceilings in 1986. Bankers Trust tested the accepted interpretation of the Glass-Steagall Act—that banks could not underwrite or distribute commercial paper—by placing commercial paper with investors for corporate customers in 1978. This led to a protest to the Federal Reserve Board, which denied the petition; an appeal to the Supreme Court, which reversed this denial in 1984; subsequent clarifications by the board; and finally a 1987 decision by the board to permit three major commercial banks, including Bankers Trust, to set up securities subsidiaries. This decision established the principle that banks and brokerage firms could cross Glass-Steagall lines through subsidiaries. The large commercial banks and investment banks aggressively lobbied Congress to repeal the Glass-Steagall Act outright, but the smaller banks and insurance companies resisted. Congressional reformers attempted to lift some Glass-Steagall restrictions in 1984 and 1988 and to repeal the act more thoroughly in 1991 and 1995 but succeeded only in 1999, when the Financial Services Modernization Act allowed banks, securities firms, and insurance companies to merge into financial conglomerates. Although the Japanese authorities engaged in an extremely protracted process of political bargaining to de-segment the financial industry (see Chapter 4), they actually beat the U.S. government to it by a considerable margin.

U.S. corporate law strongly supported a managerial model of corporate governance for most of the postwar era, giving managers control over the nomination and election of the directors who would nominally oversee management, impeding large shareholders from exercising control over management, and excluding labor from managerial functions.[52] In the 1980s, however, the Reagan administration fueled a shift toward a shareholder value conception of the firm by easing antitrust rules, thereby facilitating mergers and acquisitions, and by reducing corporate income taxes, thereby providing more capital for the merger movement.[53] Managers then waged an extraordinary series of battles in the courts and state legislatures with shareholder advocates and corporate raiders to preserve their autonomy and contain the market for corporate control. Meanwhile, the federal government vacillated between defending managers and strengthening shareholder protections. Congress enacted "tort reform" in 1995 and 1998 to reduce managers' vulnerability to securities litigation, and the Securities and Exchange Commission (SEC) promoted shareholder interests by enacting reforms to enhance managerial accountability and financial transparency. Policymakers recognized the

---

52. Cioffi 2004, 255–60.
53. Fligstein 2001, 156. We return to the question whether the "shareholder value" model actually improves the welfare of shareholders in the concluding chapter.

structural flaws in the U.S. corporate governance model, but they were pressed to act only after a stock market collapse in 2000 combined with the spectacular failure of Enron and other corporate scandals in 2001–2. Congress responded with the Sarbanes-Oxley Act of 2002, the most comprehensive corporate governance reform in the United States since the 1930s. U.S. business leaders, who had fought so hard to preserve managerial autonomy in the 1980s and 1990s, abruptly changed course and embraced selective reforms.[54] The act created a new regulatory body, the Public Company Accounting Oversight Board, to enforce much tougher accounting standards, and made corporate boards more independent and strengthened their auditing function. The federal government thereby reasserted control over an issue area that had long been dominated by the states.[55] Reform advocates remained dissatisfied because the act did not address some of the key flaws in the U.S. corporate governance system, such as managers' effective control over the nomination of directors. Corporations were alarmed by the enormous costs of compliance with the new regime and promptly set about lobbying to roll back some of the more costly provisions.[56] In May 2005 U.S. regulators issued guidelines designed to ease the costs of Section 404 of the Sarbanes-Oxley Act, which requires large companies to have auditors evaluate their internal financial controls.[57]

The U.S. government has not enacted major reforms of labor law since the 1950s, but the Reagan administration attacked union power by taking on public-sector unions itself, facilitating corporate restructuring, paring back labor protections, and cutting welfare benefits. Reagan set the tone in 1981 by firing workers from the Professional Air Traffic Controllers Organization who went on strike. The administration also appointed more business-friendly representatives to the National Labor Relations Board and enacted rule changes that made it easier for companies to decertify unions and harder for unions to win elections.[58] Golden et al. find that only the United States and Britain—among a sample of twelve industrialized countries, including Japan and Germany—experienced a clear decline in union influence in the 1980s and 1990s, and they contend that government policy played an important role in this decline.[59]

54. *New York Times* (July 14, 2002), 3/1.

55. Cioffi 2004, 265–71.

56. One academic study calculates the net private cost of compliance at $1.4 trillion by estimating the total loss in market value due to the legislation (*Economist*, May 21, 2005, 71). A Financial Executives International survey found that firms reported an average cost of compliance with Section 404 of $4.4 million (*New York Times*, May 17, 2005, C10).

57. *New York Times* (May 17, 2005), C1.

58. Cohen 2000, 133–34.

59. Golden et al. 1999, 201, 221–25.

U.S. industry has been more likely than Japanese business to view welfare spending as a threat to competitiveness; to lobby for reforms to lower welfare costs, both direct employer expenses and the tax burden; and to give employers greater flexibility in designing employee benefit programs.[60] Meanwhile, the financial industry has strongly lobbied for reforms to expand private pension plans. The U.S. government moved earlier than other industrialized countries to transfer the burden of pensions from employers to employees. It encouraged a shift from defined-benefit plans to defined-contribution plans—such as individual retirement accounts (IRAs) and 401(k) plans—by providing tax exemptions for employer contributions and making defined benefits more expensive to provide and more difficult to fund. In 1974, for example, Congress passed the Employment Retirement Income Security Act (ERISA), which introduced IRAs and increased corporations' liability for paying out benefits from underfunded defined-benefit plans, thus encouraging employers to switch to defined-contribution plans. A 1978 amendment to the law then created 401(k) plans, allowing pension funds and insurance companies to invest large proportions of their portfolios in the stock market, laying the foundation for the rise of large and powerful institutional investors.[61] The government reduced tax subsidies for pension programs in 1982 and imposed new restrictions on funding defined-benefit plans in 1987.[62] It made substantial cutbacks in social security in 1977 and 1983, although it was unable to enact more comprehensive reforms in the face of massive political resistance.[63] As employers became more wedded to private defined-contribution plans and less tied to social security, however, they became more supportive of social security reform.[64] In 2005 President George W. Bush launched a major political battle by proposing a comprehensive reform of social security that would transform the system's benefit structure and allow workers to divert some of their payroll taxes into private accounts.

Reform German Style

The German case offers a much closer comparison with the Japanese one, allowing us to examine how similar causal mechanisms operate in a different national context to produce a broadly similar pattern of reform.[65] German

---

60. See Swank and Martin 2001.
61. Lazonick and O'Sullivan 2000, 17.
62. Allen et al. 2003, 52–54; Roberts and Turner 1997, 367; Salisbury 1994, 86.
63. Pierson and Weaver 1993, 115–24.
64. Hacker 2005, 68.
65. See Vogel 2001 and 2003 for more detailed treatment of the German case, and Yamamura and Streeck 2003 for a more comprehensive comparison of German and Japanese reforms.

corporations resemble their Japanese counterparts in that they are ambivalent about liberal reforms because they do not want to undermine close working relationships with workers, banks, and other firms. They diverge on the specific substance of reforms, however, reflecting differences in the specific market institutions that shape industry preferences. For example, codetermination (the cooperative governance of firms by management and labor) is codified in law in Germany whereas it relies on private-sector practice in Japan. German unions are organized primarily by industrial sector whereas Japanese unions are established at the company level. German *Hausbanken* typically have higher ownership stakes in their corporate clients than Japanese main banks, they are represented directly on corporate boards, and they enjoy proxy voting rights for large blocks of shares. And German corporate networks are not as dense as Japan's horizontal and vertical *keiretsu*.[66] So German industry resists reforms that would undermine these specific institutions and supports reforms that preserve or reinforce them.[67] German firms have been somewhat more favorable than their Japanese counterparts toward liberal reforms, however, because they are more exposed to international practices and more integrated into international markets. In addition, the European Union (EU) has pressed the German government to enact reforms in some issue areas, such as financial regulation and antitrust policy.

German political institutions also aggregate industry preferences slightly differently, with even greater emphasis on consensual decision-making procedures at the highest levels and a more equal partnership between industry and labor.[68] German industry associations resemble their Japanese counterparts in that they represent both the competitive and protected sectors and are committed to a consensual style of governance. Hans-Olaf Henkel, president of the Federation of German Industries (Bundesverband der Deutschen Industrie, or BDI), advocated sweeping liberal reforms, including the dismantling of the collective bargaining system, but his own organization distanced itself from some of his proposals. Meanwhile, BDI was not able to take a position on many reform issues because of dissent from one or more member

---

66. See further discussion of German market institutions and corporate restructuring in Chapter 5.

67. Like their Japanese counterparts, German firms mute their support for liberal reforms for fear of backlash. "If we speak out, it would be counterproductive," explains Norbert Walter, chief economist at Deutsche Bank. "We can do our research and disseminate it, but if we tried to exert influence directly, it would backfire" (interview, July 7, 1998).

68. Pempel and Tsunekawa (1979), Wilensky (2002), and others describe this in terms of the difference between corporatism (Germany) and corporatism without labor (Japan). For a fuller treatment of the German political context, see Katzenstein 1987 and 2005 and Schmidt 2003.

industries. "We would welcome a reduction in coal subsidies," concedes Axel Schulz of the Chemical Industry Association (VDI), "but we do not say so because this is not our concern. So the government cannot make cuts because the coal industry and the unions oppose them and no one will take a stand publicly in favor of them. The BDI will not take a position. This is the real problem in Germany."[69] The Confederation of German Employers' Associations (Bundesvereinigung der Deutschen Arbeitgeberverbände, or BDA) has refrained from advocating reforms that would alienate its labor partners. "We actually support some recent government policy changes," confesses the BDA's Renate Hornung-Draus, "but we do not say so too loudly or we will get in trouble with the unions."[70] Furthermore, the BDA and its member associations oppose any major changes to the collective bargaining system because one of their primary functions is to oversee this system. Even at the sectoral level, German industry associations are internally divided over reform policies. The German Automobile Association (Verband der Automobilindustrie, or VDA), for example, represents not only the large automakers but almost five hundred small and medium-sized body and parts suppliers. The association takes great pains to reach a position acceptable to all members, or it simply defers to the BDI when it cannot reach a consensus.[71]

Germany's main conservative party, the Christian Democratic Union (CDU; and its Bavarian partner, the Christian Social Union), resembles the LDP in that it relies heavily on support from protected sectors, especially small business and service industries, so it is extremely cautious in cutting back protection and promoting competition. The CDU differs from the LDP, however, in that it enjoys substantial support from labor unions, especially moderate Christian unions, so those CDU politicians who benefit from this support are naturally wary of taking positions that would alienate these constituents. The party has a substantial bloc of parliamentarians committed to defending and supporting generous welfare provisions.

The Free Democratic Party (FDP) is more solidly devoted to a liberal policy line, but it has been unable to widen its popularity beyond 5–10 percent of the vote. Even the FDP has been forced to moderate its passion for liberal reform, given resistance among its own supporters. The FDP garners considerable support from small business owners and professionals who benefit from government regulation, so it has refrained from endorsing unbridled deregulation. When the Monopoly Commission issued a report favoring deregulation of the professions in July 1998, FDP leaders wasted no time in denouncing the

69. Interview, June 21, 1999.
70. Interview, July 8, 1996.
71. Interview, Götz Birken-Betsch, VDA, July 9, 1998.

proposal. "As liberals we knew the commission was right," noted party adviser Thomas Ilka, "but as a party we could not support the proposal."[72]

With its election victory in 1998, the Social Democratic Party (SPD) took power for the first time in sixteen years, in a coalition with the Greens. The SPD tried to recognize the new realities of the German economy and push through reforms without alienating its core supporters. The government began with relatively modest reforms but moved on to more extensive labor and welfare reforms after 2003 (discussed below), eventually undermining its political support base.

The SPD's junior partner in government, the Greens, underwent a substantial transformation while in power. Some Green parliamentarians even favored liberalization in finance, energy, and telecommunications, but when they recommended extending shopping hours for small retail stores (under five employees), they ran up against virulent opposition from their own party and dropped the proposal. "We are divided between the 'New Greens' who favor smaller government and empowerment of the individual," reported party adviser Petra Kachel, "and those who still assume that direct state action can effectively address complex problems."[73] The Green Party leadership became more pragmatic through its experience in power, yet many of the rank-and-file members remained bound to the party's earlier ideals.

After the SPD suffered a major defeat in North Rhine-Westphalia in May 2005, Chancellor Gerhard Schröder gambled on a showdown with the opposition by moving up lower house (Bundestag) elections by one year to September 2005. Despite initial predictions of a huge victory for the conservatives, the CDU/CSU defeated the SPD by the narrowest of margins. This meant that the two major parties would have to cooperate to pass legislation, making it even more difficult to enact liberal reform measures without devising elaborate compromises.

The German bureaucracy has not shaped the substance of reform as much as its Japanese counterpart. Government officials are less involved in packaging compromises among private-sector actors, and they play a smaller role in guiding private-sector coordination, relying less on regulatory powers as leverage. So they have not been as zealous as Japanese officials in designing reforms to maintain their own regulatory discretion.

The German government produced a highly publicized report in the late 1980s proposing deregulation in a wide range of sectors, yet it failed to implement many of the proposals. The government accelerated reform in the late 1990s, however, especially in more dynamic sectors such as telecommunica-

72. Interview, July 19, 1998.
73. Interview, July 3, 1998.

tions. The government initiated telecommunications reform relatively late, only beginning the process in the late 1980s in response to developments at the EU level. Few firms favored reforms to Germany's classic post, telegraph, and telephone (PTT) administration before that time. Once the reform debate began, however, several computer makers voiced support for liberalization because it would lower telecommunications costs and expand the equipment market. Most telecommunications equipment manufacturers were wary since they benefited from privileged relations with the Bundespost. A twelve-member reform commission was set up by the government in 1984, including representatives from the unions, the CDU, the SPD, the *Länder* governments, and the media. The government eventually passed reform legislation in 1990, but not without making considerable concessions to the unions. It agreed to include union representatives on Deutsche Telekom's board and to leave organizational links between Telekom and the postal service. It decided to privatize Telekom in 1993, beginning with the sale of a 25 percent share in 1996. It then liberalized telephone markets effective January 1998, bringing in an array of new entrants and prompting a rapid drop in telephone charges.

Germany has been more cautious with liberalization in retail, for political leaders are extremely sensitive to the fate of small businesses. Although large retailers would increase their market share and manufacturers would benefit from more efficient distribution, few companies have pressed for deregulation. The conservative government proceeded with a modest extension of shopping hours in 1996 despite considerable resistance from within its own coalition as well as rabid opposition from retailers and some labor and consumer groups. Then, in 2000, the government proposed extending hours further, from 8 to 10 p.m. on weekdays and from 4 to 8 p.m. on Saturdays.[74] Economists have recommended that the government abolish the complex rebate system whereby retailers cannot offer discounts greater than 3 percent of a purchase price. "A few politicians proposed reforms of the rebate system in 1994, but the CDU rejected the idea," conceded party economic adviser Stephen Hesselmann. "Now no one has the courage to take this up—not even the FDP."[75]

Germany lagged behind many other advanced industrial countries with financial reforms, especially with respect to securities markets. By the 1990s, however, the big banks supported measures to promote new financial instruments and to centralize equity trading activity in Frankfurt, which the smaller financial institutions and the *Länder* opposed. The government pushed through substantial reforms in the 1990s in response to increasing competition from other financial centers, especially London, and EU directives on

74. *Economist* (September 2, 2000), 64.
75. Interview, July 19, 1998.

financial services. In 1994 the government passed an omnibus financial reform bill to reorganize the stock exchange; to create a new regulatory agency, the Supervisory Office for Securities; to set criminal penalties for insider trading; and to establish the legal foundation for money market funds.[76] The government then consolidated financial regulation into one agency, the German Financial Supervisory Authority. At the same time, however, it sought to ensure that the financial system continues to serve the needs of German industry. For example, it redeployed credit institutes, which were originally created to provide long-term finance for industry, to provide venture capital for start-up firms.[77]

Meanwhile, the public-sector regional banks and cooperatives have remained highly popular and politically powerful. Despite pleas for reform from the private banks, political leaders and regional governments have resisted reforms that would threaten this sector. The government and the regional banks (Landesbanken) fought off challenges at the EU level, contending that the government unfairly subsidizes these banks, but ultimately agreed to phase out government loan guarantees for them after 2005. Government officials and public bank executives continued to work together to increase economies of scale through business tie-ups and mergers within the network of public banks. Political and financial leaders launched yet another initiative to make Germany a more attractive financial center in 2003, but progress was stalled by a stalemate between private- and public-sector banks.[78]

German politicians debated major corporate governance reform legislation for over a year before reaching a compromise in November 1997. The (then) opposition SPD proposed the bill to constrain bank power at the same time as it promoted economic reform. Managers were reluctant to push reform too far for fear that it might make them more vulnerable to pressures from shareholders.[79] The Control and Transparency in Business (KonTraG) bill, which emerged from this debate, reflects a delicate compromise designed to enhance the accountability and transparency of supervisory boards without dismantling codetermination or undermining the positive role of banks in providing capital to growing industrial firms and supporting firms in times of crisis.[80]

76. Vogel 1996, 250–53; Story 1996.
77. Adelberger 2000.
78. *Economist* (June 26, 2004), 77.
79. Ziegler (2000, 197–213) cites ambivalence within the German business community as a primary reason for the limited degree of reform in corporate governance. He notes that the business community was divided as well as ambivalent, but not along any identifiable lines of cleavage, such as large versus small firms, manufacturers versus banks, or exporters versus more domestic firms.
80. Hampton 1997.

Specifically, the bill increases the duties of supervisory boards, especially with respect to coordination with auditors; reduces restrictions on shareholders' ability to receive compensation for management misconduct; abolishes enhanced and maximum voting rights (special voting rights not accorded to all shareholders); restricts banks from exercising proxy voting rights in firms in which they have a greater than 5 percent ownership share; requires banks to report transfers of their own personnel to firms in which they have a greater than 5 percent stake; and allows firms to buy back up to 10 percent of their own shares. The government considered but ultimately rejected proposals to impose legal restrictions on bank share ownership.[81] In addition, Labor Minister Norbert Blüm blocked proposals to reduce the size of supervisory boards because of powerful resistance from unions that feared losing influence. In July 2000, the government passed tax reform to eliminate the capital gains tax for companies selling equity stakes in other companies, thereby making it much less costly for firms to divest their cross-holdings. The corporate governance and tax reforms combined to weaken traditional protections against takeovers, but German leaders reinforced these protections under the new Takeover Act of 2001 and confronted the EU on common rules for cross-border takeovers.[82] The German government eventually forced the EU to moderate the rules to preserve codetermination: if a third or more employees in the merged firm enjoy strong participation rights, as with codetermination, those rights will apply to the entire firm.[83] The government-sponsored Cromme commission issued new corporate governance guidelines in May 2003, but the government did not make compliance mandatory. Corporations have been especially wary of following the commission's guidelines for disclosing executive pay.[84]

Economists, journalists, and other opinion leaders have called for the abolition of the collective bargaining system altogether, but most firms feel that they benefit from the system and prefer to preserve it while introducing modest reforms to allow more flexibility. As in Japan, they have resisted labor reforms that threaten their comparative institutional advantage. Many firms are wary of abandoning the collective bargaining system because they fear that shifting wage and benefit negotiations to the plant level would under-

---

81. Cioffi (2002, 366) finds that the banks threatened to stop voting proxies for their clients if the government did not moderate or withdraw those provisions of the bill that were most threatening to bank power. The government conceded, as reform advocates recognized that this would only undermine shareholder control over managers and make shareholder votes more unpredictable.

82. Cioffi 2002.

83. *Economist* (December 4, 2004), 11–12.

84. *Economist* (August 21, 2004), 52.

mine the cooperative atmosphere on the shop floor. In addition, labor market reforms could force companies to compete for workers on the basis of wages, dilute their incentive to invest in human resources, and otherwise erode their productivity advantage.[85] The conservative government under Chancellor Helmut Kohl did not attempt to reform the collective bargaining system but took several smaller steps. It reduced legally mandated sick pay allowances from 100 to 80 percent of salary in 1996, eased requirements for terminating workers, and allowed more flexibility with short-term (one- to two-month) contracts in 1997. The SPD-Green government then reversed all these measures.

The Schröder administration adopted a tripartite dialogue among the government, employers, and unions to cope with high unemployment under the rubric of the Alliance for Jobs. It used this forum to cultivate a consensus on policies to combat unemployment and to encourage employers and unions to negotiate their own solutions, such as bargains whereby workers agree to wage moderation and greater flexibility in working hours in exchange for job security. The government introduced modest reforms to give employers more leeway but also adopted measures to reinforce the German model: strengthening works councils, limiting the duration of fixed-term contracts, and imposing tax and welfare charges on low-paid jobs.[86] In 2002, the government set up a commission—led by Peter Hartz, personnel director at Volkswagen—to propose bolder measures. The commission recommended creating new job centers, providing incentives for case managers to place unemployed workers and for workers to accept temporary or low-paid jobs.[87] The plan eased rules on firing workers for firms of five to ten employees and required unemployed workers to take jobs or lose benefits, but it also fought off opposition pressure to allow more exceptions to collective bargains.[88] In late 2003, the government then incorporated the Hartz commission recommendations into a broader roadmap for economic reforms known as Agenda 2010. In July 2004, the government passed the most controversial phase of the Hartz commission reforms—known as Hartz IV—substantially reducing government support for the long-term unemployed, cutting the level and duration of payments, and requiring recipients to meet needs tests and to actively seek employment.

German politicians, like their Japanese counterparts, have sometimes blamed foreign capital for undermining valued German practices. SPD leader Franz Müntefering set off a furor in April 2005 when he described foreign

85. Thelen 1999, Soskice 1999.
86. *Economist* (July 14, 2001), 47.
87. *Economist* (August 24, 2002), 41.
88. *Economist* (December 20, 2003), 73.

investors as "swarms of locusts that fall on companies, stripping them bare before moving on." An internal party report, which was leaked to the press, accused specific foreign firms of plundering German assets, laying off workers, and otherwise violating local norms. Müntefering and his colleagues were less concrete about the remedies for this problem, but they favored tougher rules on financial disclosure and policies that would encourage companies to create jobs and not simply maximize profits.[89]

German employers have not blindly advocated welfare cuts, preferring to maintain or enforce welfare programs that help to sustain their comparative institutional advantage. German firms' high-skill and high-quality production strategy works only within a particular institutional context, which includes generous pension and unemployment schemes that are tightly linked to employment. Firms are more willing to invest in upgrading worker skills because benefit programs foster worker loyalty; and workers are more willing to cultivate job-specific skills because they are protected from job loss. Hence German employers oppose reforms that undermine those welfare programs that support their production strategies—such as early retirement schemes, unemployment insurance, and active labor market policies—but they are more favorable toward cost-cutting efforts that focus on health care and public pensions.[90] The Schröder government has gradually confronted the problem of financing pensions with an aging population, beginning with measures to provide government subsidies to privately financed pension plans. In 2003, a reform commission chaired by economist Bert Rürup proposed capping pension contributions at 22 percent of monthly salary, raising the legal retirement age from 65 to 67, and reducing pension benefits from 48 to 40 percent of average gross earnings.[91]

The German case fits the basic model presented in Chapter 1: business leaders have been decidedly ambivalent about liberalization, the political parties and industry associations have moderated liberal reforms further as they aggregated societal preferences, and Germany ended up with an overall pattern of incremental reform designed more to revive the German model than to dismantle it. The German pattern differs from the Japanese one on specifics, however, because the German model relies on somewhat different institutions with different advantages. And Germany has moved further with microeconomic reforms than Japan because of its greater economic, political, and social integration into the broader international community.

89. *New York Times* (May 5, 2005), C1; *Economist* (May 7, 2005), 63–66.
90. Manow 2001.
91. *Economist* (August 30, 2003), 35.

4 THE VARIETIES OF REFORM

Since the mid-1990s, the Japanese government has embarked on a daunting array of reforms targeted at the microinstitutions of the economic system. Taken together, these reforms represent a comprehensive program with the potential to transform Japan into a liberal market economy (see Table 1). If we turn to the specifics, however, we find that the reforms have been designed more to preserve the essence of the Japanese model than to destroy it. In this chapter, we review these reforms in greater detail to confirm and flesh out the overall pattern described in the previous chapter and to explore variations across issue areas.

With respect to variations, we would expect more reform in those areas confronting the greatest degree of crisis. Beyond this, models of Japanese politics and political economy suggest several hypotheses about how reforms might vary across issue areas. For example, we would expect to find more reform in dynamic sectors (telecommunications, for example) than in stable ones (such as trucking) because dynamic sectors are subject to stronger market pressures for regulatory change.[1] We would expect more reform in international sectors (international capital market regulation) than in domestic ones (retail banking regulation) because international sectors are more vulnerable to international economic and political pressures. We would also expect to encounter the *gaiatsu* (foreign pressure) phenomenon in these sectors, whereby foreign actors are able to break through some of the gridlock characteristic of the standard domestic policy process.[2] We would expect more reform in technocratic areas (accounting) than in highly politicized ones (welfare) because opponents would be less mobilized and less well positioned to influence reform outcomes. And we would expect more reform in areas that do not threaten farmers, retailers, construction companies, or other core constituents of the LDP (corporate governance reform) than in those that do (agricultural liberalization, retail liberalization, cuts in public works spending). In practice, these hypotheses overlap to a considerable

1. Vogel 1996, 256–60.
2. See Calder 1988, Schoppa 1997.

degree because dynamic sectors tend to be international, technocratic, and less essential for the LDP, and stable sectors tend to be domestic, politicized, and more important for the ruling party.

In the policy case studies below, we follow the framework introduced in the previous chapter: we identify industry policy preferences; trace the aggregation of these preferences by industry associations, government ministries, and political parties; and review reform outcomes. Following the model outlined in Chapter 1 and elaborated in Chapter 3, we find that the microinstitutions of Japanese capitalism shape distinctive industry preferences on policy issues and that these preferences strongly influence the substance of reforms. In this chapter, we review reforms in three broad categories—labor, finance, and competition—before turning to some of Prime Minister Koizumi's reform initiatives.

Labor

Japanese commentators have blamed rigid labor markets for high labor costs, decreasing competitiveness, and rising unemployment, yet the government has moved very cautiously with reforms. The government has given employers more freedom with working hours, compensation, and contracts, but it has not made it any easier for employers to dismiss workers. One would expect firms, employer associations, and the conservative parties to favor labor deregulation, and workers, union federations, and parties of the left to resist it. Firms have been ambivalent, however; the employer associations have opposed many reforms outright; and the LDP has tread very carefully. As a whole, firms have sought greater flexibility to facilitate cost reductions, but they have not wanted to undermine the long-term employment system. If anything, the smaller firms in the service sector have advocated liberalization more actively while the large manufacturers in competitive sectors have been more reluctant.[3] This divergence follows the micrologic of policy preferences (Chapter 1): large manufacturers tend to rely on close working relationships with their workers to enhance productivity whereas smaller service companies are more likely to maximize flexibility and minimize costs. Nikkeiren leaders were especially cautious in their proposals, stressing the need to protect employment and to preserve worker participation in management.[4] Likewise, the LDP showed more interest in supporting employment than in enhancing labor mobility. Ministry of Labor officials tended to value the

3. Interview with Takeo Naruse, Adviser, Nikkeiren, August 1, 2000, and interview with Katsuhiro Fujisawa, Policy Division, Employment Stability Bureau, Ministry of Labor, August 2, 2000. Miura 2002 provides a more detailed account of employer preferences on labor reforms.

4. See Gronning 1998.

Japanese employment system: they felt that it provides a balance of stability and flexibility and gives employers an appropriate incentive to invest in training their workers.[5] In considering reforms, they tried to assess whether proposed changes would increase or decrease the overall level of employment. As the economic crisis deepened, this calculus gradually brought them closer to the position of the employers.[6]

The government was limited in its ability to reform the employment system because many core features, such as employer guarantees of stable employment for core employees and worker participation in management, were not codified in legislation but simply embedded in standard practices. Nevertheless, the government moved forward with several reforms in areas under its control: easing regulations on working hours, permitting more freedom in using temporary workers, and allowing private employment agencies to place workers. Members of the government's Deregulation Committee (under the Administrative Reform Council) turned to labor issues in 1995. They felt that deregulation in other sectors was likely to cause labor dislocation, so they wanted to reform labor markets to facilitate the reallocation of workers. In addition, some business leaders were starting to advocate liberalization, and private entrepreneurs were hoping to get into the employment agency business.[7] Union leaders viewed the committee's initiative as a blatant violation of the standard policy process on labor issues. Pempel and Tsunekawa describe the Japanese political system as one of "corporatism without labor" because business groups have privileged access to policymakers but labor groups do not.[8] This is accurate as a snapshot overview, but it misses the fact that labor enjoyed privileged access within the limited sphere of the Ministry of Labor's jurisdiction. By shifting the arena of debate out of the ministry, therefore, the government excluded the unions from deliberations on an important matter of labor policy.[9]

The Deregulation Committee's proposals resulted in several notable reforms. In 1997 the government amended the Equal Employment Opportunity Act to remove some special protections for female workers, such as those governing overtime and nighttime work. In 1998 it revised the Labor

5. The Ministry of Labor was folded into the Ministry of Health, Labor, and Welfare (MHLW) in 2000.

6. Interview with Isao Aoki, Deputy Director General, Employment Security Bureau, MHLW, March 25, 2002.

7. Interview with Yoshio Suzuki, President of Asahi Research and member of the Deregulation Committee, January 23, 2002.

8. Pempel and Tsunekawa 1979. In addition, as suggested above, labor's interest is represented in the political system indirectly by industry, which tends to favor stable employment and anticompetitive regulations that sustain it.

9. Miura 2002.

Standards Law to give employers more flexibility with work-hour rules, but Rengō succeeded in imposing conditions, such as requiring worker consent, that made it very difficult for employers to exercise this flexibility.[10] In July 1999, the government revised the Worker Dispatching Law and the Employment Security Law to allow employers greater freedom in hiring dispatch workers (agency temps), to permit private companies to provide employment placement services, and to increase legal protection for job seekers. The ability to hire dispatch workers could help employers adjust to market fluctuations and restrain wage costs, and the private employment agencies could provide an additional mechanism for matching employers with workers in a more fluid labor market. The government shifted from a "positive list" restriction for dispatch workers, whereby they were allowed in only twenty-six job categories, to a "negative list" system, in which they were allowed in all job categories except manufacturing, construction, harbor services (longshoremen), and a few other areas. "The unions opposed the liberalization of dispatch workers," recalls one Labor Ministry official, "but many employers had their doubts as well. They wanted to preserve a system in which they keep the best people forever. So the goals of the employers and the unions were not that different."[11] In June 2003, the government passed further revisions to the Worker Dispatching Law (effective March 2004), permitting the use of dispatch workers in manufacturing, extending the maximum contract period for which employers could hire dispatch workers without hiring them permanently from one to three years, and allowing local governments to provide job placement services for free. The government also revised guidelines for temporary employment in 2003, mandating that temporary workers performing comparable work to that of permanent workers be given comparable treatment.[12] An OECD survey of trends in employment protection legislation concludes that Japan has substantially reduced employment protection for temporary workers while preserving it for regular workers. This leaves Japan with one of the most "dualistic" labor systems among OECD countries, having an unusually large gap in protection between regular and temporary workers.[13]

Meanwhile, the government revised the Labor Standards Law to codify guidelines for dismissing workers. Court decisions had generally supported

10. Miura 2002.
11. Aoki interview, March 25, 2002.
12. Ekonomisuto (March 22, 2005), 37.
13. Organization of Economic Co-operation and Development 2005, 110–17. The report develops an index of employment protection based on multiple indicators. According to this index, Japan scores an identical 2.4 for employment protection for regular workers in the late 1980s and in 2003, but for temporary workers, it drops from 1.8 in the late 1980s to 1.3 in 2003. Also see Ekonomisuto (March 22, 2005), 37.

the long-term employment system by ruling that employers could not dismiss workers without cause unless they met fairly stringent criteria for economic hardship. The resulting case law doctrine reinforced internal labor markets and constrained external labor markets: it gave employers considerable flexibility to manage human resources within the firm by transferring employees to subsidiaries or increasing work time, while limiting their ability to lay off workers.[14] The new legislation effectively prohibited employers from laying off workers except in circumstances deemed appropriate by social custom. Employers must publish guidelines for dismissal in their employee handbooks and specify reasons for dismissal in writing on request by the employee. The Democratic Party successfully amended the language of the bill so that it would not imply that firms have a basic right to lay off workers.[15]

The government made some modest adjustments in welfare provisions for unemployed workers, but it did not undertake a broader shift toward a full-fledged social safety net.[16] It revised the Employment Labor Insurance Law in April 2000 to raise insurance premiums for employers and workers, to increase some benefits, and to give priority to those who lost jobs due to restructuring or bankruptcy. It continued to rely more on government policies and private-sector practices that maintain employment than on policies to support those who lose their jobs. The system pays out only to full-time employees, leaving about half of Japanese uncovered.[17] The government also periodically deployed job-creation packages. In 1999, for example, it authorized a special fund aimed at creating 700,000 jobs by strengthening job-training programs, providing subsidies to employers for retaining workers, and hiring jobless workers directly for government projects. In 2001, it announced emergency measures to cope with rising unemployment: providing subsidies to firms that hire unemployed workers or implement job training, and creating jobs directly by increasing public service positions.[18]

The Japanese government's overall approach to economic reform strongly reflected the goal of preserving employment. It designed fiscal stimulus packages to boost public works spending in outlying regions to support construction companies and other small businesses. It moved slowly with deregulation (see below) precisely because anticompetitive practices sustain employment in protected sectors, such as retail and distribution. And it did not force the

---

14. Yamakawa 1999.

15. *Yomiuri Shimbun* (June 2, 2003), 3.

16. Levy et al. (forthcoming) argue that Japan's failure to provide a social safety net is the single greatest factor impeding liberal reform.

17. Katz 2003, 257–58.

18. Mulgan 2002, 88.

speedy sale or liquidation of nonperforming loans for fear that this would wipe out viable small businesses.

Finance

FINANCIAL REGULATION: FROM INCREMENTAL REFORM TO THE BIG BANG

The financial authorities and institutions were reluctant to abandon a financial regime that had contributed to stability and prosperity for so long, yet the financial crisis of the 1990s undermined the legitimacy of the regime, weakened their resistance, and ultimately forced a major overhaul of financial regulation. Japanese financial institutions enjoyed a stable regulatory environment for most of the postwar era, with the Ministry of Finance strictly regulating prices, products, and market entry. The financial institutions designed business strategies for this regulatory environment, cultivating close relations with ministry officials to monitor regulatory developments and to influence regulatory decisions in their favor, so they were not eager to embrace financial liberalization. Even if they might benefit from price liberalization in other areas, they were reluctant to lobby for it because they were dependent on regulation within their own line of business. And even if they might benefit from being allowed to invade other business lines, they were reluctant to advocate it because they would not want other firms to enter their own business. Meanwhile, the large industrial corporations that would benefit most from reform were systematically underrepresented in a decision-making process centered in MOF policy councils dominated by financial institutions.

By the 1980s, the large city banks recognized that deposit interest-rate liberalization would help them to compete with securities firms over the long run, but they remained ambivalent about paying out the higher rates. Meanwhile, the smaller banks were adamantly opposed. The ministry phased in deposit liberalization in a carefully planned sequence of steps from 1979 through 1994. The city banks also favored the desegmentation of the financial system because they recognized that they had more to gain by entering the securities business than they had to lose by allowing securities houses to engage in banking. Even so, the ministry moved very deliberately, packaging elaborate political compromises between the various segments of the financial industry, such as city banks, securities houses, insurance companies, and regional banks. The government finally passed legislation in 1992 allowing financial institutions to invade each other's lines of business via separate subsidiaries.[19]

19. Vogel 1996, 167–95.

With the financial crisis and the widespread loss of faith in the ministry in the 1990s, however, political pressure for reform increased substantially. In 1995, Japan forged a financial services agreement with the United States that opened the pension market to foreign managers and eased restrictions on securities transactions and cross-border financial services. Then, in 1996, Prime Minister Hashimoto proposed a "Big Bang" reform in which the government would open foreign exchange markets; liberalize mutual fund, pension, and trust markets; deregulate brokerage commissions; loosen restrictions on new financial instruments; lift the ban on holding companies; allow banks, securities houses, and insurance companies to enter one another's lines of business through holding companies; strengthen accounting standards; and shift the MOF's supervisory duties to the new Financial Supervision Agency.[20] The government delayed implementation of several of these measures beyond the original schedule, but it completed most of the proposed reforms by 2001, with the notable exception of a few key reforms in accounting and deposit insurance. As a whole, the Big Bang reforms increased competition in the financial services sector, facilitated the reorganization of the sector, enhanced foreign access, and made it easier for firms to raise funds in capital markets.

The Japanese government was able to produce such a comprehensive reform package only because of the unique circumstances of the time. Prime Minister Hashimoto found finance to be more amenable to change than many other areas, given that the financial crisis plus a series of financial scandals left both the ministry and the financial sector with a greatly diminished capacity to resist unwanted reforms.[21] Moreover, the advocates of more broad-based liberalization felt that financial reform would form a critical wedge that would promote competition throughout the economy, because firms in protected sectors would have to become more profitable if they were forced to compete for capital in financial markets.

Nevertheless, the Big Bang did not break completely with earlier patterns of financial regulation, for the authorities phased in the measures gradually, paying special attention to their impact on domestic financial institutions.[22] The government retained considerable discretion in orchestrating the process of regulatory change and in supervising and monitoring the financial system,

---

20. See further details in the discussions of accounting, tax, and antitrust reform below.

21. Toya (2003) argues that the MOF officials actually saw the Big Bang as a means of resurrecting the ministry's tarnished reputation.

22. This approach contrasts sharply with Britain's original "Big Bang" of 1986, when authorities fostered competition to the point of virtually obliterating the domestic securities industry (Vogel 1996, 93–108).

although primary responsibilities had now shifted to the Financial Services Agency.[23] The MOF and the FSA played a critical role in allocating public funds to the banks, in monitoring troubled banks' behavior, and in orchestrating the reorganization of the financial sector.[24] They partially resurrected the MOF's traditional role in allocating credit, using bank rescue funds to extend credit to small businesses and redeploying the Japan Development Bank (now the Development Bank of Japan) to support troubled firms. In essence, the financial authorities' primary source of leverage over financial institutions shifted from the power to grant branch licenses through the 1980s, to the power to set the terms for the desegmentation of the industry in the early 1990s, to the power to set the terms of restructuring the sector ever since.

With the nonperforming loan crisis apparently under control by March 2005, the FSA unveiled a two-year plan for further financial reform. It would draft a new financial services law to facilitate the formation of financial conglomerates integrating banking, brokerage, and insurance services. It also planned to strengthen disclosure requirements for financial institutions, to enhance inspection and supervision procedures, and to allow bank branches to offer a wider range of products, including insurance.[25]

INDUSTRIAL REVITALIZATION: THE NEW INDUSTRIAL POLICY

By the mid-1990s, government officials recognized that the economic crisis had generated a vicious cycle in which the financial crisis damaged the "real" economy and industrial-sector weakness hurt the financial institutions, and they sought novel remedies to break this cycle. The financial institutions were overwhelmed by their exposure to troubled corporate borrowers, so their fortunes depended in part on the prospects for turning around the borrowers. Meanwhile, they were not able to fulfill their proper role of allocating credit to viable enterprises and promising new ventures. The government's approach was to cultivate new mechanisms to help turn around troubled corporations, and to ally with the financial sector in the process, so that the firms could return to financial health and pay off their debts.

In August 1999, the government passed the Industrial Revitalization Law (*sangyō katsuryoku saisei hō*) with strong support from the business community, both the competitive and protected sectors. Those sectors of the "old" economy that sought to reduce capacity, such as steel and chemicals, were

23. The ministry's Financial Planning Bureau was combined with the Financial Supervisory Agency into the Financial Services Agency in July 2000. See Amyx 2004, 197–233, on the relationship between the MOF and the Financial Supervisory Agency, and the creation of the Financial Services Agency.

24. Ostrom 1999.

25. *Nikkei Weekly* (April 4, 2005), 8.

especially eager for government support in the form of tax breaks and low-interest loans. The bill effectively resurrected industrial policy with a new purpose: to facilitate corporate restructuring and shift the economy into new growth sectors. It combined an array of tax breaks, regulatory breaks (such as exemptions to commercial code restrictions), subsidies, and low-interest loans to support companies that were reducing capacity and to encourage investment in high technology and other growth areas.

In December 1999, the government also passed the Civil Rehabilitation Law (*minji saisei hō*), effective April 2000, to streamline bankruptcy procedures, making it easier for companies to declare bankruptcy and pay off creditors without being forced to liquidate the enterprise. The new law lowered the requirement for creditor consent for a reorganization plan from near unanimity to a simple majority.[26] It allowed creditors to enforce a settlement under continuing court supervision rather than having to initiate new proceedings. And most critically, it allowed managers to remain in place in most cases, encouraging them to endure rehabilitation since it would not cost them their jobs.[27]

The government then revised the Industrial Revitalization Law in April 2003 to promote a distinctively Japanese collaborative approach to restructuring. It would offer tax and regulatory breaks to two or more companies working together to reduce capacity through a joint venture (the "joint restructuring" plan), to third parties providing management resources to revive a company (the "business transfer" plan), or to companies investing in new facilities to foster innovation (the "mother plant investment" plan). The companies applying for support would have to pledge to meet specific criteria for financial performance, as defined by return on assets, asset turnover ratio, or added value per employee.[28] "We do not attempt to guide industry," insists METI's Yutaka Yoshimoto. "They bring the proposals to us. We use objective criteria, and we must approve the proposals if they meet the criteria."[29] METI also used Development Bank of Japan investment to spur private funds to finance corporate turnarounds.

26. That is, a majority of creditors must consent, and they must account for a majority of claims on the firm.

27. *JEI Report* (June 9, 2000).

28. The targets differed according to the type of restructuring plan. For a joint restructuring plan or a business transfer plan, for example, companies would have to achieve an improvement of 2 percent return on equity, 5 percent asset turnover for the operational division in question, or 6 percent added value per employee for the division during the period of the plan (Ministry of Economy, Trade, and Industry 2004).

29. Interview with Yutaka Yoshimoto, Deputy Director, Policy Planning and Coordination Division, Minister's Secretariat, METI, July 15, 2004. As of May 2005, the government had approved 204 applications for support under the original IRL and 155 under the revised IRL (METI data).

In May 2003, the government launched the Industrial Revitalization Corporation Japan (IRCJ), which offers an innovative approach to turning around troubled firms by building on the main bank system. It initially allocated the IRCJ ¥10 trillion in deposit insurance funds. Government officials designed the IRCJ to address a specific failure of the main bank system. That is, the main banks tend to roll over loans to troubled borrowers because they judge that this is less costly than allowing the borrowers to fail and they have an obligation to support these borrowers. But they do not have the resources to restructure these borrowers on their own, and the other lenders (especially nonbanks) do not want to participate in restructuring schemes because they have much less at stake in the companies' survival. The IRCJ resolved this dilemma by purchasing the non-main-bank lenders' share of the nonperforming loans and then working with the main bank to reorganize the company. The IRCJ concluded its purchases of new loans in March 2005, by which time it had bought shares in forty-one corporate groups—including Daiei, Kanebo, and Misawa Home—and completed the restructuring of eight of them. The IRCJ was scheduled to be dissolved by 2008.[30]

METI has continued to be interested in promoting new ventures, despite only modest results from numerous programs to foster venture capital and spur entrepreneurship. It has used "pump-priming" capital injections from government financial institutions to spur private venture capital investments, and it has developed tax incentive programs to prompt individual "angel" investors to fund new ventures. The government also lowered the requirements for incorporation in 2003, creating the theoretical possibility of the one-yen company.[31] In 2001, METI announced a new Regional Cluster Plan to foster centers of innovation bridging government, industry, and universities. It sought to link five thousand small and medium-sized enterprises and two hundred universities with regional METI bureaus and other organizations in nineteen clusters across nine geographical regions.[32] It even began a public relations campaign to foster entrepreneurship among Japanese youth, featuring pro wrestler–entertainer Bob Sapp.[33] In April 2003, the ministry set up a study group to look at new ventures spun off from large corporations. The study group concluded that venture spin-offs would be more likely to succeed in Japan than pure (independent) ventures and that the parent company's

---

30. *Nihon Keizai Shimbun* (April 8, 2005), 7.

31. The number of startup companies rose from 84,612 in 2002 to 93,012 in 2003 and 99,384 in 2004 (Ministry of Justice data).

32. Ibata-Arens 2004.

33. The "Dream Gate" project even has its own website, at http://www.dreamgate.gr.jp.

financial and logistical support could be critical to success.[34] "We want to spur a spin-off venture movement," declares Yoshimoto, "so we are launching a public campaign."[35] Experts remain skeptical, however, because Japanese parent companies tend to exercise so much control that spin-offs lack a truly entrepreneurial spirit.[36]

METI's own publications describe its new approach to industrial policy as one in which the government tries to facilitate positive "spirals." In the macrospiral, private demand prompts innovation and technological progress, which then generates more demand. In the microspiral, restructuring and corporate revitalization generate new businesses and spinouts, and the new ventures bring further revitalization. And in a third, "semi-macro" spiral, higher-return manufacturing generates more productive services, and better services make manufacturing more profitable. "We are looking at high-potential technology, where the market mechanism alone is not sufficient to stimulate growth," explains Yoshimoto. "This differs from the old industrial policy because we are promoting promising technology rather than specific industrial sectors. And we are working with the market."[37]

ACCOUNTING: REFORM BY STEALTH

Japan's financial authorities managed to push through accounting reforms with enormous implications for corporate strategy almost by stealth: the potential opponents of these reforms did not fully grasp their ramifications and mobilize politically until many of the changes were already in place. "Most of the debate took place within the policy council," reports one official. "The ministry view was that the financial system needed to be brought up-to-date. The companies did not openly demand changes, and the politicians were not interested."[38] Professional accountants, the U.S. government, and U.S. investment banks were the strongest supporters of reform. The banks fiercely opposed some reforms, such as mark-to-market accounting, which would severely impair bank finances by lowering the value of assets from historical value to market value (that is, forcing the banks to report portfolio losses). Institutional investors and consumer groups did not speak out on the issue, and the unions simply failed to recognize the implications of these reforms before it was too late. "The accounting change was not a change in legislation, so we did not know about it," protests one labor union leader. "The MOF discussed it with the accountants and with MITI. When we realized what

34. Ministry of Economy, Trade, and Industry 2004.
35. Yoshimoto interview, July 15, 2004.
36. Rtischev and Cole 2003.
37. Yoshimoto interview, July 15, 2004.
38. Interview with a former MOF official, July 16, 2004.

was up, we were outraged. We argued that this would constrain long-term investment and undermine competitiveness."[39]

Some Japanese executives advocated reforms to accord with an international trend toward tougher standards, but others feared that reforms could leave them with less leeway to control their accounts. The reforms could make it more difficult to manipulate return-on-equity (ROE) figures, to smooth out earnings over time, to ignore contingent or unfunded liabilities, or to camouflage the cross-subsidization of business operations.[40] A *Nihon Keizai Shimbun* survey in 2003 found that 25 percent of companies felt that Japanese accounting rules should be made fully compatible with international standards while 69 percent did not.[41]

MOF officials and members of the ministerial policy council, the Business Accounting Deliberation Council (BADC), advocated reforms as part of the Big Bang program to make Japanese financial markets "free, fair, and global." They felt that other advanced countries were moving toward more stringent and sophisticated accounting standards and that Japan should follow this trend. The ministry proposed substantial reforms: consolidated reporting, mark-to-market accounting for financial instruments, recognition of off-balance-sheet liabilities, and disclosure of line-of-business profit and loss. The government revised the Securities and Exchange Law to require consolidated reporting for subsidiaries above a certain threshold of ownership and to require cash-flow statement disclosure effective March 31, 2000. In tandem with the lifting of the ban on holding companies and corollary tax revisions (discussed below), this measure constrains companies from hiding losses in subsidiaries and pushes them to assess value in terms of the corporate group as a whole. It also dilutes the incentive for corporations to favor a vertically integrated structure and gives would-be acquirers a more accurate view of a company's value.[42] The cash-flow statement requirement encourages companies to pay greater attention to net present value than market share.

Nevertheless, the ministry continued to make exceptions for the financial firms under its jurisdiction. Ministry officials came under increasing public criticism for giving banks preferential treatment without consulting the BADC, exercising too much control over the BADC, and becoming mired in

39. Interview with Tadayuki Murakami, Assistant General Secretary, Rengō, March 27, 2002, Tokyo.

40. Shinn 1999.

41. *Nihon Keizai Shimbun* (March 7, 2003), 1. The *Nikkei Weekly* (March 17, 2003, 12) reports that Japan reduced its financial contribution to the International Accounting Standards Board because of industry sentiment that the IASB was dominated by the United States and the United Kingdom and did not consider Japanese views, but Keidanren officials deny this (interview, 2004).

42. Weinstein 2001; *Oriental Economist* (November 2001), 12.

several accounting scandals. In August 2001, the power to set accounting standards was transferred to a private-sector body, the Financial Accounting Standards Foundation (FASF).

The FSA introduced mark-to-market accounting for real estate and securities held for sale effective April 1, 2000, and for other real estate and securities effective April 1, 2002.[43] Because many of these assets had depreciated substantially since the bubble of the late 1980s, this change had a devastating impact on the bottom line for many corporations. It encouraged corporations to sell off assets that were not performing and added pressure to increase returns to prevent other companies from dumping shares. Some experts suggested that this shift would open up a market for corporate control, as more shares would become available for sale and shareholders would demand higher returns for their investments.[44] In addition, the FSA decided to require Japanese companies to calculate and disclose unfunded pension liabilities, although it left companies with some flexibility in meeting this requirement. Many corporations had enormous unfunded liabilities, and this requirement forced them to take losses and to reduce costs.

In April 2003, LDP elders Tarō Asō and Hideyuki Aizawa proposed reversing key accounting reforms to help ailing insurance companies and other financial institutions and to prevent further losses in the stock market. Specifically, they sought to reverse the mandatory shift to mark-to-market accounting and to delay by two years the mandatory introduction of impairment accounting for fixed assets.[45] Asset impairment accounting could force contractors, retailers, and other firms that hold substantial fixed assets to recognize major losses because it requires them to account for the difference between the historical value and the market value of noncurrent assets.[46] Critics argued that these moves would only highlight Japan's economic weaknesses and further erode investor confidence.[47] Aizawa even proposed a more radical rollback of accounting reforms: changing the legal status of the FASF. He contended that such a change would clarify the relationship between the FSA and FASF and make accounting decisions more politically accountable.[48]

---

43. Government jurisdiction over accounting standards shifted from the MOF to the Financial Supervisory Agency in 1998 and to the FSA in 2000.

44. Kinney 2001.

45. *Nihon Keizai Shimbun* (April 8, 2003), 1.

46. *Nikkei Weekly* (April 21, 2003), 1. As it turned out, the impending rule change provided a substantial impetus for firms to write off losses and to concentrate resources on more profitable business lines. Roughly 420 companies wrote off ¥3 trillion in fixed-asset valuation losses before the rules became mandatory in April 2005 (*Nikkei Weekly*, May 16, 2005, 8).

47. *Japan Times* (April 18, 2003).

48. Aizawa subsequently lost his seat in the November 2003 election.

The Accounting Standards Board (part of the FASF) concluded that these concerns of the ruling coalition were not sufficient reason to delay implementation of these accounting reforms, and the asset impairment accounting rules became mandatory on schedule in April 2005.[49]

CORPORATE LAW: MORE OPTIONS

Japanese industry has supported selective reforms in corporate law since the 1990s, but Nippon Keidanren and the ministries have designed the reforms to give companies more options rather than to impose a shift toward U.S.-style corporate governance. The Commercial Code Subcommittee (*shōhō bukai*) of the Ministry of Justice's Legislative Council (*hōsei shingikai*), an advisory body dominated by prominent constitutional scholars, began deliberating an overhaul of the commercial code in 1975. By the mid-1990s, opinion leaders were calling for reforms to curtail corporate mismanagement and to make corporations more accountable to shareholders.[50] Meanwhile, large corporations began to show an interest because they hoped that certain reforms would help them cope with the economic downturn by supporting share prices, selling assets, reorganizing operations, or otherwise reducing costs. At the same time, they feared that some reforms would make it harder for them to pursue a long-term management strategy, undermine preferential relationships with banks, and usher in U.S.-style legalistic regulation. They were especially wary of losing managerial discretion via measures to mandate outside directors or strengthen shareholder accountability. Those corporations with close labor-management ties, such as steel producers and other large-scale manufacturers, were more reluctant to tamper with the system than service companies, which were more favorable toward reform.[51] The Japan Chamber of Commerce and Industry, which represents small businesses, insisted that Japan should not emulate the U.S. model.[52] Nikkeiren favored modest adjustments but stressed that Japan should retain the positive aspects of Japanese corporate governance, including putting a premium value on human resources and taking a long-term view.[53] Beyond these positions, corporations' stances on reform varied considerably depending on the philosophy of top managers. Fujio Mitarai, president of Canon and chair of Keidanren's Corporate Governance Committee, for example, was known as an unusually "dry" manager—meaning that he sought to reduce costs and maximize profits without undue sentimentality about long-term relation-

---

49. *Nihon Keizai Shimbun* (June 14, 2003), 12.
50. Dore 2004, 18–22.
51. Naruse interview.
52. Japan Chamber of Commerce and Industry 2000 and 2001.
53. Nihon Keieisha Dantai Renmei 1998; Inagami 2001, 228–29.

ships—yet he strongly opposed reforms that would push Japan toward a U.S.-style board system.[54] Meanwhile, Yoshihiko Miyauchi of Orix emerged as a prominent advocate of corporate governance reform.

Keidanren strived to increase companies' options without making changes mandatory and to limit directors' liability in shareholder lawsuits.[55] MITI worked relatively harmoniously with the Ministry of Justice because both ministries supported reform in principle, MOJ officials welcomed MITI's input regarding industry's needs, and MITI officials respected MOJ's legal expertise and jurisdictional primacy.[56] The MITI officials saw commercial code reform as part of a larger effort—including industrial revitalization and the accounting reforms discussed above—to facilitate corporate adjustment by modernizing Japan's market infrastructure. The MOJ officials viewed themselves as mediators between the business community and the scholars on the Commercial Code Subcommittee. They wanted to allow companies to move toward a U.S.-style governance system while preserving Japan's more "rational" (meaning less costly) legal framework. Japan did not have powerful shareholder activists or class action suits to force changes in corporate governance—and did not need them, they argued—but it did need to enhance the existing system, by strengthening auditors, for example.[57]

In 1993, the government enhanced the statutory auditor system, expanded certain shareholder rights, and reduced the fees required to file shareholder suits, greatly increasing the number of suits.[58] In 1994, it allowed companies to buy back their own shares, giving managers a valuable tool to prop up share prices and fend off hostile takeovers.[59] Then, in January 1997, Keidanren representatives met with a group of LDP Diet members to discuss their primary concerns in the realm of corporate law: supporting share prices, limiting liability in shareholder suits, and permitting stock options. The Diet members, led by Seiichi Ōta and Okiharu Yasuoka, responded with an audacious proposal: why not bypass the standard ministry deliberation process and present the reforms as a member-sponsored bill? "When we proposed this, the Keidanren group could not believe it," Yasuoka recalls. "They hadn't even

54. *Oriental Economist* (August 2001), 10.

55. Motoyoshi Nishikawa (2001), a Nippon Steel executive and Keidanren committee member, outlines Keidanren's position on commercial code reforms in greater detail.

56. This contrasts with MITI's much more heated rivalries with the Ministry of Posts and Telecommunications (over telecommunications), the Ministry of Health and Welfare (over biotechnology), and the Ministry of Education (over software).

57. Interview with Yō Ōta, Associate Senior Counselor, Civil Affairs Bureau, Ministry of Justice, March 29, 2002.

58. Also see Nakamura et al. (2004) for a comprehensive review of reforms through 2003.

59. Lincoln and Gerlach 2004, 331.

dreamt of such a thing!"[60] The MOJ officials were stunned, and the scholars on the Commercial Code Subcommittee were simply outraged. The LDP was loosely divided on corporate governance issues between a commerce group (shōkōzoku) that favored reform and a labor group (rōdōzoku) that was more skeptical, and the DPJ was split as well. The Diet passed the member-sponsored legislation later that year, simplifying procedures for mergers and introducing stock options. It limited stock options to 10 percent of outstanding shares and required that those eligible for options must work for the firms. In 2001, the government eased restrictions on the types of stock that could be issued and lifted restrictions on who could receive stock options.

In August 1999, the government passed legislation permitting companies to transfer shares as a mechanism for corporate realignment. The purchasing company would issue new shares to the company being acquired in exchange for old shares, avoiding costly transfer taxes in the process. In May 2000, the government passed the Corporate Spin-off Law (kaisha bunkatsuhō) to make it easier for corporations to spin off divisions into new subsidiaries or sell them off. If companies met specific criteria, they would be able to split without shareholder approval. In such cases, shareholders opposed to the split would have the option of selling their shares. In combination with tax revisions, such as allowing deferred capital gains taxation on spin-off deals, this bill created a considerably more favorable environment for such spin-offs.[61] The government coupled this reform with the Employment Contract Succession Law (rōdōkeiyaku shōkeihō), which requires companies to consult with workers and unions before a reorganization and encourages companies to transfer existing employment contracts to the newly created divisions. The government added a resolution stating that precedents rule that companies cannot lay off workers if the sole reason for the dismissal is corporate realignment.

Then, in 2001, the government passed another member-sponsored reform bill to strengthen the statutory auditing system and limit directors' liability in shareholder suits. Keidanren consciously linked these two measures because pressing for limits on executive liability without strengthening corporate governance would appear too blatantly self-interested. The government limited executive liability to twice annual income and ruled out lawsuits

60. Interview with Okiharu Yasuoka, Member, House of Representatives, June 19, 2003. Member-sponsored bills have a secondary advantage in that they do not undergo scrutiny by the Cabinet Legal Bureau, which has a reputation for being staunchly conservative. They are reviewed by the Diet Legal Bureau instead.

61. In practice, companies generally used this reform to spin off divisions to prepare for mergers or to create new subsidiaries rather than to sell them on the open market (see Chapter 5).

by shareholders involving corporate actions that occurred before they bought shares in the company. The Japan Federation of Bar Associations (Nichibenren) objected to the proposed limits on liability, arguing that they contradicted the goal of strengthening shareholder governance. Nichibenren also stressed, however, that Japan should not shift to a U.S. model of corporate governance, which has its own faults. In November 2001, the LDP reached a compromise with the DPJ in which liability would be limited to four times annual salary and any shareholder holding stock for six months could sue.[62] Rengō played very little role, except to request—belatedly and unsuccessfully—that the legislation stipulate that companies should have one employee-appointed director.[63]

In 2002, the government permitted large firms to adopt a U.S.-style committee system board. Firms that chose this form would abolish the statutory audit board and establish new audit, nomination, and compensation committees. Each committee would have at least three members, a majority of whom would be outside directors. Keidanren lobbied successfully against a proposal that would have required all companies (not just those adopting the committee system) to appoint at least one outside director. The commercial code's definition of outside director, however, includes employees of a parent company, a subsidiary of the parent company, or a major shareholder. This means that Japanese companies could use outside directors to *strengthen* corporate groups. Moreover, given the absence of effective judicial review of board action, U.S.-style boards will not function the same way in Japan as they do in the United States. Gilson and Milhaupt argue that because of the lack of strict judicial review plus the expansive definition of outside director, the new committee-system boards could actually reinforce "stakeholder tunneling" (the diversion of resources from shareholders to stakeholders) and managerial governance.[64]

In April 2005 a METI panel issued guidelines for takeover defenses to help companies determine which strategies would be legal and appropriate. The panel recommended that companies obtain shareholder approval before issuing equity warrants to thwart a takeover and proposed revising the commercial code to require companies to disclose takeover defense schemes in their business reports.

---

62. Yoshio Nakamura, Senior Managing Director at Keidanren (interview, October 12, 2001), notes that the MOJ officials did the primary drafting, even in the case of the member-sponsored bills, which gave them the opportunity to play a few tricks. Keidanren staff members discovered that the ministry had quietly added a requirement to report names and compensation levels of board members, and complained to the ministry. "So you noticed that!" the ministry officials conceded wryly.

63. Dore 2004, 51–52.

64. Gilson and Milhaupt 2005. Also see Shishido forthcoming.

The Diet passed a further round of commercial code revisions in June 2005 to eliminate minimal capital requirements for a stock company and turn limited liability companies (*yūgen gaisha*) into stock companies, to broaden the discretionary power of boards of directors, and to facilitate mergers and acquisitions while also expanding companies' options for takeover defenses. The bill would not allow foreign companies to acquire Japanese companies via direct stock swaps, owing largely to industry resistance, but it would allow them to do so via triangular mergers, a mechanism by which foreign firms could use their shares to acquire a Japanese company through their Japanese affiliates. A *Nikkei Sangyō Shimbun* survey found that 68 percent of Japanese company presidents viewed acquisition by foreign companies using stock swaps as a threat.[65] The bill became embroiled in a national uproar, however, when Livedoor, an upstart Internet firm, made a hostile bid for Nippon Broadcasting System (see Chapter 5). The LDP responded to this controversy by delaying implementation of the triangular-merger provision by one year. LDP leaders feared that the provision might open the floodgates for foreign investors to mount hostile bids for Japanese firms, so they decided to give companies another year to prepare their defenses. There was a flaw in this logic, however, since triangular mergers are designed for friendly takeovers, not hostile ones.[66] The United States and the European Union protested an article in the bill that prohibits "quasi-foreign corporations"—companies that are incorporated abroad but conduct their primary business in Japan—from doing business in Japan. They feared that this article would be used to shut out legitimate businesses, but the Japanese authorities insisted that it would be applied only to prevent tax evasion or other illegal activities by shell companies formed abroad.[67] The government had initially intended the bill to facilitate cross-border mergers and acquisitions as one step in fulfilling Prime Minister Koizumi's 2003 pledge to double foreign investment by 2008.

PENSIONS: WHERE WELFARE MEETS FINANCE

As the pension system came under increasing stress, government officials and corporate executives sought to devise reforms that would address funding problems while limiting collateral damage to the financial system. The pension system had played a critical role in the postwar economic model: the government used pension funds to finance industrial policy, and private corporations used them as patient capital for long-term investments. Japan's public pension program has three tiers: the Employee Pension (*kōsei nenkin*) for corporate

65. Merrill Lynch, Global Securities Research and Economic Group 2005, 5.
66. *Ekonomisuto* (April 11, 2005), 11.
67. *Nikkei Weekly* (June 27, 2005), 8.

employees, the Mutual Aid Pension (*kyōsai nenkin*) for public servants, and the National Pension (*kokumin nenkin*) for self-employed workers and others not covered by the first two plans. Before 2001, the government transferred most public pension funds to the Ministry of Finance's Trust Fund Bureau, which then allocated them through the Fiscal Investment and Loan Program (FILP). The FILP constituted a critical "second budget," which the government used to achieve public policy objectives and to reward client groups without using taxpayer funds. Private corporations used book reserve pension plans—whereby they reported liabilities but did not set aside funds in a separate account—as an internal source of working capital. They also invested in funded plans through trust banks and life insurance companies, generating a major portion of the funds that sustained stable shareholding in the postwar era.[68]

The government confronted the fundamental problem of Japan's changing demographic profile, as fewer working people would pay into the system over time and more elderly people would become eligible for benefits. One would expect firms to favor reforms that would minimize spending on employee benefits and otherwise lower the overall tax burden. But Japanese firms have not been supportive of pension cuts, feeling that pensions help to sustain labor-management cooperation and provide an important source of patient capital. Keidanren favored more funding through the tax system combined with some benefit cuts while Nikkeiren preferred to preserve an insurance-based approach.[69] As the fiscal situation deteriorated in the late 1990s, the government proposed reforms to increase contributions and scale back benefits in the public pension system. Meanwhile, private corporations experienced an explosion of unfunded liabilities in their pension plans, leading them to demand more freedom to manage these funds and restructure the plans and forcing some to dissolve the plans altogether. Accounting reforms (discussed above) forced the issue by requiring companies to report unfunded liabilities on their balance sheets.

The government gradually eased restrictions on how private corporations could invest their pension funds. In 1990, it allowed companies to hire private investment managers; in 1994, it loosened restrictions on the allocation of investments among stocks, bonds, property, and domestic versus foreign investments; and in 1998, it removed these restrictions altogether. Then, in 2001, the government restructured conventional defined-benefit plans and introduced defined-contribution systems similar to U.S. 401(k) plans (effective April 2002). For defined-benefit plans, the government created two new

---

68. Park 2004, 550–57. Also see Estevez-Abe 2004 on Japan's welfare-finance nexus.
69. Naruse interview, August 1, 2000.

types of plans, a "contract type" run by outside investment managers and a "fund type" managed internally. Companies would be required to offer pensions for employees with at least twenty years of service, to maintain a specified level of reserves to cover pension payments, and to review their pension plans at least once every five years. Existing plans would have to be converted into one of these new types of schemes within five years. The defined-benefit plans were expected to enhance labor mobility because benefits are portable from one employer to another. With nonportable plans, many Japanese workers faced a stark choice of remaining loyal to their employer or losing pension benefits. As of 2004, three thousand firms had introduced defined-contribution plans for more than one million total employees.[70]

In 1987, the government shifted control over some public pension funds from the MOF to a public corporation under the Ministry of Health and Welfare known as the Public Welfare Services Corporation (*nenkin fukushi jigyōdan*, or *nenpuku* for short). In 2001, it transferred all public pension funds to a new public corporation, the Government Pension Investment Fund, which was supposed to have autonomy in investing these funds but retained close ties to the MOF and continued to invest in MOF-managed FILP bonds.[71] Meanwhile, the government passed an initial reform of the public pension system in March 2000, despite bitter opposition from the unions and some opposition parties. The bill increased taxpayer contributions, phased in benefit reductions through 2025, loosened restrictions on fund investments, and hiked the government contribution from 35 to 50 percent. It raised the age requirement for eligibility from 60 in 2013 to 65 in 2025 for men and from 60 in 2018 to 65 in 2030 for women.

The government engaged in an even more heated political battle before passing another reform bill in June 2004, this time gradually increasing the premium for the Employee Pension system from 13.6 percent of annual income to 18.3 percent by 2017 and allowing benefits to drop to a minimum of 50 percent of average disposable income. It also raised premiums for the National Pension system from ¥13,300 to ¥16,900 in 2017. The business community opposed the reform, arguing that the government should pick up more of the financial burden by increasing the consumption tax. The Democratic Party proposed a more comprehensive reform that would integrate the three public pension plans, distribute the financial burden more equitably across occupational and generational groups, and increase government funding from consumption taxes. The DPJ and the LDP agreed to consider a more comprehensive approach to welfare reform, including health insurance and nursing care

---

70. *Nikkei Weekly* (October 25, 2004), 1.
71. Park 2004, 563–66.

insurance, and to issue recommendations by March 2007.[72] The employee pension system requires companies to pay 50 percent of the contribution for all permanent employees, but not for nonregular (temporary) workers, encouraging the trend toward increasing the proportion of nonregular workers (see Chapters 5 and 6). The government considered extending the contribution requirement to nonregular workers, but it withdrew the proposal in response to strong resistance from the private sector, especially retailers and other service industries that rely heavily on nonregular workers.[73] The entire debate in 2003–4 was colored by a scandal in which top figures from all major political parties admitted to having failed to pay into the system. As a result, DPJ leader Naoto Kan stepped down from his party post, and Chief Cabinet Officer Yasuo Fukuda resigned from the Diet. Prime Minister Koizumi conceded that he had missed payments when they were still voluntary for Diet members before 1986 but insisted that he had faithfully contributed since that time. The DPJ took advantage of voter displeasure with premium hikes and benefit cuts, making pension reform a central pillar of its campaign strategy in the July 2004 Upper House elections. In the September 2005 Lower House elections, however, the LDP largely succeeded in keeping pension reform out of the spotlight, despite the DPJ's attempts to shift the focus from postal reform to pensions and other social policies.

Competition

REGULATORY REFORM: LIBERALIZATION WITHOUT DEREGULATION

The Japanese government has taken a distinctive approach to regulatory reform: selectively promoting competition while still controlling entry and exit; packaging elaborate political compromises, including substantial compensation for the formerly regulated industries; and resisting the delegation of authority from central ministries to independent regulatory agencies.[74] As noted in the previous chapter, Japanese exporters have been less supportive of deregulation than one would otherwise expect, for they have been concerned that it might undermine strong cooperative relationships with workers, banks, suppliers, and distributors. Moreover, the proponents of deregulation have been bound to the opponents through common ties to industry associations, government ministries, and the LDP.

The Japanese government designated deregulation a national priority in 1993, when Prime Minister Morihiro Hosokawa appointed a new study group,

---

72. *Nikkei Weekly* (June 7, 2004), 2; (June 14, 2004), 7.
73. *Nikkei Weekly* (February 9, 2004), 2.
74. Vogel 1996, 207–13.

to be headed by Keidanren chairman Gaishi Hiraiwa. Government officials tried to enhance the prospects for meaningful reform by stacking deliberation councils with reform advocates, excluding opponents, and structuring the councils to impede manipulation by individual ministries. The Hosokawa administration excluded bureaucrats and former bureaucrats from the Hiraiwa commission, but the committee then found itself reliant on bureaucrats for their expertise. The government created a new deregulation headquarters in the Cabinet Office in February 1994, giving politicians greater authority to set the reform agenda relative to the ministries. It produced a five-year action program in March 1995 and established a Deregulation Committee under the new Administrative Reform Committee (*gyōsei kaikaku iinkai*, or Gyōkakui for short) to implement the program in December. It appointed notable reform advocates to leadership positions and deliberately excluded unions, consumers, and other groups that might oppose deregulation. The committee staff and members worked together to find creative ways to maximize results. They published reports outlining the costs and benefits of specific regulations, for example, and asked ministries to justify their positions publicly when they disagreed with the committee's recommendations. Committee chair Yoshihiko Miyauchi explains:

> Our committee has been all private sector and all pro reform, so we have not had any fights among ourselves. We make our recommendations to the government. Then the ministries oppose us. And then we have a debate. But government officials can be vulnerable to rational argumentation. So eventually they say they will try to convince industry. And then the industry opposes. So we have to persuade them all the way—that is the key.[75]

In 2001, the government launched a new Regulatory Reform Council with a more comprehensive mandate to investigate systemic issues as well as specific regulations.[76] In 2003, the council identified twelve priority areas, including permitting private companies to provide health insurance and nursing care and authorizing banks to sell insurance policies. It followed with a more comprehensive three-year plan in 2004. It would monitor progress with regulatory impact analysis, requiring the relevant ministries to publicize information about the costs of regulation and the benefits from reform. Meanwhile, the cabinet set up two new regulatory reform panels, one for cabinet ministers and the other for private-sector experts.[77] Despite all these efforts, the

75. Miyauchi interview, June 18, 2003.
76. Kazuaki Tanaka, a former MCA official and a member of the Deregulation Committee (interview, January 24, 2002), suggests that the new council lacked the Deregulation Committee's mechanisms for combating ministry resistance and monitoring implementation.

government made relatively modest progress in promoting competition.[78] It went further in dynamic sectors, such as telecommunications, however, than in more political sectors, such as retail.

In telecommunications, analysts have described the politics of reform as a contest between two coalitions: an old-guard coalition, comprising the monopoly service provider and its favored equipment suppliers, and a reform coalition, comprising corporate users, computer firms, and potential market entrants.[79] In Japan, however, the groups we would expect to favor reform— the computer firms, the non-NTT-family equipment manufacturers, and the potential market entrants—were virtually absent from the political debate. The non-NTT-family equipment manufacturers were members of an industry association, the Communications Industry Association of Japan (CIAJ), that was dominated by the NTT-family manufacturers. The Ministry of Posts and Telecommunications itself took the lead in pushing through privatization and liberalization, viewing the reform process as an opportunity to assert its rightful role as the primary agency in the sector.[80]

The government passed legislation to liberalize the market and privatize NTT in 1985, with the ministry closely controlling price and service changes by both NTT and its new competitors. In 1997, Prime Minister Hashimoto, the MPT, and NTT worked out a delicate compromise whereby NTT would be allowed into the international telephone service market and would be broken up into one long-distance carrier and two regional carriers, but the three units would remain joined within a single holding company. In reaching this compromise, ministry officials assured NTT that the operating companies would be able to make a reasonable profit within three years. After this settlement, some ministry officials became less aggressive in promoting competition and more protective of NTT. In March 1998, the ministry announced a three-year program of deregulation measures, including the elimination of some price regulations and the recalibration of interconnection charges (charges levied by NTT for other providers using its network). Keidanren supported

77. *Nikkei Weekly* (March 22, 2004), 2. A senior official of the Ministry of Public Management, Home Affairs, Posts, and Telecommunications (MPHPT) (interview, July 2004), notes that LDP leaders set up this vertical structure, with the cabinet committee over the private-sector committee, in order to exercise more oversight over committee chairman Yoshihiko Miyauchi (president of Orix Corporation) and his colleagues, who they felt had been in office too long and had pushed deregulation too far.

78. See Organization for Economic Co-operation and Development 1999 and 2005, 152–56, for assessments. Although the number of government regulations is at best a very crude measure of the overall level of regulation, the government's own data show an increase from 10,581 regulations in 1990 to 11,007 in 2003 (Organization for Economic Co-operation and Development 2005, 155).

79. Borrus et al. 1985.

80. Vogel 1996, 137–66.

competition in principle but refrained from commenting directly on interconnection charges or the reorganization of NTT. Participants in this debate
contend that Keidanren held back because its chairman sat on the NTT board
and NTT threatened to take its whole group of companies out of Keidanren if
the association backed bolder reforms.[81] In July 2000, the United States and
Japan concluded an agreement to reduce interconnection charges in Japan.

Meanwhile, the government and the private sector were acutely aware that
they lagged the United States in the all-important information technology
sector, and they mobilized to address this gap. The government's IT Strategy
Council unveiled an ambitious reform program in December 2000 designed
to propel Japan to global leadership in the IT sector by 2005. The plan combined liberalization of the telecommunications market, heavy investment in
telecommunications infrastructure, improvements in the legal apparatus to
support electronic commerce, and measures to promote electronic government. The Ministry of Internal Affairs and Communications (MIC) seized this
opportunity to press NTT to lower interconnection charges and to lease
unused copper and fiber-optic lines.[82] This fueled a remarkable price war in
digital subscriber line (DSL) services (see the Softbank case in Chapter 6),
giving Japan the lowest prices in the world for these services. NTT responded
by demanding higher interconnection charges and new restrictions on access
to its fiber-optic network. When the government subsequently allowed NTT
to raise its interconnection rates, NTT's competitors took the extraordinary
step of challenging this decision in court. By 2003, the government shifted its
policy focus from infrastructure to content. It targeted seven areas for development: medical services, food, lifestyle, financing for small and midsize
firms, "intelligent" work, employment, and administrative services.[83]

The Japanese government has been more cautious with liberalization in
retail, as in other politically sensitive sectors, because of the potential impact
on small businesses. Although manufacturers would benefit from more efficient distribution, they did not actively press for deregulation. Keidanren
included retail in its deregulation proposals but did not make it a priority. The
large retailers pressed for liberalization, however.[84] The Chamber of Commerce, which represents small businesses, and the LDP opposed reform. MITI

81. Interviews, August 2000.

82. The MPT was folded into the Ministry of Public Management, Home Affairs, Posts,
and Telecommunications (MPHPT) in 2000, and the MPHPT's English-language name was
changed to the MIC in 2004.

83. See Kushida forthcoming for a detailed review of developments in telecommunications policy.

84. Interview with Noriyuki Watanabe, Chairman, Seiyu Ltd., and Chairman, Japan
Chain Stores Association, January 23, 2002.

found itself torn between its basic stance in favor of deregulation and its role as the supervising ministry for the retail sector.

MITI announced an initial proposal for reforming the Large-Scale Retail Store Law in 1989, and the U.S. government pressed for reform through the Strategic Impediments Initiative (SII) talks.[85] The government phased in reforms gradually from 1990 through 1994, streamlining the approval process for large stores but allowing small merchants to exercise considerable control. In practice, local regulatory boards required most large store operators to reduce planned floor space before accepting their proposals. Moreover, the government compensated small retailers with a new budget line of ¥10 billion a year to support the modernization of local shopping districts.[86] These reforms led to a substantial expansion of large stores and a crisis of overcapacity by 2000.[87] In May 1998, the government replaced the Large-Scale Retail Store Law with a new regulatory regime (effective in 2000) that devolved authority to local governments. The new system was designed to encourage competition while allowing local authorities to promote social values such as preserving the environment. Critics argued, however, that it left considerable discretion in the hands of both MITI and the local governments and that it might actually constrain competition in practice.[88]

In 2002, Kabun Mutō and his anti-deregulation forces (see Chapter 3) mobilized to roll back the deregulation of liquor stores by limiting discounts and imposing zoning restrictions on general merchandise stores selling liquor. "We have to use antitrust policy to protect smaller enterprises," insisted Mutō. "The strongest should not always rule." Although Keidanren favored deregulation in principle, Mutō obtained assurances from Keidanren leaders that they would not interfere on this particular issue.[89] Mutō and his colleagues prevailed in 2003, as the ruling coalition passed emergency legislation to soften the impact of deregulation by prohibiting large retailers from opening stores in locations where competition was found to be "excessive." By 2004, 1,274 zones (37.7 percent of total zones nationwide) had been designated "reverse special zones" in which new liquor retailers were barred from entry for one year to protect the existing liquor stores.[90]

The Regulatory Reform Council also waged a major battle against the Ministry of Health, Labor, and Welfare (MHLW) and pharmacists over permitting general retailers to sell over-the-counter drugs. Council members

85. Schoppa 1997, 155–63.
86. Schoppa 1997, 174–80.
87. Katz 2003, 269; McKinsey Global Institute 2000.
88. Satō 1998.
89. Interview with Kabun Mutō, Member, House of Representatives, April 4, 2002.
90. *Nikkei Weekly* (September 13, 2004), 15.

even staged a public debate with the ministry in March 2003.[91] The council recommended liberalization, but that left the ministry to determine the list of products the general retailers could offer. The ministry decided to exclude cold medicines and analgesics, arguing that these items can have dangerous side effects.[92]

ANTITRUST: THE HOLDING COMPANY RETURNS

Large corporations, industry associations, and MITI had been interested in lifting the ban on holding companies for years, but they feared that this move would be viewed as a blatant expansion of corporate power and a threat to the postwar antitrust regime. In the 1990s, however, they seized their opportunity. The U.S. occupation forces had enacted the ban to break up the prewar industrial groups (*zaibatsu*). Corporate executives felt that holding companies could help them with financial management by allowing them to offset profits in one company with losses in another. They could also reduce labor costs by differentiating wages and benefits across companies; reorganize internally by turning divisions into separate companies; and merge with other companies more easily by using a holding company structure.[93] MOF officials had explored the holding company option as a mechanism for allowing cross-entry among different types of financial institutions in the late 1980s, but they ruled it out because they judged that it would not be politically feasible.

A MITI policy council proposed lifting the ban in February 1995. The issue came up in a Diet question, so staff members in the Industrial Organization Policy Division rushed to brief MITI minister Ryūtarō Hashimoto on the proposal. They were astonished when Hashimoto instantly embraced the idea, and they began to explore ways to push it through. LDP politicians sought to link the proposal to ongoing efforts to strengthen the Fair Trade Commission, Japan's antitrust regulator: they would support a tougher antitrust regime in exchange for allowing holding companies. The FTC then shifted in favor of lifting the ban, and an FTC report issued that summer recommended allowing holding companies under certain circumstances, subject to FTC discretion. The LDP, MITI, and industry protested, arguing that holding companies should be allowed in principle and banned by exception, not the other way around.[94]

91. *Nikkei Weekly* (March 10, 2003), 4.

92. *Nikkei Weekly* (December 29, 2003), 28.

93. Interviews with Hideo Watanabe, Managing Director, Mitsubishi Chemical Corporation, February 27, 1996, and Kazumasa Abe, Senior Counsel, Legal Department, Nippon Steel, April 15, 1996.

94. Interview with Shigeaki Koga, Director, Industrial Organization Policy Division, Industrial Policy Bureau, MITI, April 2, 1996.

The unions did not grasp the implications of the proposal until late 1995, when they suddenly enlisted the support of the Social Democratic Party of Japan (SDPJ) in demanding amendments to the draft legislation. They hoped to ensure that the holding companies themselves would have a duty to negotiate with unions rather than be able to pass it off to member companies. The unions feared that holding companies would use the structure to undermine the balanced distribution of wages and benefits across member companies— and of course, this is precisely what the corporations had in mind. The government coalition, which included the SDPJ at the time, was sympathetic to the unions yet determined to push through the bill so it could use the holding company structure for the reorganization of NTT. The government agreed to review the unions' demands in a ministerial council, but the council eventually determined that the unions did not need further protection since companies have an obligation to bargain in good faith under existing law.[95] Few firms other than NTT and a small number of financial institutions formed holding companies after the reform passed in 1997, in part because they could not fully take advantage of this structure until the government introduced a consolidated tax system in 2003 (see below).

The FTC and Nippon Keidanren began to clash publicly over proposals to strengthen antitrust regulation after Kazuhiko Takeshima took over as FTC chairman in 2002. The U.S. government had raised the antitrust issue under the rubric of the SII talks in the late 1980s and made it a priority in bilateral talks in the 1990s. The FTC gradually increased its staff from 150 in 1990 to 672 in 2004 and its budget from ¥5.24 billion in 1995 to ¥7.81 billion in 2004, yet enforcement remained relatively lax by international standards.[96] In regulated sectors, such as telecommunications and electricity, the FTC took a more active role in promoting competition, issuing its own progress reports. The government also revised the Anti-Monopoly Law, effective April 2001, so that consumers and companies could directly seek court injunctions on violations of the law rather than ask the FTC to take action on their behalf. Meanwhile, the FTC was merged into the Ministry of Public Management, Home Affairs, Posts, and Telecommunications (MPHPT) under the administrative reform of 2000, and then separated again in 2003.

The FTC prepared legislation to strengthen antitrust policy by expanding its investigative powers, doubling penalties for price fixing to 12 percent of sales obtained from anticompetitive practices, and offering leniency to firms that blow the whistle on their partners in collusion. Nippon Keidanren strongly

95. Interview with Takuya Seryū, Executive Director, Department of General Planning, Rengō, August 10, 2000.

96. Katz 2003, 243–44; FTC data.

opposed these measures, however, arguing that the government was acting too quickly; that the penalty increase was unreasonable; that the penalties were unconstitutional because they could subject executives to double (civil and criminal) punishment; that the FTC would be acting as both prosecutor and judge if firms filed appeals with the FTC; and that the proposals failed to address the government's own role in collusion, especially via public procurement practices.[97] The LDP was especially concerned about small business opposition to the reforms and delayed action on the proposal from spring 2004 to spring 2005. The Diet finally forged a compromise in April 2005, passing a bill to increase fines to 10 percent for large companies and 4 percent for smaller companies; to encourage whistle-blowing by waiving fines for the first company to admit illegal activity and reducing fines for the second and third; and to strengthen the FTC's powers to conduct criminal investigations.[98]

TAX REFORM: MULTIPLE AGENDAS, MULTIPLE ARENAS

Tax reform nicely illustrates the complex interconnections among different policy reforms. Lifting the ban on holding companies was incomplete, for example, without changing the tax system so that companies could benefit from reorganization. With consolidated taxation, holding companies would be able to subtract losses from unprofitable subsidiaries from overall profits, thereby reducing their tax bill. The MOF resisted this change, however, because it feared a reduction in tax revenues. The ministry announced its intention to introduce consolidated taxation in April 2001 but then announced in November that it would have to postpone implementation because it could not prepare legislation in time. Several cabinet members joined the business community in protest, and eventually the ministry agreed to honor the original schedule even if the legislation was not fully in place. The MOF then came up with a classic bureaucratic compromise. It would levy a 2 percent surcharge tax on corporations using consolidated taxation and add further measures to offset the projected ¥800 billion tax shortfall, eliminating tax-deductible retirement payment reserves (¥300 billion) and restricting loss carry-forwards for subsidiaries prior to the introduction of the consolidated tax system (¥500 billion). One ministry official conceded that this was a case of ministerial "aestheticism" (*bigaku*) run amok, for the compensating tax increase would undermine the original goals of the reform.[99]

97. Interview with Yoshio Nakamura, Senior Managing Director, Nippon Keidanren, July 20, 2004; *Nihon Keizai Shimbun* (May 2, 2005), 11.

98. *Nihon Keizai Shimbun* (May 2, 2005), 11.

99. Interview with Shigeki Morinobu, Executive Vice President, Policy Research Institute, Ministry of Finance, January 21, 2002.

In April 2002, Prime Minister Koizumi announced plans for comprehensive tax reform to shift toward a less progressive tax system; to redesign tax incentives to promote corporate restructuring; to adjust tax policy to changes in other areas, such as finance and corporate governance; and to stimulate the economy via selective tax reductions. The debate was centered in three committees with overlapping jurisdiction: the LDP's Tax Committee (*zeisei chōsakai*), the cabinet's Tax Council (*seifu zeisei chōsakai*), and the Council on Economic and Fiscal Policy, or CEFP (*keizai zaisei shimon kaigi*). The LDP committee was inherently oriented toward party constituents, favoring selective tax cuts. The MOF exercised substantial control over the cabinet council, emphasizing revenue generation but also playing the classic role of balancing interests. The CEFP, a more academic advisory council, advocated corporate tax cuts plus tax relief in specific policy areas.[100] The net result was an unusually disjointed process of negotiation. Business groups pushed for lower corporate taxes, higher consumption taxes, and other measures that would move the system in a more regressive direction. This strategy, however, bore the risk of further stifling consumer demand and preventing economic recovery.[101] Nippon Keidanren chairman Hiroshi Okuda even devised a plan to raise the consumption tax by 1 percent a year beginning in 2004 until it hit 16 percent in 2014. Insiders suggest that Okuda could not possibly have come up with this proposal on his own—the Ministry of Finance must have gotten to him.[102] In March 2005, the ruling coalition decided to reduce the 1999 cuts in income and residence taxes by half and to consider eliminating the cuts altogether the following year.[103]

Koizumi's "Structural" Reforms

As noted in Chapter 3, Prime Minister Junichirō Koizumi understood that the public was fed up with the old LDP machine, especially wasteful public works spending, and he turned this potential liability into an asset as he vowed to dismantle the system. Analysts depict a battle between Koizumi and the LDP's old guard, but the reality is considerably more complex. On the core agenda for economic reform—fighting deflation and resolving the nonperforming loan crisis—Koizumi became bogged down by contradictory advice from his own experts (see Chapter 2). Koizumi himself had less passion and

100. Mulgan 2002, 198–200.

101. Katz 2003, 278–83.

102. Interview, March 2003. The MOF advocates a shift toward consumption taxes in order to prevent a deterioration of the fiscal balance as the Japanese population ages and wage earners (who pay more taxes via income) decrease in proportion to retirees (who pay more taxes via consumption).

103. *Japan Times* (March 31, 2005), 3.

less expertise on these issues, and many key advisers counseled him against the prescriptions most widely recommended by economists. Meanwhile, Koizumi put more energy into his own favored "structural" reforms, focusing especially on the special public corporations, the postal system, and regional structural reform zones. These reforms have major ramifications for the ongoing evolution of Japan's economic model because dismantling the public works machine would undermine an important mechanism of redistribution and employment maintenance, and effective postal reform would fundamentally restructure the financial system.

THE SPECIAL PUBLIC CORPORATIONS: KOIZUMI VERSUS THE PARTY MACHINE

Koizumi recognized that he could not control wasteful public works spending without reforming the special public corporations that do much of the spending. The government was allocating ¥6 trillion in subsidies plus ¥24 trillion in loans annually to these corporations from postal savings money channeled through the FILP. The government had created the FILP as well as many of the special public corporations in the early postwar years, and they had served as critical mechanisms for both sides of Japan's "dual" political economy: an industrial policy designed to direct personal savings into productive investment in growth sectors, and a redistributive strategy aimed at compensating less favored regions and sectors.[104] Koizumi and his advisers argued that the system had outlived its utility and now posed an excessive burden on government finances and distorted financial markets. They earmarked the seventy-seven special public corporations plus three thousand–odd subsidiaries for reform, with special emphasis on the four highway corporations and the Housing Loan Corporation.

LDP members quickly mobilized a working group to fight Koizumi's proposals. Keidanren supported Koizumi's overall reform program yet was unable to forge a unified position on special corporation reform. "We have too many members in the construction sector and other areas who benefit from this system, so we simply cannot take up the issue," conceded one official.[105] The government ministries, which were reluctant to embrace reform of those special corporations under their jurisdiction, responded with a list of only four corporations for liquidation, all of which had been previously earmarked. Koizumi's own state minister for administrative reform, Nobuteru Ishihara, proposed reforms for only about one-third of the corporations.[106] Ishihara

104. Woodall 1996, Park 2005.
105. Nakamura interview, October 12, 2001.
106. *Oriental Economist* (December 2001), 7.

describes the political dynamics with some resignation: "The regions and the organizations that benefit from the special public corporations naturally resist the elimination or privatization of these corporations. They need the second budget all the more when economic conditions are bad. Diet members valiantly defend them. And of course, money politics gets mixed in as well."[107] Koizumi responded by focusing on a few of the most prominent cases. He pledged to liquidate the Housing Loan Corporation altogether but subsequently settled for a privatization scheme. He initially pressed for reform of all nine government-run financial institutions, including the Development Bank of Japan. By privatizing these institutions, the government would eliminate an important mechanism of industrial and regional policy. It scaled back proposals, however, because these institutions were playing a critical role in maintaining lending while the troubled private banks pulled back.

Koizumi waged a particularly heated battle over highway reform. He cut ¥300 billion from the fiscal 2002 budget for highway construction, threatened to freeze new highway construction entirely, and slated the four highway corporations for privatization. Under the government's initial proposal, the Japan Highway Public Corporation, the largest of the four, would be split into three regional entities, making it harder to cross-subsidize unprofitable highways with profitable ones. The government would drastically cut back on new highway construction and gradually pay off the corporations' ¥40 trillion in debt. The LDP old guard and the Ministry of Land, Infrastructure, and Transport fought back, however, and sabotaged the reforms before they passed the Diet in June 2004. The government would retain about one-third of the new corporations' shares and would have the power to approve business plans, issue stock, and appoint chief executives. Moreover, an administrative entity would own the road assets and bear the corresponding debts, and the new corporations would simply lease and manage the highways. The government maintained its commitment to paying off the debt but refused to scale back planned highway construction projects.[108] Two members of the government's own reform highway reform panel resigned in protest of these concessions to the opponents of reform.[109]

POSTAL REFORM: KOIZUMI'S CORE MISSION

Koizumi earned his reputation as a maverick by proposing the privatization of the postal system—including mail delivery, postal savings, and postal insurance—as minister of posts and telecommunications in 1992, violating

107. Interview, June 19, 2003.
108. *Oriental Economist* (April 2004), 8–9.
109. *Nikkei Weekly* (December 19, 2003), 2.

the standard that a minister should protect the interests of his own ministry. This threatened the LDP's political machine, for the "special" (franchise) post-masters play a critical role in mobilizing votes for the party in rural areas.[110] Private financial institutions lobbied hard for reform, however, because the postal savings system has built-in competitive advantages that squeeze them out of business. The postal savings and life insurance systems held about one-quarter of all personal assets in Japan, and this share had been rising steadily.[111] Reform proponents contended that Japan would never develop a truly market-based financial system without privatizing or eliminating the postal savings system. Koizumi himself came from a district with few special post offices and garnered considerable support from financial institutions, especially the Bank of Yokohama.[112] The Democratic Party itself was divided between proponents and opponents of reform, as members with labor constituencies sided with the postal unions. In November 2001, Diet members formed a nonpartisan alliance to oppose postal reform, with 165 members in the Lower House and 150 in the Upper House. The LDP committee leaders with jurisdiction on the issue were strongly opposed to the reform, so Koizumi took the extraordinary step of submitting the proposal to the Diet without the committee's approval, although he managed to get the informal consent of Hiromu Nonaka, the top Postal Tribe (*yūseizoku*) boss. Nonaka and his colleagues insisted that Koizumi put off any consideration of privatization until after the postal system was organized, and they negotiated amendments before allowing the bill to pass in July 2002.[113] The legislation turned the postal service into a public corporation, Japan Post, and permitted private mail carriers to deliver mail. It imposed a requirement, however, that new mail carriers would have to provide nationwide service at uniform rates, effectively ensuring that no new entrants would emerge. Moreover, it gave the ministry the right to appoint the president of the new public corporation and to define what constituted postal mail, thereby specifying the terms of private-sector participation in the postal business.[114]

The government then devised three alternatives for further reform: create a semipublic corporation that would provide mail service but reduce its role in postal savings and life insurance by lowering limits on individual accounts; privatize the postal service as a holding company, with savings and life insurance handled by regional subsidiaries; or privatize the mail service and

110. Maclachlan 2004.

111. ¥350 trillion of the ¥1,400 trillion total personal financial assets in Japan as of 2005 (*Nikkei Weekly*, April 11, 2005, 7).

112. Mulgan 2002, 136–37.

113. Mulgan 2002, 223–24.

114. Mulgan 2002, 102.

abolish postal savings and insurance by refusing new accounts.[115] In an interim report in April 2004, the Council on Economic and Fiscal Policy recommended gradually privatizing Japan Post over ten years, beginning in April 2007. During the transition period, the government would give Japan Post greater managerial freedom but also would require it to pay corporate taxes and contribute to deposit insurance premiums.[116] The Postal Tribe remained committed to stopping privatization, the private banks hoped to restrict the new entity so that it would not emerge as an even more dominant competitor, and MOF officials sought to maintain Japan Post's role as a stable buyer of government bonds.

Koizumi engaged in an extraordinary battle with members of his own party as he pressed forward with privatization, threatening to dissolve the Diet if the bill did not pass. The cabinet approved a bill in April 2005 that made substantial concessions to privatization opponents. It would break Japan Post into four units under a holding company: postal savings, postal life insurance, mail delivery, and post office network management. The government would retain a one-third share of the holding company after completing privatization in 2017, but it would sell off 100 percent of the savings and life insurance operations. The government would allow the postal firms to own one another's shares after privatization. It would permit the savings and life insurance units to protect themselves from hostile takeovers by limiting voting rights for a portion of their shares. And it would maintain a ¥1 trillion fund to preserve post offices and postal financial services in sparsely populated areas.[117] The Lower House passed the bill by a narrow margin, as thirty-seven LDP members voted against the bill and another fourteen abstained. The Upper House defeated the bill by a vote of 125 to 108, however, as twenty-two LDP members voted against the bill and eight abstained or were absent. Koizumi promptly made good on his threat to dissolve the Lower House, setting up the September 2005 election in which Koizumi ousted the Lower House rebels from the party, framed postal privatization as a litmus test for reform, and won a spectacular victory at the polls (Chapter 3).

THE STRUCTURAL REFORM SPECIAL ZONES: ONE COUNTRY, TWO SYSTEMS?

The Koizumi administration also launched a program of special reform zones that would be exempt from various government regulations in June 2002. Proponents saw this as a creative way to cut through resistance to

---

115. *Daily Yomiuri* (August 29, 2002), 18.
116. *Nikkei Weekly* (May 3, 2004), 2.
117. *Nikkei Weekly* (April 11, 2005), 1.

deregulation by experimenting with reforms that were limited in geographi-cal scope and by cultivating local support. As of March 2004, the government had approved 328 zones in ten categories, with the largest number focusing on agriculture, community life, or education. The government's "evaluation committee" not only selects specific proposals but also may recommend that reforms initiated in special zones be extended nationally.[118] Ministry bureau-crats were wary of offering regulatory exceptions to these zones, however, and denied many requests and imposed conditions on others. For example, the government allowed private companies to engage in farming, but only if they would lease the farmland rather than buy it, and to enter the medical field, but only for services not covered by national health insurance pro-grams.[119] The program became mired in the contradiction between the reformers' original goals and LDP politicians' instinctive desire to use the program to reward constituents. The Regulatory Reform Council insisted that the government not provide any financing for these zones, yet politicians saw no point in the program unless it offered financial benefits.[120]

Variations across Issue Areas

It is difficult if not impossible to "measure" policy change, yet it is impor-tant to make some qualitative assessments about change and continuity pre-cisely because there has been a combination of major reforms in some areas and deadlock in others. Let us briefly consider three possible criteria by which to assess policy change. If we focus on the sheer scale of reform activity—the level of political effort expended, the quantity of legislation passed, and the number of regulations revised—then corporate law reform and Koizumi's structural reforms probably top the list. It is striking, however, that by this definition the level of reform has been relatively high in all the issue areas reviewed in this chapter. This finding underscores the argument, presented in Chapter 2, that the Japanese government has not failed to reform. The government's shortcomings have been in the substance and not in the scale of reform. Alternatively, we might judge reform by comparing a policy regime at one time (2005, for example) with an earlier point in time (1995, for example) and then evaluating the degree of change. By this metric, the gov-ernment has accomplished the most with the Big Bang, corporate law, account-ing, and telecommunications reforms. In each of these areas, the government overturned basic principles of regulation that had survived with relative sta-bility through most of the postwar era. In contrast, reforms in labor, pensions,

118. Organization for Economic Co-operation and Development 2005, 156–59.
119. *Nikkei Weekly* (April 28, 2003), 7.
120. Mulgan 2002, 116–17.

industrial policy, and retail did not fundamentally overturn the existing policy regimes. Finally, looking forward to the following chapters, we might also evaluate the reforms in terms of their impact on corporate behavior. We might begin by making a distinction between reforms that simply give corporations more options and reforms that impose mandatory changes in corporate behavior. The labor market and corporate law reforms and many of the industrial revitalization measures, for example, were designed to give corporations more choices. Several of the key accounting reforms, in contrast, forced corporations to alter their practices. In addition, certain reforms virtually mandate changes in behavior, not directly via legal rule but indirectly via the market mechanism. For example, the Big Bang reforms and telecommunications liberalization transformed the competitive environment so radically that corporations had no choice but to revise their basic strategies.

These judgments fall short of an objective ranking of issue areas from most to least reformed, but they give us enough of a sense of the variation across issue areas to revisit the hypotheses presented at the beginning of the chapter. The most striking finding is that there is no clear correlation between the level of crisis in a particular issue area and the level of reform. The Japanese government moved slowly and cautiously in those areas where the crisis was most obvious and the economic stakes were highest—resolving the banking crisis and combating deflation, for example—while it moved more aggressively in areas where problems were less obvious and the link between reform and economic performance was far more tenuous, such as accounting and special public corporation reform.

The other hypotheses noted at the outset of this chapter fare reasonably well across the cases reviewed here. The Japanese government has gone further with reform in dynamic, international, and technical issue areas (financial regulation, accounting, corporate law, telecommunications, antitrust) than in stable, domestic, and highly politicized areas (labor, pensions, retail). In addition, we find that external influence has been critical in pushing many of the reforms forward. The U.S. government and international organizations have pressed Japan toward some reforms (lowering interconnection charges); international market pressures have propelled others (liberalizing stock commissions); and the diffusion of international norms of best practice has driven others (accounting). In addition, some of the boldest reforms have come in those areas relatively insulated from the political process, such as accounting and corporate law. In accounting, the MOF and the FSA were able to make major changes via agency decree, thus avoiding the legislative process altogether. In corporate law, the MOJ and METI collaborated quietly, in consultation with Keidanren.

These political dynamics affect the sequence as well as the substance of reforms. The Japanese government tends to move from external liberalization to internal liberalization and from "stealth" liberalization to more overt measures. Reform advocates understand this and try to manipulate the sequence of reforms accordingly, deploying politically feasible measures as levers to achieve broader reform over the long run. In finance, for example, the Big Bang's supporters reasoned that lifting foreign exchange restrictions—one of the first steps in the program, and one that faced little opposition—would give Japanese investors more access to foreign markets, which in turn would increase market pressure for further reforms in domestic markets. Furthermore, they believed that the Big Bang financial reforms would drive reform in other sectors beyond finance.

If reform is moving further in some sectors than others, this raises the question of how tightly the different parts of the Japanese system are linked. As noted in Chapter 1, the complementarity between the components of the Japanese model affects the trajectory of change. Among the reforms reviewed in this chapter, the core financial reforms—financial liberalization, accounting reform, and pension reform—have the greatest potential to drive systemwide adjustments. Financial liberalization presses corporations to compete for capital and therefore to maximize returns. Accounting reform forces them to pay greater attention to short-term returns and gives them more incentive to sell off unproductive assets and to focus on their most productive operations. And pension reform could reorient the financial system more toward equity markets. Among these three areas, the government has moved furthest with financial liberalization and accounting reform, but it could move ahead with pension reform in the years to come. The logic of complementarity suggests that firms are able to make long-term commitments to their workers only because the financial system shields them from shareholder demands for short-term profits.[121] If this were true, then financial reforms should force Japanese firms to abandon the long-term employment system. Yet scholars in the Varieties of Capitalism and New Institutional Economics schools overstate how tightly the components of the system are linked: financial reforms certainly press firms to adjust, but they do not dictate *how* the firms adjust. Although changes in finance have pressured companies to reduce costs and raise returns, firms have not been forced to abandon the core features of the labor-relations system. In the logic of our original model, new challenges may push firms to reassess valued institutions but can also make firms embrace these institutions in new ways.

121. Aoki 1994.

The reforms reviewed in this chapter have substantially altered the strategic options available to Japanese corporations. They have allowed greater freedom in labor relations and corporate organization, imposed new requirements in accounting, introduced new tax breaks and subsidies, and transformed the competitive environment in many sectors. In the next two chapters, we examine how corporations have responded to these changes.

5 CORPORATE RESTRUCTURING JAPANESE STYLE

Japanese companies have restructured in the face of economic pressures since the early 1990s, yet they have done so in a distinctively Japanese fashion. Takayoshi Nakano, a senior manager at Nippon Steel, explains:

> Our definition of restructuring differs from that of American consultants. The Japanese model of long-term employment and the main bank system have reached their limits. All the big companies face the challenge of becoming more competitive—but we hesitate. We ask: Has the Japanese model lost all meaning? We cannot simply focus on financial results. We have stakeholders, we have an obligation to our workers, and we have a responsibility for regional development. So the question is: How far do we go?[1]

Japanese firms will emerge from this process with systems of labor relations, corporate finance, and corporate networks that differ from both Japanese institutions of the past and U.S. institutions of the present. This chapter seeks to grasp the unfolding substance of this transition.

Labor Relations

Japanese firms have responded to increased pressure to cut costs in remarkably predictable ways, given the enormous diversity across sectors and companies. Following the logic laid out in Chapter 1, Japanese firms have favored voice over exit: they negotiate restraints on wages or reductions in working hours rather than lay off workers. They do not simply weigh the cost of shrinking the workforce versus the benefit of reducing operating expenses but consider how layoffs might impair their ability to mobilize remaining workers to enhance productivity, to recruit new workers in the future, and to project a positive image in the business community.[2]

1. Interview, August 3, 2000.
2. Ahmadjian and Robinson (2001, 6) argue that companies learned from their experience in the 1970s, when those that reduced their workforce suffered a decline in labor-management relations and corporate image.

Nissan's "Revival Plan" of 1999 was one of the most aggressive restructuring schemes in recent Japanese history, yet even Nissan managers did not consider laying off workers. One manager reports:

> We had to take into account the union; the local community, including local businesses and suppliers; and our image overall. Some of the stakeholders resisted because they felt this would hurt us in the long run, after we recover. But the larger problem concerned our public image. The Murayama plant closure was featured on the front page of the news, so this really hurt our reputation. Our image among college students, our potential recruits, dropped considerably.[3]

An NEC executive depicts the reasoning slightly differently: "We could not lay off workers in Japan. This is not due to the law, but to social responsibility. We have 150,000 workers, and most of them have families. We have to think about them. If we laid them off, the local government would get after us, and the media too."[4] The Nissan and NEC managers appear to calculate within all three of the circles of rationality outlined in Chapter 1: they consider immediate costs, the longer-term damage to comparative institutional advantage, and the broader loss of reputation.

Japanese employers are not only reluctant to lay off workers but ambivalent about workforce reductions of any kind. A Japan Institute of Labor survey found that more respondents thought workforce reductions would improve productivity (35.9 percent) than felt reductions would reduce productivity (14.3 percent), yet more judged that reductions would undermine morale (51.5 percent) than expected reductions would enhance morale (13.6 percent). In addition, 11.3 percent worried that reductions would make it more difficult to recruit new employees, and 17.2 felt reductions would lead more employees to quit.[5]

Moreover, the Japanese model provides troubled corporations with other options: they can collaborate with workers to raise productivity, call on their main bank to obtain more credit, or work with suppliers to reduce procurement costs. As a result, Japanese firms adopt a fairly predictable pattern of adjustment. They focus first on raising productivity and lowering nonlabor costs. Even when they are concerned about labor costs, they tend to focus more on enhancing productivity than cutting wages or workers. A MHLW survey reports that firms deal with high labor costs primarily by increasing

3. Interview with Masahiko Aoki, Senior Vice President, Nissan Motor Co., Ltd., January 15, 2002.

4. Interview with Yoshio Izumi, Vice President, Internet Business Development Office, NEC Corporation, August 3, 2000.

5. Japan Institute of Labor 2002, 21.

sales or cutting nonlabor costs rather than by reducing labor costs directly: 36.9 percent focus on sales growth and product development, and 15.6 percent cut general costs, while 12.7 percent introduce more performance-based wages, 11.6 percent add part-time and temporary workers, and 8.1 percent cut wage costs or reduce workers by attrition.[6] And even when they turn to workforce reductions, they generally avoid outright layoffs. They negotiate with their workers to reduce labor costs per worker, adopting some combination of the following steps: (1) reducing overtime, (2) cutting bonuses, (3) restraining base wages, (4) increasing the proportion of lower-cost "temporary" workers, and (5) reducing work hours ("work sharing").[7] And if necessary, they reduce the workforce by (1) cutting new recruits, (2) transferring workers to affiliated companies, (3) phasing out some nonregular workers, or (4) introducing voluntary early retirement programs.[8] Some firms also compensate for the constraints on employment adjustment at home by downsizing more rapidly abroad. Table 2 shows that nonrenewal of contracts and outright dismissals have accounted for a very small, but growing, share of job separations.[9] Table 3 gives a fuller picture of the relative frequency of the various labor adjustment strategies, plus trends over time. In a comparative study of U.S. and Japanese employment systems through the mid-1990s, Brown et al. found that Japanese labor market institutions change more slowly; Japanese firms require a much deeper economic crisis before they make adjustments to reduce costs; and Japanese firms' adjustments tend to be marginal compared with those of their U.S. counterparts.[10]

Japanese firms have responded to shareholder pressures for restructuring while preserving their commitment to workers by announcing more downsizing than they have actually implemented. Gary Evans of HSBC reviewed restructuring plans from the 1998–99 recession and found that fewer than half the companies came close to fulfilling their plans. Firms made it look as if they were cutting workers by shifting them to new, unlisted subsidiaries or by forming 50–50 joint ventures in which neither partner had a controlling stake (so neither partner had to claim the workers as its own).[11]

6. MHLW 2003 Survey on Wage Increases (*chingin hikiage tō no jittai ni kansuru chōsa*).

7. In general, companies have preferred to restrain wages by reducing overtime and bonuses rather than by cutting base wages. At the aggregate level, base wages have slowly increased since 1990 while overtime and bonus pay has dropped significantly (OECD 2005, 177).

8. Chuma (2002) compares employment adjustment in the 1990s with that of the 1970s and finds that in the 1990s, companies were even more prone to use "soft" modes of adjustment, such as natural attrition and transfers, and less likely to eliminate regular workers.

9. See Chapter 6 for a discussion of the cross-sectoral variation in Table 2.

10. Brown et al. 1997, 61.

11. *Economist* (July 20, 2002), 57.

TABLE 2. *Reasons for Job Separation, 1990–2003 (in Percent)*

Industry	Year	Expiration of contract	Operational reasons			Retirement	Individual's responsibility (dismissal)	Personal reasons
			All	Temporary transfers	Return from secondment			
Total	1990	6.1	6.1	1.5	0.9	3.7	3.7	78.4
	1995	10.1	8.7	2.0	1.1	5.5	5.0	68.2
	2000	10.5	9.3	1.8	1.1	5.2	6.3	67.0
	2003	11.2	10.1	1.8	1.2	6.3	2.4	68.4
Construction	1990	—	—	—	—	—	—	—
	1995	26.1	7.4	1.6	0.5	2.4	5.4	55.1
	2000	21.2	13.1	1.8	0.8	4.0	7.8	51.6
	2003	17.0	22.2	1.5	0.9	8.0	2.1	48.7
Manufacturing	1990	8.0	4.6	1.5	0.5	4.7	3.5	77.0
	1995	8.5	11.1	2.9	0.8	8.8	5.7	63.4
	2000	11.7	13.8	3.3	1.0	10.0	6.1	56.5
	2003	10.7	18.5	3.1	0.8	12.3	2.3	54.0
Electric	1990	4.4	4.2	2.1	0.6	6.4	2.0	80.3
machinery	1995	2.9	12.1	4.5	1.2	8.8	2.8	70.7
	2000	8.6	17.9	4.3	3.1	9.3	6.8	55.6
	2003	10.0	21.0	6.4	1.6	13.7	1.6	51.9
Transport	1990	20.2	3.1	1.0	0.2	4.5	1.3	69.1
equipment	1995	11.2	7.5	2.6	0.8	16.5	7.3	55.1
	2000	14.0	12.7	3.8	1.9	19.9	4.1	47.9
	2003	15.1	8.4	1.8	0.6	21.0	1.2	50.0
Transportation and	1990	4.7	5.8	1.4	1.1	9.7	5.0	72.9
communication	1995	6.8	10.5	3.1	0.2	7.5	8.2	64.8
	2000	8.2	10.4	3.0	0.8	11.7	5.6	61.8
	2003	15.6	9.2	4.1	0.7	9.7	3.6	60.2
Retail	1990	1.3	6.1	1.4	0.9	1.8	3.8	85.0
	1995	5.2	6.8	1.2	0.5	4.5	4.3	76.4
	2000	4.3	6.5	1.1	1.0	2.6	6.8	78.7
	2003	8.0	4.3	0.9	0.5	2.6	3.4	80.4
Finance and	1990	1.6	7.6	3.8	0.8	5.0	1.8	81.8
insurance	1995	3.8	2.5	2.0	0.2	4.2	1.3	87.0
	2000	13.3	3.9	1.5	0.7	5.2	4.1	71.3
	2003	9.1	4.8	2.2	1.2	3.4	0.1	79.0

Source: MHLW, Survey on Employment Trends.

TABLE 3. *Types of Labor Adjustment, 1993–2004 (in Percent)*

Year	Limit overtime	Increase holidays and vacations	Nonrenewal of contracts of nonregular employees	Reduce or cease midcareer recruiting	Transfers (reassignment)	Temporary transfers (*shukkō*)	Temporary layoffs	Voluntary retirement	No labor adjustment implemented
93	26.0	6.0	7.0	18.0	11.0	8.0	4.0	2.0	62.0
94	22.0	4.0	4.0	12.5	9.8	7.8	3.3	2.0	67.3
95	18.3	3.3	2.3	10.8	9.3	7.5	2.0	1.3	71.0
96	13.3	3.0	1.8	6.0	7.0	5.8	1.0	1.5	77.5
97	9.8	3.5	1.5	3.8	6.0	5.0	0.5	1.3	80.5
98	16.8	4.8	4.0	7.8	9.3	6.0	2.0	2.8	71.0
99	17.8	3.8	3.5	8.3	9.5	6.8	3.0	3.8	69.5
00	12.5	2.8	2.0	5.0	7.3	6.0	1.3	2.3	76.8
01	14.0	4.3	3.8	6.0	7.8	5.3	1.5	3.8	73.5
02	14.0	3.8	3.5	5.0	8.5	5.5	2.0	4.5	72.5
03	8.8	3.3	2.5	3.5	6.3	3.8	0.8	2.3	80.0
04	6.0	2.5	1.3	2.0	4.8	2.5	0.0	1.8	84.5

Source: MHLW, Survey on Labor Economy Trends.

Note: 1993 figures based on data from October through December, 2003 and 2004 figures not seasonally adjusted.

In essence, Japanese firms have preserved the long-term employment system for regular workers by making adjustments elsewhere. A Policy Research Institute report indicates that 84.1 percent of firms maintained long-term employment practices as of 2002, down from 90.3 percent in 1999.[12] Average job tenure for regular workers actually increased from 10.9 years in 1990 to 12.1 years in 2004.[13] And employers have not substantially increased midcareer hiring.[14] Japanese firm practices imply that corporations have absorbed some of the cost of economic stagnation, with the net effect of preserving employment at relatively high levels. Unemployment rose steadily from 2.1 percent in 1991 to 5.5 percent in 2003 (compared with 6.0 percent in the United States and 9.5 percent in Germany) before dropping to 4.7 percent

12. Ministry of Finance, Policy Research Institute 2003b, 114.

13. MHLW Basic Survey of Wage Structure (*chingin kōzō kihon tōkei chōsa*).

14. If anything, the MHLW Survey on Employment Management (*koyō kanri chōsa*) shows a decrease in midcareer hires from 1989 to 2004. In 1989, 12.6 percent of firms hired midcareer managers (versus 13.7 percent in 2004); 35.0 percent hired midcareer administrative workers (27.5 percent in 2004); 19.8 percent hired midcareer technicians and researchers (18.4 percent in 2004), and 68.7 percent hired midcareer operational workers (50.8 percent in 2004).

in 2004.[15] Yet Japan's unemployment rates remained remarkably low given its dismal economic performance during this period.

Japanese firms naturally take advantage of the flexibility built into the labor system during an economic downturn. Japan's postwar labor system has been characterized by a starkly tiered system of employment, with regular workers (*shain*), who are considered full members of the corporate community, and nonregular workers, who receive lower wages, fewer benefits, and no long-term employment guarantee. The nonregular workers fall into three main categories: "part-time" workers (*paato*), many of whom actually work full time in relatively high-skilled positions; short-term workers (*arubaito*), such as students and other casual workers; and dispatch workers (*haken rōdōsha*) such as agency temps. Many firms have reduced wage costs by not renewing the contracts of nonregular workers. They have also shifted the burden of adjustment to smaller subcontractors outside the system of long-term employment guarantees by pressing these suppliers for price reductions.

Firms not only reduce labor costs by shedding nonregular workers in the short term, however, but also increase their flexibility and lower their wage costs per worker by increasing the share of nonregular workers in the workforce over the long term. Service-sector firms have been especially likely to adopt this strategy.[16] In fact, according to data from the OECD, which defines part-time employment as less than thirty hours per week, the Japanese part-time employment rate is considerably higher than that of the United States and Germany and has been rising steadily, from 19.2 percent in 1990 to 25.5 percent in 2004 (Figure 6).[17] With the liberalization of the agency temp business (Chapter 4), firms expanded their use of dispatch workers from 257,000 in 1997 to 721,000 in 2002.[18] Since regular workers are overwhelmingly male whereas nonregular workers are mostly female, firms have in essence preserved jobs for men at the expense of women by cutting nonregular workers first.[19] As firms shift the composition of the workforce more toward nonregu-

---

15. IMF World Economic Outlook Database, September 2003.

16. See Chapter 6 on cross-sectoral variations.

17. The MHLW Survey on Employment Trends (*koyō dōkō chōsa*) defines part-time more narrowly, but it reports a similar rising trend, from 11.1 percent in 1990 to 19.8 percent in 2003.

18. The MIC's 2002 Employment Status Survey (*shūgyō kōzō kihon chōsa*) reports the following breakdown for 54.7 million total workers: 3.9 million managers, 34.6 million regular employees, 7.8 million part-time workers (*paato*), 4.2 million short-term workers (*arubaito*), 0.7 million dispatch workers, 2.5 million contract workers, and 1.0 million others.

19. As of 2004, 76.9 percent of men were regular workers whereas only 49.6 percent of women were regular workers (MIC, Establishment and Enterprise Census [*jigyōsho kigyō tōkei chōsa*]).

FIGURE 6. *Part-Time Employment Rate in Japan, the United States, and Germany, 1990–2004*

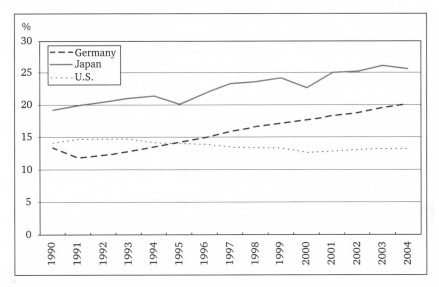

Source: OECD, Employment Outlook.

lar workers, however, they create more new job opportunities for women. Thus women are more likely to lose their jobs but also more likely to find new ones. Overall job mobility has increased slightly since 1996 but remains substantially lower than in most industrialized countries. The shift toward non-regular workers plus net job losses among the regular workers—job separations not matched by new hires—account for this rise.[20]

Firms have also leveraged their cooperative relations with workers to renegotiate the terms of the employment relationship. Japanese unions are organized at the company level, so they have a strong sense of common purpose with management. In essence, the firms have preserved employment security in exchange for wage restraint. Firms have asked for greater flexibility in working hours and workplace location and for cooperation in reducing costs and enhancing productivity. They have maintained a sense of equity by restraining compensation for managers even more than for blue-collar and clerical workers. Wage increases from 1990 to 2004 varied inversely by rank, for both men and women, with the highest increases going to entry-level

20. The MHLW Survey on Employment Trends bears out these developments. From 1996 to 2003, the job placement rate for permanent employees declined from 12.2 percent to 11.5 percent while the separation rate increased from 12.3 percent to 13.3 percent. Meanwhile, the placement rate for temporary workers increased from 23.7 to 27.6 percent, and the separation rate increased from 23.3 to 27.8 percent.

TABLE 4. *Wage Differentials by Rank and Gender, 1990–2004*

Wages (thousands of yen)		1990	1995	2000	2004	Increase (%) 1990–2004
Men	General manager	573.0	627.8	636.3	633.3	10.5
	Manager	458.6	512.0	517.3	515.1	12.3
	Section chief	346.1	385.9	401.0	388.7	12.3
	No rank, 20–24 years old	174.1	197.5	204.3	203.0	16.6
Women	General manager	522.4	531.2	574.5	584.9	12.0
	Manager	361.1	404.0	436.8	428.8	18.7
	Section chief	289.7	332.0	344.0	345.6	19.3
	No rank, 20–24 years old	156.7	182.7	190.6	191.5	22.2

Wage Differentials (No rank/20–24 years old = 100)		1990	1995	2000	2004
Men	General manager	329	318	311	312
	Manager	263	259	253	254
	Section chief	199	195	196	191
	No rank, 20–24 years old	100	100	100	100
Women	General manager	333	291	301	305
	Manager	230	221	229	224
	Section chief	185	182	180	180
	No rank, 20–24 years old	100	100	100	100

Source: MHLW, Basic Survey on Wage Structure.
Note: Companies have more than 100 employees, from all industrial sectors and educational backgrounds.

workers and the lowest increases going to senior managers. Hence the ratio of wages for general managers over entry-level workers (20–24 years old) decreased from 3.29:1 for men and 3.33:1 for women in 1990 to 3.12:1 for men and 3.05:1 for women in 2004 (Table 4). The results of Japan's firm-level bargains for wage restraint show up clearly at the aggregate level, with real wage growth declining from 1996 to 1998 and stalling from 2001 through 2004.[21] Nevertheless, the labor share of national income actually increased over the 1990s, from 66.8 percent in 1990 to a peak of 74.5 percent in 2001

21. MHLW Basic Survey on Wage Structure.

(and then stabilized at 71.2 percent in 2003 and 2004), because overall economic growth was so low.[22]

Japanese firms have increasingly deployed "performance-based" wage systems, beginning in the late 1990s and accelerating since then.[23] They have always incorporated both seniority and performance in wage calculations, but they have shifted the weight toward the latter. A 2004 Japan Institute of Labor survey found that 55.8 percent of companies had adopted performance-based pay schemes and another 26.7 percent planned to adopt them.[24] A Keidanren survey found that companies have increased the performance-based component of bonuses from 43.3 percent in 1999 to 52.0 percent in 2003 for managers, and from 25.7 percent to 29.7 percent for other employees.[25]

In many cases, however, firms have used these new compensation systems as cover for wage restraint. That is, they reduced the base wage and increased the performance-based component, but on average they did not pay out performance bonuses sufficient to offset the lower base.[26] In practice, most firms maintained relatively modest discrepancies in wages among a particular cohort.[27] In manufacturing firms, employers have tended to adopt performance-based wages for white-collar but not blue-collar workers: teamwork is so critical on the production line that individual assessments are neither desirable nor practical.

Those firms that have adopted performance-based pay systems have encountered mixed results. A survey by JMA consultants found that fewer than 30 percent of personnel managers at major companies reported that these systems had the intended results, and 53 percent stated that the systems were less successful than expected. Managers were ill prepared to evaluate the workers, and employees were concerned about the standards for evaluation.[28] The Japan Institute of Labor survey found that 29.9 percent of workers were less satisfied with how evaluations affected their compensation than they had been three years earlier while only 9.7 percent were more satisfied.

22. MIC, Statistics Bureau, National Accounts for Fiscal Year 2003.

23. See Japan Institute of Labor 2000 for a detailed analysis of how corporations evaluate performance, plus survey results.

24. Japan Institute of Labor 2004b.

25. Nippon Keidanren 2004.

26. A similar adjustment occurred in the 1970s when firms introduced qualification-based wage systems as a way to cut costs. Companies were able to cut back on promotions by offering smaller pay increases for a given job category, but the contradictory goals of the program—rewarding qualifications and reducing wages—generated inconsistencies in implementation and discontent among employees (Holzhausen 2000, 225).

27. The Nippon Keidanren survey (2004) reported that bonuses for managers varied by 30 percent or less at 61.4 percent of firms, and bonuses for regular employees varied by 30 percent or less at 69.7 percent of firms. Also see Dore 2000, 107–10.

28. *Nikkei Weekly* (October 28, 2002), 1.

Meanwhile, 20.0 percent reported that they were less satisfied with the fairness of evaluations while 10.9 percent were more satisfied.[29] Even where firms allowed for larger wage discrepancies based on merit, actual wages tended to cluster around the mean because supervisors avoided giving very high or very low evaluations. Fujitsu made a name for itself by promoting a rigidly performance-based pay scale in 1993 but later pulled back, modifying it in 2001. Fujitsu managers found that employee morale deteriorated because so many employees received average ("B") or lower ("C") evaluations, and some employees actually compromised their job performance by focusing too narrowly on those measures rewarded by the evaluation system.[30]

Some companies have experimented with multiple tracks of compensation. For example, they have used more contract workers for specific job categories such as research and design. They typically offer these special-category workers higher wages, with a larger performance-based component in total compensation, but no job guarantee beyond the term of the contract. Others have tried to regionalize their wage structure by guaranteeing certain employees that they would not be transferred out of their region in exchange for lower wages.[31]

Japanese companies have also reorganized to facilitate the differentiation of wage scales across units and to reduce the overall wage bill. Japanese unions tend to push for relatively uniform wage scales within a given company, but reorganization offers employers a way to escape from this constraint. Firms can maintain a relatively high scale in the main company while shifting to lower wages in subsidiaries. A Policy Research Institute survey found that 73.7 percent of firms viewed flexibility in personnel management as a primary benefit from separating subsidiaries.[32]

By 2001, employers and unions recognized that standard forms of wage restraint had run their course, yet the economy continued to stagnate and many firms still needed to reduce costs. They began to look for ways to extend the bargain in the form of "work sharing." In the Japanese case, work sharing refers not so much to actual job sharing as to a wide range of measures that entail a bargain of less work for less pay. Japanese employers and unions had never been as eager as their German counterparts to arrange a bargain around shorter workweeks. They did not feel as much pressure to reduce working hours because they did not have the high unemployment common in Europe,

29. Japan Institute of Labor 2004b.
30. Japan Institute of Labor 2004a. Also see the NEC case in the next chapter.
31. Mitsukoshi and Seiyu have adopted this strategy (Chapter 6).
32. Ministry of Finance, Policy Research Institute 2003a, 53.

and they feared that shorter working hours might make them less competitive with U.S. producers.[33]

When Japanese firms reduce their workforce, they do so predominantly by reducing new hires and transferring workers to affiliated companies.[34] By reducing or eliminating new hires, they are able to achieve substantial reductions via natural attrition. When asked why his bank was not laying off workers, a personnel director at Mizuho offered a disarmingly simple response: "Because we don't have to." Turnover was sufficiently high, he explained, that Mizuho could meet its targets for shrinking the workforce through attrition.[35] By preserving jobs for incumbent workers at the expense of new recruits, however, employers have clumped unemployment among Japan's youngest eligible workers. They have also created a demographic imbalance in their workforce, with the younger cohort being underrepresented or absent among permanent employees.

In many cases, firms have resorted to voluntary retirement programs. Paying generous premiums to volunteers, they have often exceeded their target numbers for reductions. Even so, some union leaders worry that "voluntary" retirements are less than voluntary. They have dealt with this concern by negotiating with firms to develop fair and transparent mechanisms for obtaining workers' consent.

The most distinctive feature of Japanese employment adjustment has been the redeployment of corporate groups as employment networks. Firms use short-term transfers (*shukkō*) to facilitate coordination across companies and permanent transfers to reemploy workers after retirement. In hard times, however, they use transfers to downsize. In fact, some companies have diversified with precisely this goal in mind: to create subsidiaries and affiliates that could absorb excess workers.[36] As companies have expanded this practice, the long-term employment guarantee has shifted from employment within the firm to employment within the group.[37] The have also moved from "temporary" transfers (*tenkin*), whereby the main company continues to pay the full

33. Interview with Tadayuki Murakami, Assistant General Secretary, Japan Trade Union Confederation (Rengō), March 27, 2002.

34. Kato 2001.

35. Interview with Nobuhiro Ishikawa, Director, Personnel Planning Division, Mizuho Holdings, January 16, 2002. Japan's commercial banks reduced their workforce steadily from 448,934 (at 134 banks) in 1995 to 273,412 (at 123 banks) in 2004, with annual reductions ranging from 1.2 percent in fiscal 1996 to 10.3 percent in 2002 (Teikoku Data Bank).

36. When Japanese companies outsource information technology functions, they prefer to form a joint venture so they can preserve their employees' jobs in the new venture (*Economist*, April 19, 2003, 55–56).

37. Sako and Sato 1997, Ariga et al. 2000.

salary of the transferred employee, to permanent transfers (*tenseki*), whereby the affiliate takes over the responsibility of paying the worker. Even with a permanent transfer, however, the main company typically honors its obligation to pay the employee full salary and benefits by making up the difference. In some cases, companies in financial distress have downgraded this commitment by paying only a portion of the difference or by paying a lump sum that covers the difference for only a specified amount of time.

Bank Relations

Japanese companies and their main banks have continuously renegotiated their relations in the face of disintermediation (the shift from lending to capital market financing), internationalization, and economic stagnation, yet they have not abandoned each other. In fact, this evolving partnership has continued to shape distinctively Japanese corporate adjustments to changing market conditions. Japan's largest corporations began to wean themselves from their main banks (*ginkō banare*) in the 1980s. They were increasingly able to finance investments from retained profits or to secure outside financing more efficiently in international capital markets. Japanese banks were not universal banks, so the migration of their best clients to capital market financing posed a serious threat to their business. Not surprisingly, they responded by lobbying to enter the securities business, gaining the right to underwrite debt through separate subsidiaries with the financial system reform of 1992 and through holding company structures following the Big Bang reforms of 1996.

Even in the heyday of the bubble economy of the late 1980s, most large companies continued to borrow small amounts from their main banks. They felt that it was important to maintain the main bank as a partner that could provide a wide range of services and assist in times of need. Many also sought to maintain ties with their main bank because their subsidiaries and affiliates continued to rely on bank loans.[38] Nevertheless, the balance of power shifted in favor of the clients. Instead of firms pleading to banks for credit in an era of scarce capital, banks were appealing to firms for business in an era of abundant capital. Some have argued that this dynamic fueled the bubble economy, as banks pushed firms to borrow and invest more than they would have otherwise.[39] In this context, the banks tried to expand the range of services they provided to preserve the loyalty of their main bank clients. They offered privileged access to their information resources and international

---

38. Interview with Hideto Ozaki, General Manager, Finance Division, Toyota Motor Corporation, June 9, 1998; Lincoln and Gerlach 2004, 309.

39. Watanabe 1999, 170. Also see Yoshitomi 1998.

contacts, performed full-service consultancy, and arranged client-client alliances and mergers. They tried to strengthen main bank ties with small and medium-sized companies even as their ties with larger companies were loosening. While large manufacturers became less dependent on bank debt, small manufacturers became more dependent. The large manufacturers' bank debt as a percentage of total assets dropped from 30.2 percent in 1980 to 20.4 percent in 1998 (compared with 10.4 percent in the United States in 1998), but small manufacturers' bank debt rose from 28.5 percent in 1980 to 35.5 percent in 1998 (compared with 19.4 percent in the United States in 1998).[40]

Once they were allowed into the securities business, the banks hoped to use their newfound ability to provide the full range of financial services as a way to hold on to valued clients. In particular, they sought to leverage their main bank relationships to expand into the corporate bond market.[41] They also embraced syndicated loans, which allow banks to spread the lending risk across a team of lenders. They tried to preserve a quasi–main bank relationship with their valued corporate clients by marketing commitment lines, which allow borrowers to deploy credit on a continuous basis.[42] The clients, meanwhile, exercised voice but not exit: they did not abandon their main banks but squeezed them. They demanded lower margins, lower fees, and better services, and they pressed the banks to upgrade their capabilities in the securities arena as a quid pro quo for not shifting their business to securities firms.

As the economy deteriorated in the late 1990s, many companies were forced back to their main banks (*ginkō gaeri*) because their bond ratings plummeted so low that they could not issue corporate bonds. Weak firms also found themselves turning to their main banks for essential credit, for help with alliances and mergers, or for outright bailouts. Company reliance on bank borrowing as a proportion of debt, which had dropped from 70 percent in 1986 to 54 percent in 1991, rebounded to 71 percent by 2000. Likewise, the percentage of firms that relied exclusively on bank borrowing dropped from 58 percent in 1980 to 28 percent in 1991 and then rose back to 47 percent in 2000.[43] Arikawa and Miyajima find that the percentage of firms in their sample with a main bank relationship, defined as having a lead bank that remains

40. Hoshi and Kashyap 2001, 315–16. The MOF Financial Statement Statistics of Corporations (*hōjin kigyō tōkei chōsa*) reports that large manufacturers' bank debt as a percentage of total assets declined further, to 13.5 percent in 2003.

41. Hoshi and Kashyap (2001, 320–22) are skeptical that Japanese commercial banks can succeed as universal banking groups.

42. Ministry of Finance, Policy Research Institute 2003b, 35; Amyx 2004, 238. Formal commitment-line contracts were not permitted before the 1999 passage of an exception to the Interest Rate Control Law and the Funding Law (Amyx 2004, 120).

43. Arikawa and Miyajima 2005.

stable over five years, actually rose from 65 percent in 1990 to 82 percent in 1997—at the peak of the financial crisis—before dropping to 74 percent in 1999. They also report that banks sent slightly fewer outside directors to their main bank clients and marginally decreased their ownership stake in these clients over the 1990–99 period, but that the clients became substantially more reliant on loans from their main banks (as a proportion of total assets) over the same period. Arikawa and Miyajima also note increasing heterogeneity in main bank relations, with some companies strengthening ties with their main banks during this period and others loosening them (see further discussion below).[44]

The economic slump produced a peculiar moment in the evolution of main bank relations, as companies needed bank assistance more than ever yet the banks were less able to bail out the companies. Banks continued to play a role in corporate restructuring, but they were less capable of providing funds. When they did intervene, they carefully gauged their commitment in terms of the client firm's loyalty as a banking customer, the bank's exposure to the firm and its affiliates, and the level of cross-ownership. Hirota and Miyajima find that bank interventions as a proportion of financially distressed firms declined from the 1970s (45 interventions among 132 cases of distressed firms, or 34.1 percent) to the 1980s (16 of 70, or 22.9 percent) to the 1990s (16 of 99, or 16.2 percent).[45] Moreover, banks that participated in corporate turnarounds played a more modest role in the process, refraining from sending bank executives to serve directly as corporate managers. They increasingly deployed debt-for-equity swaps, sometimes in partnership with investment funds, and some sold off their equity stake when the share price increased.[46] Meanwhile, government financial institutions took up some of the slack as private banks restrained lending, raising the public-sector share of lending substantially.[47]

Some analysts have argued that with the banks unable to fulfill their traditional rescue role, the main bank system is all but dead.[48] It would be more accurate to suggest that the main banks have shifted from performing their insurance function through active rescues to relying on passive life-support operations. Yet the main bank system's impact on the economy has been greater than ever, for the banks have kept many near-failing companies afloat by rolling over bad loans, extending lines of credit, and maintaining very low margins in their lending activity (hence low profits). In this sense, the banks'

44. Arikawa and Miyajima 2005.
45. Hirota and Miyajima 2000.
46. *Nikkei Weekly* (September 29, 2003), 9.
47. Katz 2003, 197.
48. Hoshi and Kashyap 2001.

behavior—seen as so perverse by investors and commentators—reflects the stubborn resilience of main bank relations rather than their demise. The banks found themselves in dire straits precisely because they remained loyal to their main bank clients.

The banks have even turned to their clients for help with recapitalization. One survey found that 79 percent of firms that were asked to purchase new stock issued by large banks in spring 2003 agreed to do so. Most complied in order to maintain good relations with the banks. Those who refused to comply, many of which were large multinationals, cited fears of criticism from shareholders.[49]

The main bank system has not dissolved but rather fragmented into a wider range of relationships. The *Nihon Keizai Shimbun* finds that 95.6 percent of listed firms still report that they have a main bank.[50] According to a MOF Policy Research Institute survey, 73.3 percent of firms intended to continue raising funds from their main banks at current levels, 8.1 percent planned to increase this fundraising, and 12.0 percent expected to decrease it. Companies with bond ratings above BBB and with commitment lines from their banks were significantly more likely to report plans to decrease fundraising from the main bank. Respondents cited the following reasons for maintaining or strengthening relations with their main bank: the bank provides needed capital (68.8 percent); the bank offers supplementary services, transactions, or information (42.6 percent); the bank provides low-cost financing (27.7 percent); the bank will rescue the firm in a crisis (11.6 percent); the bank provides financial or other personnel (3 percent); and the bank protects the company from takeover (2.5 percent).[51]

Stronger companies have grown more independent from their main banks while weaker ones have gone back to their main banks and smaller companies have strengthened main bank ties. The healthier corporations have also become more selective in their banking relationships, actively reducing the number of banks from which they borrow. One survey found that 43 percent of companies had reduced the number of banks from which they borrow in the three-year period ending March 31, 2003. Many did so because they had less need to raise funds; others noted a linkage with the unwinding of cross-shareholding with the banks.[52] Some firms shifted toward corporate group financing—or "internal" capital markets—whereby firms provide capital to other firms within the group.[53]

49. *Nikkei Weekly* (September 15, 2003), 9.
50. *Nikkei Weekly* (September 15, 2003), 9.
51. Ministry of Finance, Policy Research Institute 2003b, 36.
52. *Nikkei Weekly* (September 8, 2003), 8.
53. Ministry of Finance, Policy Research Institute 2003a, 117–18.

The relationship managers at the banks have shifted from a relatively uniform formula to a more intricate system of classifying relations with corporate clients. Nobuo Tanaka of Fuji Bank (now merged into the Mizuho group) describes four categories of clients.[54] The "traditional" main bank clients, mostly members of a related industrial group, are the most loyal. The "functional" main bank clients, the largest group, act as loyal clients in some service areas (such as borrowing) but not in others (such as capital market financing). The "core bank" companies retain a relatively stable share of business but have a larger group of core banks, so they give the top bank a smaller share of their business. The "independent" clients have no loyalty and may even compete with the bank in some areas. They do some business with the bank but strictly on a price basis. These clients include newer companies without strong corporate group ties. Tanaka emphasizes that client loyalty depends heavily on the past history of favors and obligations. It also varies with the give-and-take of specific reciprocal obligations. For example, computer manufacturers have to remain loyal bank customers if they wish to sell computer systems to the bank. Tanaka's strategy is to focus primarily on preserving ties with the "traditional" and "functional" main bank clients but also to market specific services to the "core" and "independent" clients.[55]

Tadashi Ishikuro, a younger-generation rising star and co–head of corporate banking at Shinsei Bank—a foreign-owned bank that has abandoned any pretense of acting as a traditional main bank—also differentiates carefully among clients, but he deploys a very different strategy. He describes a two-by-two matrix, with traditional and progressive companies and traditional and progressive managers. The traditional-traditional companies seek a main bank relationship, so they are not likely to work with Shinsei. The traditional companies with progressive managers are looking for new ways to finance, so they may be open to proposals. The progressive-progressive companies are the most open to new ideas, but they also demand competitive terms. The fourth box is virtually empty, Ishikuro notes, because progressive companies do not tolerate traditional managers. So Shinsei targets the second and third groups as its primary client base.[56]

Under a traditional main bank relationship, the two parties generally cemented the partnership by holding each other's shares. Often these stakes represented the accumulated legacy of business transactions, with stakes increasing as a result of specific deals. With the softening of the economy and

54. See Chapter 6 for case studies of Mizuho and Shinsei.

55. Interview with Nobuo Tanaka, Deputy General Manager, Global Business Planning Division, Fuji Bank, January 17, 2002.

56. Interview with Tadashi Ishikuro, Director and Corporate Executive Officer, Co-Head of Corporate Banking, Institutional Banking Group, Shinsei Bank, June 11, 2003.

FIGURE 7. *Trends in Cross-Shareholding in Japan, 1987–2003*

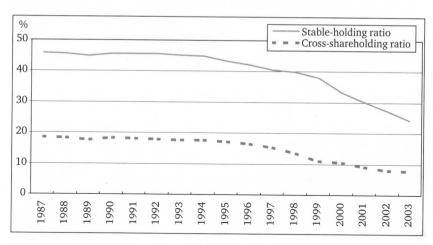

Source: NLI Research Institute.

the banking crisis plus the accounting changes described in the previous chapter, however, both sides came under severe financial pressure to reduce cross-holdings. Using data from the Nippon Life Insurance (NLI) Research Institute, Figure 7 shows long-term shareholding and cross-shareholding as a proportion of total market capitalization for corporations listed on the Tokyo Stock Exchange.[57] The institute finds steep declines in the levels of cross-shareholding after 1995, but the percentage of companies having some cross-held shares remained relatively high.[58] The institute ceased publishing these data after 2003 because the overall reduction in cross-holding made it increasingly difficult to determine whether declines reported in the statistics were due to real declines in cross-ownership or to data limitations, or some combination of the two.[59] The reconfiguration of corporate groups (see discussion below) has further complicated this picture. Many companies, especially non-financial corporations, have actually begun to *increase* cross-shareholding in response to the threat of takeover, but it is impossible to determine whether this activity has reversed the long-term decline at the aggregate level.[60]

57. The NLI institute restricts the term *cross-shareholding* to *reciprocal* cross-ownership. See Lincoln and Gerlach 2004, 328–30.

58. This figure was steady at about 95 percent from 1987 to 1997 before dropping to 83.2 percent by 2003 (NLI Research Institute 2004).

59. The institute presents this explanation in an April 2005 addendum to NLI Research Institute 2004.

60. Merrill Lynch, Global Securities Research and Economics Group 2005, 26; *Nikkei Weekly* (April 18, 2005), 9.

With regard to the process of selling off cross-held shares, Japanese bankers describe an elaborate ritual in which the banks and their clients renegotiate their mutual stakes. Under the framework introduced in Chapter 1, we might think of this ritual as partial exit coupled with a substantial element of voice. The guiding principles are twofold: prior consultation and reciprocity. If a bank wants to sell shares of a corporation, it consults the corporation first. As a result, it would expect to lose a proportionate share of the corporation's banking business. Likewise, a corporation that shifts some of its banking business to other financial institutions would expect the bank to divest some shares. In either case, the bank would not divest all its shares, and the corporation would not completely drop the main bank, so the long-term relationship would continue. Moreover, both sides would be careful to sell off their shares in more peripheral business partners first and divest shares in main bank or industrial group partners last. And when firms do sell shares, they often make sure to sell them into friendly hands or repurchase them at a later time.[61]

Meanwhile, both banks and their clients have attempted to differentiate the functional aspects of main bank relationships from the excesses. In some cases, they have mutually agreed to shift some main bank functions from complimentary to fee-based services. Mizuho, for example, now charges main bank clients for business introductions (see the Hikari Tsushin case in Chapter 6).[62] "There has been a 'rationalization' of the financial system in two senses," concludes Thierry Porté, vice chairman of Shinsei Bank. "Bank relationships with main bank clients are becoming more rational, and the financial sector is being rationalized [slimmed down]."[63]

After the government announced stricter requirements for Tier 1 capital (the types of capital considered most reliable and liquid, primarily equity) in 2003, the banks accelerated their sales of shares, feeling that the government's policy meant that they could do so without unduly antagonizing their clients.[64] The banks also sought to raise lending margins, but they encountered substantial resistance from their corporate borrowers. Some tried to finesse this issue by setting low rates but inserting a clause that allows them to raise rates if the company's financial health erodes.[65] According to a *Nihon*

---

61. Lincoln and Gerlach 2004, 327, 329. The Policy Research Institute report (Ministry of Finance, Policy Research Institute 2003a, 112–14) finds that financially weaker companies have been *more* likely to hold on to shares.

62. Following a June 2003 regulatory change, the government recognized these services under the Banking Law (Amyx 2004, 237).

63. Interview, July 14, 2004.

64. Interview with senior bank executives, June 2003.

65. *Nikkei Weekly* (December 15, 2003), 9.

Keizai Shimbun survey, only half those companies asked by their banks to agree to a review of lending terms had complied with this request.[66]

The major city banks responded to the Big Bang reforms by forging new alliances both within and across industrial groups. They consolidated the affiliated trust banks, securities houses, and insurance companies within their groups so that each holding company would have a subsidiary focusing on each of these business lines. They also formed new "mega-banks" via mergers across industrial group lines, such as the Bank of Tokyo-Mitsubishi, Mitsui-Sumitomo, and Mizuho (a merger of Fuji, Daiichi Kangyo, and the Industrial Bank of Japan).

The reconfigured mega-banks have been left with the complex task of renegotiating main bank relationships with the traditional clients of their component banks. Mizuho's Tanaka explains:

> I used to work on the Canon account, and the Fuji and Canon people had tight personal relationships all the way from section chiefs to the president. They could be very direct with each other—maybe even kid around a bit—and they would go out drinking. But once you bring Daiichi Kangyo and IBJ people into the mix, then that complicates things. When you encounter people from a different corporate culture, you feel more nervous and reserved.[67]

The banks have dealt with this dilemma by leaving the management groups from the old relationship intact at first and then gradually transferring personnel across the groups. Mizuho's Corporate Banking Division No. 1, for example, was initially populated almost entirely by former IBJ employees charged with maintaining relations with former IBJ main bank clients.[68] Some clients may want to reduce their business ties, however, if the merger makes them too reliant on one bank. A company that did 40 percent of its business with Fuji and 10 percent each with Daiichi Kangyo and IBJ, for example, would find itself 60 percent reliant on the new Mizuho. In some cases, the merged bank finds itself in the difficult position of serving as the main bank for arch-rivals. Mizuho, for example, is the main bank for both Nippon Steel and JFE. Nippon Steel, which was accustomed to exclusive treatment from IBJ, views Mizuho differently. A Mizuho executive predicts that Nippon Steel will watch Mizuho very closely for any signs of favoritism in

66. *Nikkei Weekly* (September 8, 2003), 8.
67. Interview with Nobuo Tanaka, Manager, Utsunomiya Branch, Mizuho Bank, July 22, 2004.
68. Interview with Takehiro Mikoda, General Manager, Corporate Banking Division No. 1, Mizuho Corporate Bank, June 13, 2003.

either direction—but his team will do its best to keep both companies happy.[69]

The reorganization of the largest banks is closely linked to the ongoing transformation of Japan's industrial groups (or horizontal *keiretsu*). During the postwar period, the major industrial groups such as the Mitsui or Sumitomo group followed the "one-set" principle, with one firm in most major industrial sectors but not two or more that would directly compete. This was particularly true in the financial sector, where most groups had one major commercial bank, one trust bank, one securities firm, and so on. The commercial bank was the main bank for most group firms. In fact, common membership in the group solidified the ties of loyalty between the main bank and its most valued clients. In several cases, bank mergers across groups have been followed by additional mergers along the same group lines. For example, the Mitsui-Sumitomo bank merger was followed by Mitsui-Sumitomo mergers in other financial services and construction plus an alliance between the two trading companies.[70]

Corporate Governance

Some analysts predict that the main bank system will eventually be replaced by a shareholder model of governance.[71] Yet in some respects the weakening of the main bank system has only strengthened the hand of managers in the absence of a wholesale shift toward shareholder sovereignty. Popular commentators have blamed the Japanese system of corporate governance for Japan's economic stagnation since 1990, just as others praised it for Japan's economic rise before that. The weakness of the economy has driven substantial changes, as lower share prices and poor bond ratings have made Japanese managers more sensitive to these indices. Foreign shareholders— who tend to be less loyal than their Japanese counterparts—took a much larger stake in Japanese firms (Table 5). And some representatives of foreign shareholders began to demand that Japanese firms raise their returns on equity upward toward U.S. levels (see Figure 8). Meanwhile, Japanese executives lost confidence in their own management systems and began to experiment with U.S. practices. Corporate governance reform had become a widespread movement by the late 1990s.

Corporate executives rushed to bolster investor relations activities and to announce reforms that would please investors, but they were more cautious in making fundamental changes in the way they do business. Some took

69. Mikoda interview, June 13, 2003.
70. Lincoln and Gerlach 2004, 315–17. Mitsui Chemical and Sumitomo Chemical announced a merger in 2001 but subsequently abandoned it.
71. Hoshi and Kashyap 2001.

TABLE 5. *Ownership of Listed Corporations in Japan, the United States, and Germany*

	Japan		United States		Germany	
	1990	2004	1990	2003	1990	2004
Banks	20.9	16.2	—	8.0	9.4	6.6
Nonfinancial firms	30.1	21.9	—	—	41.4	42.9
Government	0.3	0.2	0.0	—	6.0	6.6
Insurance firms	15.9	7.6	1.9	—	3.2	4.3
Pension funds	0.9	4.0	24.4	21.0	—	—
Investment firms and others	7.0	6.1	15.8	24.0	3.3	4.1
Individuals	20.4	20.3	51.0	37.0	18.3	14.5
Foreign	4.7	23.7	6.9	10.0	18.6	21.0

Sources: Tokyo Stock Exchange; New York Stock Exchange; Deutsche Bundesbank.
Note: For Japan, investment firms and others includes investment trusts, securities companies, and other financial institutions. For the United States, it includes bank personal trusts, mutual funds, and other nonhousehold investors.

FIGURE 8. *Return on Equity in Japan and the United States, 1975–2004*

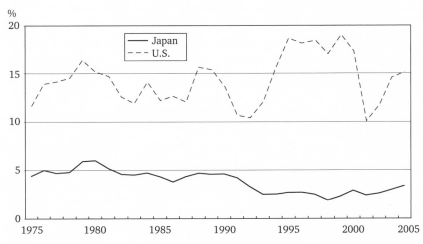

Sources: Ministry of Finance, Statistics of Corporations; Morgan Stanley Capital International.

advantage of corporate law reforms (see Chapter 4) to introduce stock options, share buybacks, spin-offs, and U.S.-style corporate boards. A *Nihon Keizai Shimbun* survey of publicly held corporations found that 36 percent had issued stock options by 2004.[72] Most of the issuing firms have limited stock options to a small number of executives and restricted them to relatively small bonuses.

Companies have increasingly used share buybacks to appeal to investors and combat declining share prices. Yet Japanese executives also view buybacks as a mechanism to insulate themselves from shareholder pressures by maintaining share prices at an acceptable level and as a way to protect the firm from hostile takeover.[73] They often announce buybacks right before the end of the financial year to maximize the impact on the share price. A 2002 survey found that 43.6 percent of firms had bought back shares and another 22.3 percent planned to do so. Respondents cited the following reasons: to facilitate the unwinding of cross-held shares (52.0 percent), to increase profits per share (51.3 percent), to enhance capital efficiency (46.0 percent), to offer stock options (30.8 percent), to prevent hostile takeover (10.4 percent), and to prepare for corporate reorganization (7.0 percent).[74] Following the government's October 2001 move to allow companies to buy back shares for unspecified purposes rather than exclusively for share retirement or stock options, about 30 percent of all listed firms announced buyback limits between April and July 2002, for a total of ¥9.5 trillion, or 3 percent of total market capitalization. Yet market participants estimate that the firms actually exercised only about 20 percent of these limits.[75]

Firms have experimented with various forms of reorganization, beginning with the introduction of semiautonomous business divisions, then with more autonomous internal "companies," and most recently with holding company structures. One survey found that 69.4 percent of firms had introduced a divisional structure by 1995, 25.8 percent had adopted an internal company system by 2000, and 8.4 percent planned to institute a holding company structure (Figure 9).[76] Firms have also taken advantage of the spin-off law,

72. *Nihon Keizai Shimbun* (June 24, 2004), 17, cited in Shishido forthcoming. METI's 2002 Basic Survey of Japanese Business Structure and Activities (*kigyō katsudō kihon chōsa*) found that 4.6 percent of a much larger sample of 25,594 companies had issued stock options by 2001. The gap between the two surveys implies that large corporations are much more likely than small companies to issue stock options.

73. Lincoln and Gerlach 2004, 331.

74. Ministry of Finance, Policy Research Institute 2003b, 32–33.

75. *Nikkei Weekly* (July 29, 2002), 12.

76. METI's 2002 Basic Survey of Japanese Business Structure and Activities found that 2.5 percent of companies had adopted holding companies and 9.6 were considering adoption.

FIGURE 9. *Corporate Reorganization in Japan since 1990*

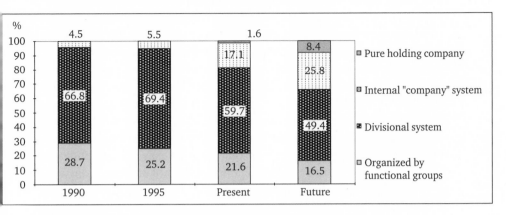

Source: Ministry of Finance, Policy Research Institute 2003b, 21.

selling off divisions to cut labor costs by reducing wages and benefits at the newly separated subsidiaries. They have sold stakes to strengthen their balance sheets or to redefine their relations with affiliated companies. According to a Daiwa Institute of Research study, however, these companies did not sever ties with their affiliates along the lines of a U.S.-style spin-off but rather transformed them into wholly owned subsidiaries or separated them in preparation for a merger.[77]

Japanese firms have also turned their attention to corporate board reform. Many firms have reduced the number of board members and introduced outside board members, measures that are commonly viewed as positive signals by shareholders. The average number of directors at major companies declined from 20.7 at the end of fiscal 1999 to 18.8 in 2000 and 17.3 in 2001.[78] In many firms that have consolidated their boards, those executives removed from the board are designated "corporate officers," thereby clarifying the separation between executive and supervisory roles. Some firms have also favored a corporate officer system as a way to limit the personal liability of these officers.[79] As of 2002, 32.9 percent of companies had introduced a corporate officer system, another 2.7 percent planned to do so, and 25.8 percent were considering doing so.[80] As of 2004, 630 of 2,108 listed companies (or 30 percent) had outside directors, up 28 percent from the previous year.[81] The

77. *Nikkei Weekly* (October 15, 2001), 9.
78. *Nikkei Weekly* (June 24, 2002), 3.
79. *Nikkei Weekly* (January 13, 2002), 12.
80. Ministry of Finance, Policy Research Institute 2003b, 38.
81. *Nikkei Weekly* (September 13, 2004), 21.

Policy Research Institute found, however, that the majority of "outside" directors were not true outsiders: 29.8 percent came from business partners, 17.7
percent from group firms, 16.0 percent from the parent company, 4.6 percent
from the main bank, and 1.7 percent from another bank. In addition, 8.8
percent came from other companies; 3.6 came from life insurance companies;
3.4 percent were consultants, advisers, or attorneys; 1.1 percent were government officials; and 13 percent came from other organizations.[82] A Corporate
Governance Forum survey reports that 17.7 percent of responding firms had
outside auditors who participate in all decisions, 44.2 percent had outside
auditors who participate in some decisions, 9.2 percent were considering
having outside auditors, and 26.7 percent were not considering having them
at all.[83] Yet many of these "outside" auditors have actually come from within
the main bank group.[84]

With the commercial code reforms of 2002, a few firms have adopted U.S.-
style committee-based boards, but most have preferred to stick with the traditional Japanese structure. A Japan Statutory Auditors Association survey
reports that only 1.2 percent of firms planned to adopt the new system, 1.2
percent were considering it, and 83.5 percent had no plans to adopt it. Among
the latter group, 44 percent argued that they could improve governance under
the existing system and 13.4 percent reported that it would be difficult to find
outside directors.[85] In the year ending March 2004, the first year in which
companies could adopt the U.S.-type board, 71 companies (less than 3 percent
of eligible companies) chose to do so.[86]

Japanese institutional investors have gradually become more vocal. M&A
Consulting has waged several high-profile proxy fights. Some large institutional investors are monitoring performance more closely and adopting more
active strategies to maximize returns. The vast majority of shareholders
remain passive, however, leaving managers with considerably leeway to run
their companies as they see fit.[87]

Japan has experienced a gradual increase in mergers and acquisitions, as
Japanese firms have joined forces to increase market share and facilitate
restructuring or have partnered with foreign firms. Foreign corporations have
also begun to buy out troubled Japanese firms. Britain's Cable and Wireless
acquired IDC, an international telephone service company, in 1999; and Japan

82. Ministry of Finance, Policy Research Institute 2003b, 40–41.
83. Corporate Governance Forum 2001.
84. Miyajima 1998, 60.
85. *Nikkei Weekly* (May 19, 2003), 12.
86. Gilson and Milhaupt 2005.
87. On recent developments in Japanese corporate governance, see Itami 2000, Inagami
2000, Inagami 2001, Patrick 2004, Dore 2004, Gilson and Milhaupt 2005, Jackson 2005b,
and Shishido forthcoming.

FIGURE 10. *Mergers and Acquisition Transactions in Japan, 1986–2004*

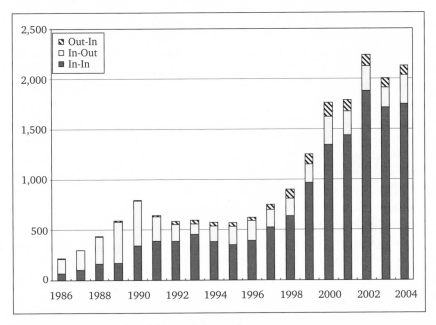

Source: Nomura Securities Financial Research Center.

Boehringer Ingelheim took over SS Pharmaceuticals in 2000. Figure 10 shows merger and acquisition transactions divided into three categories: domestic mergers ("in-in"), Japanese acquisitions of foreign firms ("in-out"), and foreign acquisitions of Japanese firms ("out-in"). Shareholder activist Yoshiaki Murakami and his firm M&A Consulting mounted a bid for Shoei in 2000, but Shoei's banks came to its defense. In August 2004, the Sumitomo Mitsui Financial Group stunned the business community by making a rival bid for UFJ despite the fact that Bank of Tokyo-Mitsubishi had already reached a merger agreement with UFJ. The Bank of Tokyo-Mitsubishi prevailed, forming the world's largest bank in terms of assets, but not before several months of legal wrangling at considerable cost.

Then, in the spring of 2005, the Japanese public became enthralled with an extraordinary takeover drama pitting enigmatic entrepreneur Takafumi Horie and his Internet start-up, Livedoor, against Japan's media establishment. Livedoor used after-hours trading to buy up a controlling share of Nippon Broadcasting System (NBS), an affiliate of Fuji Television that also held a stake in Fuji via cross-holdings. NBS tried to defend itself by issuing share warrants to Fuji, but the Tokyo District Court ruled this move illegal since it would devalue shares without the shareholders' consent. Fuji then asked about fifty business partners to come to its aid by buying its shares. Ironically, Softbank Investment, a renegade firm in its own right (see Chapter 6), led the rescue effort, borrowing NBS's stake in Fuji, along with its voting rights, so that Livedoor could not use its majority stake in NBS to gain influence at Fuji.[88] In April, Livedoor and Fuji brought their battle to a close by announcing a very traditional Japanese business alliance: Fuji would make an equity investment in Livedoor; it would promote links between its conventional broadcasting and Livedoor's Internet business; and it would transform NBS into a fully owned subsidiary.[89]

The Livedoor saga not only made for great entertainment but frightened Japanese corporations into devising defense strategies. By the time of the Fuji-Livedoor settlement, over 60 percent of senior executives at major corporations reported that they were considering takeover defenses or had already implemented them. Among their favored strategies, they mentioned boosting the share price, adopting poison pill provisions (which grant shareholders the right to buy more shares at attractive prices in the event of a hostile bid), and increasing cross-shareholdings.[90] Meanwhile, investment banks, accountancies, and consulting firms rushed to offer their services in devising M&A defenses.[91]

Supplier Relations

Large manufacturers have also favored voice over exit with their suppliers: they have been reluctant to drop loyal suppliers despite the severity of Japan's economic crisis, but they have not hesitated to squeeze them. They have pressed suppliers to lower costs and have reduced the total number of suppliers while strengthening relations with the most important ones.[92] In this way, they have passed along the burden of adjustment to the suppliers, which have experienced sharper downturns in sales and more drastic reductions in workforce.[93] At the aggregate level, small companies have given smaller wage increases and larger wage cuts than larger firms.[94] Manufacturers have

88. *Oriental Economist* (April 2005), 13–14.

89. *Economist* (April 23, 2005), 64.

90. *Nihon Keizai Shimbun* (April 23, 2005), 1.

91. See Nomura Securities, IB Consulting Division 2004 for a "how to" guide on takeover defenses.

92. METI's Basic Survey of Japanese Business Structure and Activities shows a gradual consolidation of corporate groups, with the average number of subsidiaries and affiliates per firm decreasing from 2.36 in 1991 to 2.23 in 1999 and 2.01 in 2002.

93. In 2002, for example, large companies preserved level sales and increased profits by restructuring while smaller firms lost sales and profits (*Economist*, June 14, 2003, 75).

94. MHLW, Monthly Labor Survey (*maitsuki kinrō tōkei chōsa*).

become more price-oriented in procurement for more standard parts, expand-ing imports and experimenting with electronic procurement. Meanwhile, they have reinforced ties with suppliers when closer collaboration could help to reduce overall costs, spur innovation, or enhance quality. They have con-sulted extensively with suppliers before making any changes, they have given suppliers time to adjust, and they have offered considerable support for the suppliers—even finding new customers and arranging alliances.[95]

For Toyota, the logic is quite simple: the company benefits from its close relations with its suppliers, so it has responded to competitive pressures by strengthening—not loosening—these ties.[96] Toyota increased its ownership stake in affiliates Daihatsu and Hino to fend off foreign suitors and placed top executives in core suppliers to further cement these relationships.[97] Toyota executives stress how collaboration with suppliers can promote a permanent drop in production cost, as opposed to a temporary reduction in price, benefit-ing both Toyota and the supplier. They describe how they discovered that Volkswagen was producing the handles above the passenger side window at a cost advantage of 70 to Toyota's 100. Toyota then worked with a handle manufacturer to analyze the problem and develop a solution. They eventually designed a handle of equal quality to the Volkswagen model at a substantially lower cost.[98] Ahmadjian and Lincoln note that Toyota has differentiated between suppliers, moving toward hierarchical control in some cases and toward more arm's-length transactions in others. Toyota consciously sought to move production of some high-technology electronic parts in-house begin-ning in the late 1980s and to reduce its dependence on its top supplier, Denso Corporation. It was strategic in deciding which parts to manufacture on its own, focusing especially on high-value technology such as traction control and antilock brake systems, where developing its own capacity would con-tribute to organizational learning. At the same time, it moved toward more market-based relations with suppliers for less sophisticated parts, seeking to contain costs by reducing the overall number of parts, exploiting economies of scale, and shifting from customized to standardized parts.[99]

In contrast, Nissan has taken a more price-based approach toward procure-ment since 1999. Nissan sold off its ownership stake in many suppliers and publicly announced that it would base all purchasing decisions on price and quality, not past relations. The Nissan union, which covers group companies

95. See Ahmadjian and Lincoln 2001.
96. See Chapter 6 for the Toyota and Nissan case studies.
97. Lincoln and Gerlach 2004, 340–41.
98. Interview with Hidehiko Tajima, General Manager, Global Purchasing Planning Division, Global Purchasing Center, Toyota Motor Corporation, Toyota City, January 18, 2002.
99. Ahmadjian and Lincoln 2001.

and not just the head company, expressed reservations because it feared that it would weaken the suppliers over time.[100] In practice, however, Nissan managers were extremely cautious in managing the sale of ownership stakes, consulting closely with affiliates to gain their consent and carefully brokering new alliances with the buyers.[101] Likewise, they have been especially sensitive to the impact of their procurement decisions on major suppliers because the Nissan union covers the workers at many of these suppliers.[102]

Shimizu, a large construction company, has also responded to competitive pressures by strengthening ties with suppliers. "We work together with our suppliers to cut costs," reports one executive. "We try to promote best practice among our subcontractors through information-sharing. We bring the best cost-reduction experts among them to our headquarters, and then we channel what we learn back to the others."[103] An executive at Kajima, another general contractor, views his company's loyalty toward its steel suppliers in terms of reciprocity. "We see this as a give-and-take relationship," he explains. "We buy a lot of their steel, and they give us a lot of business. We will buy a little bit extra when we want a contract. If we buy Korean, then the steel companies might not hire us for any more projects."[104]

The large suppliers have also moved toward more careful differentiation among their corporate customers. "The companies that are related to us— through mutual shareholding ties, for example—have been more loyal customers," explains a steel company executive. "But after all, that was the purpose of building up these ties in the first place." Those companies with looser ties have been less loyal, he adds, but they also expect less service. So the company set up a second tier of lower prices with no service, particularly for low-grade steel such as that used for construction.[105] Meanwhile, the steel companies have tried to use quality and service to maintain customer loyalty in the higher end of the business, such as specialty steel used by auto manufacturers.

As Japanese manufacturers shifted production abroad beginning in the late 1980s, they often brought their suppliers with them, creating regional

100. Interview with Kōichirō Nishihara, President, Federation of All Nissan and General Workers' Unions (Nissan Rōren), and Vice President, Japan Automobile Workers' Unions, March 28, 2002.

101. Interview with Seiji Uehara, Senior Manager, Purchasing Administration Department, Nissan Motor Co., June 20, 2003.

102. Nishihara interview, March 28, 2002.

103. Interview with Shūji Takagi, General Manager, Planning Department, Corporate Planning Division, Shimizu Corporation, June 5, 1998.

104. Interview with Naoki Atsumi, Managing Director, Kajima Corporation, June 4, 1998.

105. Interview, April 1996.

supply networks in Southeast Asia.[106] They designed these production networks strategically, shifting lower value-added production abroad while retaining critical technology and R&D at home. They also remained loyal to their Japanese suppliers for critical components while purchasing some of the more standard parts from local suppliers. They encountered increasing pressure from local governments, however, to increase purchases of local components.

Japanese subcontracting relationships are evolving, yet they remain distinctive in comparative terms. A 1999 MITI survey found that 55 percent of small and medium-sized manufacturing firms were primarily engaged in subcontracting for large parent corporations. And among these, 81.6 percent reported that their largest trading partner had remained unchanged over the entire lifetime of the company.[107]

Restructuring American Style

U.S. corporations have different comparative institutional advantages than their Japanese counterparts, so naturally they have taken a different approach to restructuring. They tend to have a more hierarchical relationship between managers and workers, relying more on managers for production innovation and investing less in upgrading shopfloor skills. They are more likely to select financial intermediaries on the basis of price and performance than relationships, and they employ more capital market financing and less bank borrowing. They favor suppliers that provide goods and services at low cost more than suppliers that serve as reliable long-term partners or that have the greatest potential for innovation.[108] In short, they are less reliant on long-term cooperative relations with workers, banks, and suppliers, so they are less reluctant to undermine these ties. They are less likely to exercise voice with these partners and more likely to exercise exit.

This does not mean that U.S. companies operate exclusively within the first circle of rationality introduced in Chapter 1 (simple economic calculus). Rather, they are highly sensitive to their own distinctive comparative institutional advantage (second circle), which tends to lie with flexible labor markets, efficient capital markets, and low-cost suppliers. And they are acutely aware of broader social norms (third circle), which favor more of a shareholder conception of the firm than in Japan and place less value on loyalty to workers, banks, and suppliers. In fact, U.S. managers may internalize social norms that actually make them *more* prone to downsizing their workforce than they

---

106. Hatch and Yamamura 1996.
107. Lincoln and Gerlach 2004, 334.
108. Lazonick and O'Sullivan 2000, 15; Hall and Soskice 2001, 27–33.

should be based on a simple economic calculus alone, an argument we consider in Chapter 7.

The U.S. model itself is a moving target, as we discovered with our survey of major U.S. policy reforms in Chapter 3. Here we turn to private-sector reforms to see how U.S. restructuring differs from the Japanese variety. Before the 1980s, the U.S. model was characterized by a managerial rather than a shareholder orientation. Managers had substantial autonomy from shareholders, so they retained and reinvested earnings rather than maximizing distributions to shareholders. Prominent economists built on agency theory to criticize this model. They viewed shareholders as principals and managers as agents and contended that managers had too much discretion to stray from their core task of maximizing value for shareholders. They argued that managers would more faithfully represent shareholder interests if their compensation were more closely tied to stock performance (through stock options, for example) and their companies were more vulnerable to takeover.[109]

By the 1980s, the United States had developed a full-fledged market for corporate control. Investment banks were facing more competition and tighter margins in their traditional business lines in the wake of financial liberalization, so they actively sought new business that could generate higher fees, and they especially targeted mergers and acquisitions. In the process, they cultivated new techniques for transferring corporate control. The most important innovation was the leveraged buyout (LBO), which enables investors to purchase a company by borrowing against the company's own assets. The investors then use asset sales or operational revenues to pay off the debt. Investment bankers at Drexel Burnham Lambert and elsewhere developed the junk bond market as a source for investments in LBOs, fueling the expansion of the takeover market.[110]

Meanwhile, financial market developments (see Chapter 3) fueled a shift in the composition of shareholdings from individuals to institutions. Institutional investors used their market power plus direct appeals to press companies to deliver higher returns. Corporations became less concerned with their own institutional survival and more focused on maximizing returns, to the point where they actively sold off operational divisions.[111] They also used share buybacks to increase value for shareholders. Corporations' payout ratios to shareholders (the ratio of dividends to after-tax-adjusted corporate profits)

109. Lazonick and O'Sullivan 2000, 15–16.
110. O'Sullivan 2000, 161–75; Fligstein 2001, 147–69.
111. Fligstein 2001.

TABLE 6. *Rates of Corporate Downsizing in Germany, Japan, and the United States*

Country	10% cut 2001 (%)	10% cut 1991 (%)	Cumulative likelihood for each firm, 1991–2001
Germany	9.3	9.9	0.402
Japan	5.9	2.0	0.213
United States	20.6	9.2	0.445

Source: Adapted from Jackson 2005b, 424.

Notes: Sample covers listed corporations with over 2,000 employees. Downsizing is counted as a negative shift in total employment of 10 percent over a one-year period. Cumulative likelihood is calculated as the probability of each firm within the sample undergoing one or more employment cuts within the time period. $N = 33,094$ firm-years for 13 OECD countries. Only Germany, Japan, and United States reported here.

soared from 42.4 percent in the 1960s and 42.3 percent in the 1970s to 49.3 percent in the 1980s and 49.6 percent in the 1990s.[112]

The shift to the shareholder model directly affected U.S. corporations' approach to restructuring, fueling a shift toward downsizing: selling assets and shrinking the workforce.[113] U.S. companies spun off less profitable and nonessential divisions, undoing the excesses of the conglomerate movement of the 1960s. In the face of intense competition in product markets, they shifted production abroad, outsourced noncore functions, and sometimes simply exited business lines rather than seeking to enhance productivity. They also invested in the capabilities of narrower and more concentrated skill bases, with considerable success in high-technology sectors such as semiconductors and biotechnology.[114]

U.S. companies began large-scale downsizing of their workforce in the late 1970s, accelerating in the 1980s and 1990s. They initiated the trend during an economic downturn but continued through upturns to the point where better economic conditions in the 1990s actually correlated with *more* downsizing. The U.S. job loss rate reached 10 percent in the 1980s and then increased to 14 percent in the 1990s. Gregory Jackson calculates that U.S. firms were three to four times as likely as Japanese firms to have workforce reductions greater than 10 percent in 1991 and 2001 (Table 6). When controlling for company size

112. Lazonick and O'Sullivan 2000, 22.
113. Useem 1996.
114. O'Sullivan 2000, 186–231.

and performance, he finds that Japanese firms were 32 percent as likely and German firms 56 percent as likely as U.S. firms to cut employment by 10 percent or more in 2001.[115] While Japanese job tenure was increasing during hard times, U.S. job tenure was decreasing in good times: from 5.0 years in 1983 to 4.7 years in 1998.[116] Larger firms were more likely to downsize in the United States whereas smaller firms were more likely to shed workers in Japan. Meanwhile, U.S. executive compensation soared as stock options expanded and the stock market boomed. The pay packages for CEOs of U.S. corporations jumped from 44 times those of factory workers in 1965 to 419 times in 1998.[117] By 2000, CEOs at large companies earned 531 times as much as their hourly workers, compared with 11 times in Germany and 10 times in Japan.[118]

If we compare individual U.S. companies with their Japanese counterparts, we find that the U.S. firms have a much more aggressive approach to restructuring, especially with respect to laying off personnel. Here we briefly review the restructuring programs of one company from each of the four sectors to be examined in the Japanese case studies in the following chapter: autos, electronics, banking, and retail. I selected representative companies that have confronted major competitive challenges and undergone substantial restructuring. I cannot control for level of corporate performance or other factors with such a small sample, but even these four cases illustrate some major differences between restructuring U.S. style and Japanese style. Table 7 portrays these companies' corporate performance in terms of sales and return on assets, and provides one measure of their restructuring—reductions in total workforce.[119]

The Ford Motor Company, plagued by declining revenues and a plummeting share price, announced a restructuring program in January 2002 that makes Nissan's Revival Plan look timid. Ford declared that it would earn $7 billion before taxes by 2006 by cutting 35,000 jobs worldwide (about 10 percent of total workforce), closing five plants, eliminating four car lines, divesting $1 billion in assets, and pressing suppliers to lower prices. The program generated intense conflicts with U.S. and Canadian auto unions and substantially delayed plans for introducing new car models.[120] By 2005, Ford

115. Jackson 2005b, 424.

116. Lazonick and O'Sullivan 2000, 14–27.

117. Lazonick and O'Sullivan 2000, 25.

118. *New York Times* (January 25, 2004), 3/1.

119. Some workforce increases in Table 7 reflect the mergers discussed below: Hewlett-Packard and Compaq, 2001–2; Chase Manhattan and Chemical, 1994–95; JPMorgan and Chase, 1999–2000; and Daimler and Chrysler, 1997–98. As noted below, Kmart filed for bankruptcy protection in 2002, which affects results after that point.

120. *New York Times* (January 29, 2002), 3/1; *Financial Times* (October 1, 2003).

TABLE 7. *Total Employment at Four U.S. and Four German Companies, Consolidated Basis, 1990–2004 (with percentage annual change in employment and sales, and return on assets)*

U.S. Firms

Year	Ford				Hewlett-Packard				JP Morgan Chase				Kmart			
	Employees	Δ Emp (%)	Δ Sales (%)	ROA	Employees	Δ Emp (%)	Δ Sales (%)	ROA	Employees	Δ Emp (%)	Δ Sales (%)	ROA	Employees	Δ Emp (%)	Δ Sales (%)	ROA
1990	368,547	—	—	0.5	92,000	—	—	6.5	—	—	—	0.4	373,000	—	—	5.4
1991	331,977	-10	-12	1.3	89,000	-3	10	6.3	43,169	—	77	0.1	349,000	-6	5	5.4
1992	325,333	-2	17	-0.3	92,600	4	13	6.4	39,687	-8	-14	0.8	358,000	3	10	5.0
1993	322,213	-1	8	1.3	96,200	4	24	7.0	41,567	5	2	1.1	344,000	-4	9	-5.6
1994	337,778	5	17	2.4	98,400	2	23	8.2	42,130	1	2	0.8	348,000	1	-9	1.8
1995	346,990	3	3	1.7	102,300	4	26	10.0	72,696	73	17	1.0	307,000	-12	0	-3.8
1996	371,702	7	7	1.7	112,000	9	22	9.3	67,785	-7	84	0.7	265,000	-14	1	-1.5
1997	363,892	-2	4	2.5	121,900	9	12	9.8	69,033	2	11	1.0	261,000	-2	-9	1.8
1998	345,175	-5	-3	9.3	124,600	2	10	8.8	72,683	5	7	1.0	278,525	7	2	3.7
1999	364,550	6	15	2.6	84,400	-32	-10	8.8	74,801	3	4	1.3	271,000	-3	5	2.7
2000	345,991	-5	3	1.9	88,500	5	15	10.5	99,757	33	78	0.8	252,000	-7	7	-1.6
2001	354,431	2	-7	-2.0	86,200	-3	-7	1.9	95,812	-4	-16	0.3	234,000	-7	3	-17.0
2002	350,321	-1	2	0.1	141,000	64	25	-1.3	94,335	-2	-14	0.2	212,000	-9	-2	-28.6
2003	327,531	-7	3	0.3	142,000	1	29	3.4	110,453	17	2	0.9	158,000	-25	-24	-10.1
2004	324,864	-1	6	1.2	151,000	6	9	4.6	160,968	46	28	0.4	133,000	-16	-15	12.8

TABLE 7—cont.

German Firms

	DaimlerChrysler				Siemens				Deutsche Bank				KarstadtQuelle			
Year	Employees	Δ Emp (%)	Δ Sales (%)	ROA	Employees	Δ Emp (%)	Δ Sales (%)	ROA	Employees	Δ Emp (%)	Δ Sales (%)	ROA	Employees	Δ Emp (%)	Δ Sales (%)	ROA
1990	376,785	—	—	10.9	373,000	—	—	—	68,552	—	—	0.3	—	—	—	3.8
1991	379,252	1	11	2.7	402,000	8	—	—	71,400	4	11	0.3	—	—	14	3.7
1992	376,467	-1	4	2.6	413,000	3	—	3.8	74,256	4	10	0.4	—	—	8	3.0
1993	366,736	-3	-1	1.7	391,000	-5	4	3.7	73,176	-1	42	0.4	75,951	—	1	2.9
1994	330,551	-10	6	0.7	382,000	-2	4	3.7	73,450	0	-7	0.5	108,286	43	29	0.4
1995	310,993	-6	-1	1.0	373,000	-2	5	3.6	74,119	1	-4	0.3	105,129	-3	<.1	0.1
1996	290,029	-7	3	-6.3	379,000	2	6	3.4	74,356	0	12	0.3	99,991	-5	<.1	0.5
1997	300,068	3	17	2.5	386,000	2	14	2.7	76,141	2	13	0.1	94,463	-6	-1.0	1.4
1998	441,500	47	32	3.5	416,000	8	10	0.8	95,847	26	-44	0.3	89,399	-5	-61	1.9
1999	466,938	6	-3	3.3	443,000	6	14	3.0	93,232	-3	22	0.3	113,490	27	59	2.8
2000	416,501	-11	8	4.0	430,200	-3	-42	10.0	98,311	5	103	0.5	113,120	0	3	3.0
2001	327,470	-21	-6	-0.3	450,000	5	11	2.3	94,782	-4	0	<.1	112,141	-1	5	2.2
2002	365,571	12	-2	2.5	426,000	-5	-3	3.3	77,442	-18	-26	0.1	104,536	-7	-2	1.6
2003	362,063	-1	-9	0.3	417,000	-2	-12	3.1	67,682	-13	-22	0.2	100,956	-3	-3	1.2
2004	384,723	6	4	1.3	434,000	4	1	4.3	65,417	-3	4	0.3	92,546	-8	-12	-18.0

Sources: Hoover's Online; Mergent Online; SEC 10-K filings.

Note: Fiscal years end in December of the year listed, except Hewlett Packard (Oct.), Siemens (Sept.), Kmart (Jan; listed in table as preceding calendar year).

had abandoned the profit target as domestic sales slumped, especially for larger sport utility vehicles such as the Explorer and Expedition, and Standard & Poor had downgraded Ford's debt rating below investment grade.[121] Meanwhile, Ford reclaimed twenty-four plants from Visteon, the parts division it had spun off in 2000, and prepared many of them for sale. Ford officials predicted that this would lead to cost savings of $600–700 million by promoting competition among parts suppliers.[122] Toyota chairman Hiroshi Okuda generated both consternation and bemusement when he stated that Toyota might have to give Ford and General Motors some "breathing room," possibly offering technical assistance or raising prices in the United States.[123]

When Hewlett-Packard (HP) CEO Carly Fiorina announced a merger with Compaq in September 2001, Director Walter Hewlett attempted to block the merger in a highly publicized proxy war that lasted through March 2002. Hewlett argued that Fiorina viewed the merger as an opportunity to raise profits by laying off workers, and he claimed that this strategy would violate the "HP Way": the corporate culture that his father, cofounder Bill Hewlett, had so carefully nurtured. Despite enjoying a stronger financial position than NEC (Chapter 6), HP engaged in a more ruthless brand of restructuring. After winning the proxy battle, Fiorina announced in May 2002 that HP would save $2.5 billion by eliminating 15,000 jobs worldwide (over 10 percent of the total), reducing product lines, and leveraging its increased bargaining power to press suppliers to lower prices. HP encountered stiff resistance in Europe— especially Germany—where strong unions and local employment protection laws slowed down the downsizing process.[124] A year after the merger, HP had exceeded its own target, with $3.1 billion in savings and 17,900 fewer jobs.[125] In February 2005, however, Fiorina was abruptly ousted. The firm's stock had performed well below that of its major rivals during her tenure, and many analysts blamed the merger. The stock price jumped 7 percent on the announcement, and Fiorina herself was rewarded with a $21.4 million compensation package that vastly surpassed what she would have earned if she had stayed.[126] Under her successor, Mark Hurd, the company announced plans in July 2005 to eliminate another 14,500 jobs—about 10 percent of the total workforce—over the following year and a half. The plan would reverse several of Fiorina's initiatives: redividing the printer and personal computer divisions and eliminating the Customer Solutions Group, a sales unit targeted at large

121. *New York Times* (April 21, 2005), C3.
122. *New York Times* (May 26, 2005), C1.
123. *Asahi Shimbun* online, April 25, 2005.
124. *San Francisco Chronicle* (July 18, 2002), B1.
125. *San Francisco Chronicle* (May 4, 2003), I1.
126. *New York Times* (February 10, 2005), C1.

corporations and government agencies. The layoffs and reorganization were expected to cost $1.1 billion, with much of the expense going to severance packages.[127]

JPMorgan Chase has gone through not one but three major mergers within a decade. In stark contrast to the Mizuho Financial Group (Chapter 6), it has undergone rapid downsizing each time. When Chase Manhattan merged with Chemical Bank in 1995, the new entity eliminated 12,000 of 75,000 total jobs. Then, in 2000, Chase merged with JPMorgan, announcing that it would save $2 billion annually by streamlining operations and eliminating 5,000 of 32,000 workers in wholesale and investment banking. By November 2001, it had achieved an estimated cost savings of $3.6 billion annually and cut 7,500 jobs. JPMorgan Chase then bought out Bank One in January 2004, declaring that it would eliminate 10,000 jobs and save $2.2 billion over three years. It took this route despite the fact that large mergers in the financial services industry had a very dubious track record, and both partners had lost value after their previous mergers.[128] The new entity jumped to second place in the U.S. market in both deposits and assets, from fourth (JPMorgan) and seventh (Bank One), respectively.[129] James Dimon, the new president, pledged $2.2 billion in cost cuts and predicted a sustained rise in the share price.[130]

Kmart engaged in perpetual restructuring throughout the 1990s in a losing battle to compete with industry leaders Wal-Mart and Target, shrinking from 365,000 employees in 1990 to 234,000 in 2002. In contrast, Japanese retailers tended to maintain workforce levels and increase store capacity despite poor results in the 1990s. Charles Conaway, who was hired as chairman and chief executive to perform a turnaround in 2000, devised a plan to consolidate stores, upgrade technology, and lower prices. Wal-Mart prevailed in a brutal price war, however; Kmart's finances quickly went from bad to worse; and the company filed for bankruptcy protection in January 2002.[131] The company later launched an investigation to determine whether the executives who ran Kmart before the bankruptcy filing had mishandled accounts and why they were paid huge bonuses to stay on while business soured.[132] Edward Lampert

127. *New York Times* (July 20, 2005), C1.
128. A *New York Times* feature (May 26, 2002, 3/1) reviews eight cases of commercial banks buying out investment banks, concluding that these mergers have a particularly disappointing track record.
129. *New York Times* (January 15, 2004), A1, C8.
130. *New York Times* (June 27, 2004), 3/1.
131. This case contrasts with Daiei, a Japanese discount retailer that was not allowed to fail and was eventually restructured by the IRCJ. In another controversial case, the Japanese government first decided to bail out Sogo, a major department store, and then reversed that decision (see Chapter 6).
132. *New York Times* (May 3, 2002), C1.

bought up a 53 percent stake in Kmart through his hedge fund, ESL Investments, while the firm was under bankruptcy protection. His associates cut overhead, inventories, and capital investments and sold off properties to competitors.[133] By the time it emerged from bankruptcy in May 2003, Kmart had closed 599 stores and laid off 57,000 workers.[134] The share price boomed from $15 in May 2003 to $109 in November 2004, when Kmart announced that it would acquire Sears to become the nation's third largest retailer. Executives expected to save $200 million by cross-selling merchandise and converting some Kmarts to Sears stores, and another $300 million by streamlining the supply chain.[135]

Restructuring German Style

German corporations, like their Japanese counterparts, rely on close cooperative relations with workers, banks, and other corporations, so they are more likely to exercise voice within these relationships than to exit. The German model differs from the Japanese model in subtle ways, however. German companies' corporate networks are not as extensive as their Japanese counterparts, for example, so German employers have not used job transfers within corporate groups to reallocate workers. Instead, they have leveraged their relationships with workers to enhance productivity, to shorten work hours, and to design early retirement plans. With these strategies exhausted, they have agreed to preserve job security or to forgo plans to move production abroad in exchange for greater flexibility in working hours. Or they have developed elaborate schemes in which they pay workers constant wages over a year but the workers' actual hours vary to better match production cycles. In the process of negotiating these deals, German employers have reinforced the role and status of the firm-based works councils.

German employers have experimented with more performance-based pay, but the performance component has often come on top of existing pay schemes rather than replacing them, and the new systems have been implemented in a manner consistent with collective bargaining.[136] As we have seen, many Japanese employers have used performance pay as cover for wage restraint, replacing automatic seniority pay hikes with contingent performance-based raises, but in practice the variations in compensation between high and low performers have remained relatively small. Thus both German and Japanese employers have deployed performance-based pay in ways that are consistent with the existing employment system, but they have done so differently.

133. *Economist* (November 20, 2004), 64–65.
134. *New York Times* (August 17, 2004), C2.
135. *New York Times* (November 18, 2004), 1.
136. Jackson 2005a.

Meanwhile, Germany's peak employer and labor organizations have agreed to allow greater flexibility in collective bargains. They have established clauses permitting companies that meet certain hardship criteria to diverge from the bargains. Employers and unions have worked toward a longer-term compromise solution that would preserve collective bargaining but permit more leeway at the plant level. The system has come under increasing stress, however, as a growing number of employers have ignored the agreements or defected from the associations altogether. Even firms that are not covered by the bargains often use these agreements as a reference point in determining wages and benefits.

As German firms sought to reduce costs and bolster profits, they naturally looked to lowering financing costs. Large firms markedly decreased their reliance on loans as a source of funding over the past two decades, shifting to capital markets and self-financing.[137] As in the Japanese case, industry clients have separated into distinct tiers, with the larger and most cosmopolitan firms weaning themselves from reliance on bank loans, and smaller and medium-sized enterprises continuing to rely on a close working relationship with their primary banks (*Hausbanken*). In Germany, however, a substantial group of the smaller firms remain in private hands, and the scale of the stock market remains considerably smaller than that of Japan.

As in Japan, even the large corporations have not simply severed their long-term relationships with their banks. German banks have always been universal banks, so they did not have to lobby their way into the securities business as their Japanese counterparts did. They could adapt to their clients' changing needs more smoothly, gradually shifting from making loans to underwriting debt.[138] Although underwriting implies less oversight and control than lending, it allowed the banks to continue to play a role in meeting industry's financial needs. To hold on to corporate clients, German banks, like Japanese banks, have tried to provide enhanced services, to leverage their insider knowledge to tailor new services, and to capitalize on personal relationships.[139] The banks have retained other channels of influence over industrial corporations, including substantial shareholding positions, representation on supervisory boards, and proxy voting rights. Some banks have decreased their ownership stakes in client firms and pulled back from positions on supervisory boards. For the most part, the bankers who have left supervisory boards have been replaced by other insiders, including retired executives and managers from affiliated firms, thereby strengthening mana-

137. Deeg 1993.
138. Roe 1994.
139. Interview with Dr. Armin Unterberg, Vice President, Economic Research, Dresdner Bank, Frankfurt, July 8, 1998.

gerial control.[140] Meanwhile, the German system of co-determination—with mandatory worker representation on the supervisory boards of large corporations—remains intact.

Rather than abandon each other, German corporations and banks have been more likely to manipulate the changing business environment to renegotiate the terms of their relationships. The banks have generally retained some equity stake in their long-term business partners, but they have pressed the firms to increase profitability. The corporations still give the bulk of their banking business to their long-term banking partners but demand lower costs and better service in exchange. Meanwhile, banks have tried to reduce the financial burden of bailing out client corporations in trouble without giving up this role altogether.[141] Bankers argue that they often serve their own enlightened self-interest in doing so, for they may lose more by allowing a firm to fail than by bailing it out because its failure could affect other corporate clients. In any case, banks remain critical intermediaries in most mergers, acquisitions, and other forms of corporate restructuring.

German corporations' well-publicized newfound attention to "shareholder value" has gone further in rhetoric than in reality. Some of the most prominent firms have set targets for profitability, decentralized business units, outsourced noncore functions, created departments for investor relations, adopted international standards of accounting, issued stock options, and otherwise sought to make themselves more attractive to international investors. Sigurt Vitols contends, however, that German managers initiated some of these measures to make their firms more competitive in product markets rather than in response to financial pressures.[142] Despite a few high-profile cases of hostile takeovers, such as the Vodafone takeover of Mannesmann, Germany still lacks an active market for corporate control. Most German companies have a substantial proportion of their shares in stable hands and relatively little in foreign hands. This means they can continue business as usual without being punished too brutally by fickle international investors. And of course, German firms are prevented from making some of the moves that would most please their shareholders—such as shedding excess workers—by the constraints of the labor relations system.

Overall, German companies have been bolder with downsizing than their Japanese counterparts but more cautious than the Americans (Tables 6 and

---

140. Hackethal et al. 2003.

141. For example, Unterberg (interview, July 8, 1998) explained that German banks would provide capital to valued corporate clients in crisis, and thereby preserve the business relationship, but instead of holding on to low-performing shares, they would gradually sell them off in securities markets as the firm recovered.

142. Vitols 2000.

7). Turning to four individual companies in the same sectors as the U.S. cases above, we find that Germany's large companies are more international than their Japanese competitors, but like the Japanese, during their restructuring they have made considerable effort to preserve valued institutions at home. Jürgen Schrempp, who took over as chairman of Daimler-Benz in 1995, oversaw a restructuring program that included shifting to lower-cost Asian suppliers, eliminating 8,800 jobs at Daimler-Benz Aerospace, dismantling an industrial goods subsidiary, and introducing a stock-options scheme for top managers. Yet Daimler-Benz also negotiated carefully with its works councils, promising to invest DM 14 billion in expanding production and improving productivity and to concentrate almost all the new investment in Germany. In exchange, the works councils agreed to more flexible hours and pledged to collaborate on reducing production costs. "We must close the productivity gap with the Americans and the Japanese," one manager declared. "We can achieve this by reducing the workforce, investing in new facilities, and investing in technology. If you focus only on cutting workers, then you are not prepared for the future."[143]

Daimler-Benz acquired Chrysler in 1998, opting for a more American approach to restructuring in North America. The deal was advertised as a merger between equals, but Daimler-Benz executives quickly asserted control. The restructuring plan for the Chrysler division included eliminating 26,000 jobs, closing six plants, and trimming production at seven more.[144] DaimlerChrysler took a 34 percent share in Mitsubishi Motors in 2000 but refused to bail out Mitsubishi when its condition deteriorated in 2004, leaving a Japanese management team to come up with its own restructuring program. By 2004, the Chrysler division had revived, but the Mercedes division was plagued with quality problems and declining sales. DaimlerChrysler made a landmark pact with its workers in southern Germany in which the workers agreed to lower wages and longer working hours in exchange for job security through 2012.[145]

In 1998, Siemens chief executive Heinrich Von Pierer announced a tenpoint program that included selling off one-seventh of the Siemens corporate empire, representing DM 17 billion in sales and 60,000 jobs.[146] Yet the most drastic cuts came abroad, in France, Austria, Singapore, Malaysia, and Portugal. Siemens was more deliberate in reducing personnel in Germany, where it gradually cut the workforce from 253,000 in 1992 to 180,000 in 2000,

143. Interview with Dr. Peter-R. Puf, Vice President, Economic Policy Research, Daimler-Benz, Stuttgart, July 2, 1996.

144. *Economist* (February 3, 2001), 66.

145. *Economist* (July 31, 2004), 51.

146. *Financial Times* (November 5, 1998), 16.

phased out twenty of the top one hundred management jobs, and avoided dismissals altogether. In 2004, Siemens preceded DaimlerChrysler in forging an agreement with its union to extend the workweek from thirty-five to forty hours at two plants. Managers argued that this measure would save two thousand jobs that would otherwise move to Hungary.[147] Von Pierer's strategy was to withdraw from low value-added segments while investing further in high value-added business lines. Although he actively sought to raise profits and enhance shareholder value, he did not believe that companies should cater to financial markets and he shunned the propensity of other firms for mega-acquisitions. "We are an engineering company: we know how to build ourselves from the inside. We do not need to make large, overpriced acquisitions that prove difficult to integrate," he explained. "And hostile takeovers are the worst thing you can do."[148] And when Von Pierer retired as CEO in 2005, he was ensured an ongoing role in the firm as the new chairman of the supervisory board.[149]

Deutsche Bank—the quintessential German industrial bank—may have gone the furthest in departing from the German model. Top managers made a conscious decision to transform the bank into something closer to an international investment bank while most of their domestic competitors stuck with more traditional strategies. They began reducing the bank's equity stakes in German firms in the mid-1990s and then proceeded to shift stakes in some companies into a cluster of tax-efficient asset-management subsidiaries. The bank announced job cuts of 2,000 in Germany in 1996, 9,000 worldwide in 1998 (5,000 in Germany), and 2,600 worldwide in 2001. Meanwhile, managers aggressively expanded international investment banking operations, moving the investment banking headquarters to London (the bank had bought out Morgan Grenfell in 1989) and acquiring Bankers Trust in 1998. Even so, Deutsche Bank's approach to unwinding its shareholdings has been almost Japanese in style. "You have to have a mutual understanding between the bank and the company," explains Norbert Walter, chief economist. "We always inform the company, and usually we discuss it with them in advance."[150] Furthermore, the bank still values its long-term relationships with corporate clients and continues to bail out valued clients in distress. "On corporate rescues, we perform a formal quantitative analysis and then we send it up to top management, and the board makes the decisions on a case-by-case basis. But of course, there is not a direct relationship between the formal analysis

147. *Economist* (July 17, 2004), 52.
148. *Financial Times* (November 27, 2000), 18.
149. A former executive became chair of the supervisory board at seventeen of Germany's top thirty listed companies (*Economist*, January 29, 2005, 63).
150. Interview, Frankfurt, July 7, 1998.

and the final decision," Walter notes. "If we have a long-term relationship or we know the firm well, then that can make the difference."[151] Deutsche Bank came under public attack in 2005 when it announced plans to lay off 6,400 workers during a period of rising unemployment. Franz Müntefering, the chairman of the Social Democratic Party, described the layoffs as "asocial."[152]

KarstadtQuelle, a major department store chain with a substantial mail-order business, announced a far-reaching restructuring program in October 2000 under its new chief executive, Wolfgang Urban, who had just come over from supermarket giant Metro. Karstadt would save DM 500 million over three years by centralizing administration, reducing warehouse space, closing stores, and cutting personnel by 7,000 (15 percent of the total).[153] After talks with its works council, Karstadt scaled back its personnel cuts, and it did not even announce store closings until it had engaged in extensive negotiations with community leaders. The company's fortunes deteriorated in 2004, as catalog sales dropped, and it posted a €1.6 billion loss. Managers pieced together a restructuring plan that included negotiating a refinancing scheme with their primary lenders, forging a pact with the union to reduce the work-force via natural attrition, and selling off or closing seventy-seven smaller stores and other specialty outlets.[154] Taking over Karstadt in May 2005, super-visory board chairman Thomas Middelhoff crafted yet another restructuring scheme, selling off selected business lines and negotiating layoffs with the union. Despite the company's dire financial situation and his own background as an investment banker, Middelhoff pledged that his mission was to turn the company around, not break it up and destroy it.[155]

Even the largest and most cosmopolitan Japanese, U.S., and German com-panies retain some distinctive national characteristics in their approaches to restructuring. Within the broad national patterns, however, there are consid-erable variations across sectors and among particular companies. In the fol-lowing chapter, we examine the variations within Japan in greater detail.

151. Interview, Frankfurt, July 7, 1998.
152. *New York Times* (August 26, 2005), C1.
153. *Financial Times* (October 18, 2000), 34; (January 16, 2001), 35.
154. *Economist* (October 9, 2004), 61; (October 23, 2004), 61–62.
155. *New York Times* (May 13, 2005), C4.

6 THE VARIETIES OF RESTRUCTURING

Why do some troubled Japanese companies restructure so timidly? And why do others, which are in better financial shape, restructure more aggressively? In this chapter, we look at ten companies to verify the overall patterns described in the last chapter, to examine the specifics in greater detail, and to explore variations across sectors and companies. We focus especially on how two variables—foreign ownership and industrial sector—affect restructuring. This will help us to discern how companies combine the three different levels of rationality introduced in Chapter 1: how they reduce costs to increase efficiency (market calculus), how they reorganize to enhance their comparative institutional advantage (institutional calculus), and how they respond to changing norms and the emergence of new models (social calculus). We do not expect to find that one logic trumps another but rather explore how these mechanisms interact with one another.

We can approach this task by examining specific hypotheses about how foreign ownership and industrial sector affect restructuring. With respect to foreign ownership, we investigate two distinct causal mechanisms. First, companies with higher levels of foreign share *ownership* should cater more to the demands of foreign investors, and this should lead them to press further with restructuring and corporate governance reform. Second, companies under foreign *management* should restructure even more aggressively because foreign managers are less likely to share Japanese social norms and are less bound by social ties to Japanese partners (workers, banks, suppliers) and therefore less constrained from loosening or breaking these ties.

With respect to variations across industrial sectors, the "two Japans" thesis would predict that firms in exposed and competitive sectors, such as autos and electronics, would restructure more than those in protected and uncompetitive sectors, such as banking and retail. Firms in exposed sectors would be forced by competitive pressures to adjust more quickly and boldly whereas firms in protected sectors would be insulated from these pressures.[1] A sectoral Varieties of Capitalism logic (see Chapter 1), however, might lead us to

1. Katz 2003, 218.

postulate that service firms would restructure more than manufacturing firms. Service firms require less investment in firm-specific skills, rely less on close labor-management collaboration to improve productivity, and depend less on close collaboration with suppliers to improve quality and reduce costs, so they should be less cautious in restructuring relations with these partners. These two theses contradict each other in the Japanese case because most manufacturing sectors fall into the exposed/competitive category and most service sectors (as well as utilities and agriculture) belong to the protected/ uncompetitive group.

We might also draw on the sectoral VOC perspective to predict smaller variations across different types of manufacturing. For example, we might hypothesize that auto companies would be less likely to restructure their supply networks than electronics companies. Auto manufacturing requires a more integrated production process in which critical parts and subsystems are designed to work together as a coherent system. Electronics manufacturing favors a more modular approach in which components and subsystems can be designed and manufactured as separate modules and then connected at the assembly stage.[2] This means that auto manufacturers rely more heavily on close coordination with their core suppliers, so we would expect them to be more cautious in making adjustments that might undermine their cooperative relationships with these suppliers. We might also expect variations across different elements of restructuring. For example, we would expect the difference between integrated and modular production to affect auto and electronics manufacturers' approach to their relations with suppliers, but this difference should not affect their relations with banks.

We begin with eight primary company cases to examine how these two factors, foreign ownership and industrial sector, affect restructuring outcomes. We examine two key sectors in manufacturing (autos and electronics) and two in services (banking and retail). These also correspond to competitive export sectors (autos and electronics) and protected domestic sectors (banking and retail). By comparing autos and electronics, we explore the distinction between a more integrated production model and a more modular production model. By comparing banking and retail, we investigate how the financial sector differs from other service industries. Within each sector, we look at one firm with high foreign ownership (Nissan, Sony, Shinsei, Seiyu) and one more purely Japanese firm (Toyota, NEC, Mizuho, Mitsukoshi).

2. Aoki and Andō (2002) and their collaborators document how manufacturing has shifted toward more modular production across a range of industrial sectors.

Among those with high foreign ownership, one has high foreign portfolio investment and a high international profile (Sony) and the other three have varying levels of foreign managerial control (Seiyu, Nissan, and Shinsei, from lowest to highest). We also compare these cases across time (the same company at two different points in time), with special attention to before-and-after comparisons for those companies that have come under foreign management. We then add two newer companies in the IT sector (Softbank and Hikari Tsushin) to see if these companies approach restructuring differently from the more established companies. At the end of the chapter, we reexamine these same hypotheses by analyzing data from more than 2,600 publicly listed companies.

I have selected representative companies to fit these categories.[3] All these companies encountered major challenges in the period since 1990, and all have engaged in substantial restructuring. I have not attempted to control for corporate performance in the case studies, although we will control for it in the data analysis at the end of the chapter. Instead, I have allowed corporate performance to vary across cases precisely so that we can consider whether the level of financial distress alone determines the level of restructuring or whether other factors—such as foreign ownership and industrial sector—influence restructuring outcomes as well. Tables 8 and 9, like Table 7 for the U.S. and German companies, provide basic performance indicators, sales growth, and return on assets (by fiscal year, on a consolidated and unconsolidated basis), plus changes in workforce.[4] It is interesting to note that many of the Japanese companies, unlike their U.S. and German counterparts, reported negative returns on assets for multiple years. Table 10 outlines some of the major restructuring highlights discussed in the case studies. For each case, we focus on how managers assessed the costs and benefits of restructuring, and we review the specific measures adopted in the areas surveyed in the previous chapter: labor, finance, corporate governance, and supplier relations.

3. The companies in the case studies are all relatively large corporations, but we shall examine how they interact with smaller companies, especially via supplier networks. The data analysis at the end of this chapter includes smaller publicly listed companies.

4. Mitsukoshi relisted in September 2003 after it absorbed four regional companies. I have not included the two banks, Mizuho and Shinsei, because they are so new that they have data beginning only in 1999 (Shinsei) and 2000 (Mizuho). In addition, Mizuho formed the Mizuho Financial Group in 2002, so numbers from 2000–2001 are not comparable with numbers after that. I provide some of the relevant data for Mizuho and Shinsei in the text below.

TABLE 8. *Total Employment at Eight Japanese Firms, Consolidated Basis, 1990–2004 (with percentage annual change in employment and sales, and return on assets)*

	Nissan				Toyota				Sony				NEC			
FY	Employees	Δ Emp (%)	Δ Sales (%)	ROA	Employees	Δ Emp (%)	Δ Sales (%)	ROA	Employees	Δ Emp (%)	Δ Sales (%)	ROA	Employees	Δ Emp (%)	Δ Sales (%)	ROA
1990	138,326	7	6	2.1	102,423	6	7	5.2	112,900	18	25	2.4	117,994	3	7	2.3
1991	143,946	4	8	0.8	108,167	6	3	4.8	119,000	5	6	2.6	128,320	9	2	1.4
1992	143,754	<1	-3	1.5	109,279	1	0	2.5	126,000	6	2	2.5	140,969	10	-7	0.4
1993	143,310	<1	-6	-0.8	110,534	1	-8	1.9	130,000	3	-6	0.8	143,320	2	2	-1.1
1994	145,582	2	1	-1.2	142,645	29	-13	1.3	138,000	6	7	0.4	147,994	3	5	0.2
1995	139,856	-4	4	-2.4	146,855	3	32	1.3	151,000	9	15	-7.7	152,719	3	17	0.9
1996	135,331	-3	10	-1.3	150,736	3	14	2.3	163,000	8	23	1.1	151,966	<1	13	1.7
1997	137,201	1	-1	1.1	159,035	6	-5	3.0	173,000	6	19	2.5	152,450	<1	-1	1.9
1998	143,681	5	0	-0.2	183,879	16	9	3.3	177,000	2	1	3.5	157,800	4	-3	0.8
1999	136,397	-5	-9	-0.4	214,631	17	1	2.4	189,700	7	-2	2.8	154,787	-2	5	-3.2
2000	133,833	-2	2	-11.1	215,648	0	4	2.5	181,800	-4	9	1.8	150,000	-3	8	0.2
2001	125,099	-7	2	5.1	246,702	14	13	2.7	168,000	-8	4	0.2	142,000	-5	-6	1.2
2002	127,625	2	10	5.2	264,096	7	6	3.1	161,100	-4	-1	0.2	145,807	3	-8	-6.2
2003	119,350	-6	9	6.4	246,410	<1	12	5.3	162,000	1	<1	1.0	143,393	-2	6	1.0
2004	169,644	42	15	5.2	265,753	1	7	4.8	151,400	-7	-4	1.7	147,753	3	-2	1.7

TABLE 8—cont.

FY	Mitsukoshi Employees	Δ Emp (%)	Δ Sales (%)	ROA	Seiyu Employees	Δ Emp (%)	Δ Sales (%)	ROA	Softbank Employees	Δ Emp (%)	Δ Sales (%)	ROA	Hikari Tsushin Employees	Δ Emp (%)	Δ Sales (%)	ROA
1990	11,457	—	10	1.6	—	—	10	0.6	—	—	—	—	—	—	—	—
1991	11,867	4	2	1.0	—	—	5	0.8	—	—	—	—	567	—	—	—
1992	12,332	4	-3	-0.2	—	—	2	0.8	590	—	—	—	477	-16	—	—
1993	12,225	-1	-4	-1.3	10,870	—	-5	0.6	630	7	—	—	420	-12	—	—
1994	11,930	-2	-2	-1.6	10,646	-2	2	0.5	909	44	—	—	489	16	—	—
1995	11,400	-4	0	-0.8	8,768	-18	-3	0.1	4,375	381	77	2.1	910	86	—	—
1996	10,784	-5	2	-0.4	8,208	-6	<1	-0.4	5,600	28	110	1.0	1,224	35	—	—
1997	10,076	-7	-2	-0.1	7,924	-3	-5	-0.2	7,743	38	43	0.8	1,279	4	—	—
1998	9,622	-5	-4	-6.2	14,593	84	-9	-4.2	6,865	-11	3	0.9	1,090	-15	—	—
1999	8,342	-13	-2	-2.0	13,528	-7	-9	0.2	7,219	5	-20	4.0	8,471	677	—	—
2000	7,852	-6	1	1.3	12,437	-8	5	-1.6	4,312	-40	-6	0.7	10,684	26	-61	1.7
2001	13,002	66	0	1.0	11,331	-9	4	0.0	4,375	1	2	3.2	2,140	-80	-42	-25.7
2002	12,617	-3	-33	1.5	11,300	<1	3	0.6	4,966	14	<1	-7.6	2,445	14	75	-9.5
2003	11,829	-6	-27	1.1	9,313	-18	-18	-1.1	5,108	3	27	-7.5	3,172	30	18	10.5
2004	11,425	-3	88	-0.6	6,943	-25	14	-1.9	12,949	154	62	-3.5	4,588	45	17	13.2

Sources: *Hoover's Handbook of World Business*; Development Bank of Japan Databank; *Kaisha Nenkan* company data.

Note: ROA calculated as after-tax profits/total assets.

TABLE 9. *Total Employment at Eight Japanese Firms, Unconsolidated Basis, 1990–2004 (with percentage annual change in employment and sales, and return on assets)*

	Nissan				Toyota				Sony				NEC			
FY	Employees	Δ Emp (%)	Δ Sales (%)	ROA	Employees	Δ Emp (%)	Δ Sales (%)	ROA	Employees	Δ Emp (%)	Δ Sales (%)	ROA	Employees	Δ Emp (%)	Δ Sales (%)	ROA
1990	56,837	3	4	2.2	70,841	4	7	5.4	18,130	7	22	2.8	38,487	1	7	2.0
1991	55,566	-2	2	1.5	72,900	3	4	3.2	19,811	9	5	0.8	39,905	4	3	1.3
1992	53,071	-4	-9	-0.4	75,266	3	1	2.5	22,972	16	-6	1.0	42,036	5	-6	0.5
1993	51,398	-3	-8	0.2	73,046	-3	-10	1.8	23,245	1	-9	1.2	42,287	1	1	0.5
1994	49,177	-4	-5	-1.9	69,748	-5	1	2.3	22,841	-2	11	1.4	41,078	-3	4	1.0
1995	44,782	-9	3	0.1	68,641	-2	-3	2.8	22,199	-3	3	1.1	40,875	-1	15	1.6
1996	41,266	-8	5	1.6	70,524	3	14	4.3	21,937	-1	12	1.4	40,788	<1	17	1.8
1997	39,969	-3	-4	0.5	69,753	-1	-15	5.2	21,559	-2	11	2.5	40,084	-2	1	1.2
1998	39,467	-1	-6	-1.0	67,912	-3	-3	3.7	21,308	-1	1	1.2	38,791	-3	-10	-3.7
1999	32,707	-17	-10	-22.2	65,290	-4	-2	4.2	19,187	-10	7	0.9	37,078	-4	3	0.6
2000	30,747	-6	-1	5.2	66,005	1	7	4.0	18,845	-2	16	1.3	34,878	-6	8	0.6
2001	30,365	-1	1	4.7	66,820	1	5	5.6	17,090	-9	-12	0.8	31,922	-8	-13	-8.7
2002	31,128	3	13	1.9	66,551	0	5	7.4	17,159	<1	-4	-0.8	23,872	-25	-22	-0.6
2003	31,389	1	2	2.0	65,346	-2	3	6.6	17,672	3	11	-2.7	23,510	-2	-10	0.9
2004	32,177	3	7	2.6	64,237	-2	3	5.8	15,892	-10	3	1.5	23,168	-1	-3	1.0

TABLE 9—*cont.*

	Mitsukoshi				Seiyu				Softbank				Hikari Tsushin			
FY	Employees	Δ Emp (%)	Δ Sales (%)	ROA	Employees	Δ Emp (%)	Δ Sales (%)	ROA	Employees	Δ Emp (%)	Δ Sales (%)	ROA	Employees	Δ Emp (%)	Δ Sales (%)	ROA
1990	11,457	1	10	1.8	10,832	-4	4	1.7	—	—	—	—	—	—	—	—
1991	11,867	4	1	1.2	10,656	-2	4	1.7	—	—	—	—	567	—	—	2.9
1992	12,332	4	-4	0.3	10,833	2	1	1.3	—	—	—	—	477	-16	27	4.4
1993	12,225	-1	-5	-0.8	10,870	0	-5	0.9	690	—	—	3.0	420	-12	5	3.7
1994	11,930	-2	-4	0.3	10,646	-2	-2	0.4	690	0	50	2.2	489	16	-100	6.3
1995	11,400	-4	-1	0.5	8,768	-18	-1	0.7	802	16	45	1.7	910	86	115	5.8
1996	10,784	-5	1	0.8	8,208	-6	-2	0.8	952	19	40	1.8	1,224	35	117	7.5
1997	10,076	-7	-4	-8.2	7,924	-3	-1	-4.1	1,064	12	4	2.4	911	-26	31	8.3
1998	9,622	-5	-7	-6.4	7,205	-9	-5	-2.6	1,002	-6	-1	2.0	2,120	133	62	7.0
1999	8,142	-15	-1	1.0	6,797	-6	-8	-4.7	8	-99	-47	8.3	2,120	0	8	2.3
2000	6,689	-18	2	0.8	5,901	-13	-5	0.6	75	838	-100	0.7	621	-71	-83	-18.6
2001	6,441	-4	0	1.0	6,476	10	-6	0.0	70	-7	0	-4.5	303	-51	-58	-7.6
2002	6,230	-3	-2	1.1	6,025	-7	<1	-23.0	70	0	0	-5.0	381	26	61	-6.2
2003	8,206	32	-34	0.8	5,499	-9	-18	-1.6	67	-4	0	1.6	331	-13	9	2.3
2004	7,904	-4	89	-1.6	4,107	-25	14	-2.9	89	33	0	-1.5	485	47	55	3.6

Source: Development Bank of Japan databank; *Kaisha Nenkan.*

Note: ROA = Profit after taxes/total assets.

TABLE 10. *Restructuring Highlights at Ten Japanese Companies*

	Toyota	Nissan	NEC	Sony	Mizuho
Foreign ownership (%) 4/05	21.3	64.3	33.1	40.1	20.4
Share price high(s)	¥5,730 in 2000	¥1,700 in 1990	¥2,290 in 1991, ¥3,450 in 2001	¥9,500 in 1990, ¥17,260 in 2000	¥560,000 in 2004
Share price low(s)	¥2,455 in 2003	¥290 in 1999	¥601 in 1993, ¥333 in 2003	¥3,350 in 1993, ¥2,720 in 2003	¥58,300 in 2003
Share price 8/31/05	¥4,500	¥1,156	¥589	¥3,700	¥614,000
Major restructuring plans		1993, 1999	1999, 2001	1999, 2003	2001
Major reorganizations	—	Renault investment 1999	Created "company" system 2000, disbanded it 2002	Many	Merger and holding company 2002
Major changes in supplier relations	Increased stake in key group companies 2000	Sold affiliates 1999–2001; 1,145 in 2000 to 595 in 2002	Disbanded association 2000, reduced	4,700 in 2002 to 2,400 in 2004	Integrated IT systems beginning 2002
Stock options	Directors 1997, others 2001	2000	For 150 managers 2003	For senior managers	No
Performance-based pay	For white-collar 1999	2003	For white-collar 2002	Managers, others 2004	Yes
Board consolidation	58 to 27 in 2003	37 to 10 in 1999	37 to 19 in 2000	38 to 10 in 1998	51 to 36 in 2001
Outside directors	No	1 of 9	3 of 15	8 of 12 in 2005	2
Committee-system board	No	No	No	2003	No

Source: Development Bank of Japan; *Kaisha Shikihō*; company data.

Note: Foreign ownership calculated on an unconsolidated basis.

The Company Cases

TOYOTA: REFORM WITHOUT RESTRUCTURING

Toyota Motor Corporation embodies the Japanese model more than any other company.[5] It developed the "Toyota system" of just-in-time supply management, quality control, incremental process improvement, and flexible pro-

---

5. The Toyota case stands out from the others in that Toyota did not encounter a major crisis in financial results and/or declining sales, but Toyota managers would argue that this reflects their efforts to reform preemptively before problems develop. Moreover, the Toyota case is critical for our purposes because it has served as a model for so many other companies.

	Shinsei	Mitsukoshi	Seiyu	Softbank	Hikari Tsushin
Foreign ownership (%) 4/05	74.0	7.6	49.9	13.5	6.5
Share price high(s)	¥904 in 2004	¥2,740 in 1990	¥3,330 in 1990	¥198,000 in 2000	¥241,000 in 2000
Share price low(s)	¥511 in 2005	¥265 in 2000	¥167 in 2005	¥827 in 2002	¥895 in 2002
Share price 8/31/2005	¥681	¥513	¥225	¥5,610	¥7,780
Major restructuring plans	1999	1999, 2005	1997, 2003	—	2000
Major reorganizations	Nationalized 1998, sold to Ripplewood 1999	Absorbed 4 regional companies 2003	Wal-Mart invests 2002	Holding company 1999, recentralized 2000	—
Major changes in supplier relations	New IT system 2000	6,200 in 1999 to 4,600 in 2003	Joint business plan, Retail Link 2004	—	—
Stock options	2004	For board 2004	Directors 2000, Wal-Mart 2002	1998, for all in 2003	For all employees 1997
Performance-based pay	2000	1999, 2003	1995	1998	Since founding
Board consolidation	No	24 to 17 in 1999, 10 to 6 in 2004	34 to 11 in 2003	No	No
Outside directors	12 of 15	1 to 2 in 2003	8 (5 from Wal-Mart) 2005	2 of 8	No
Committee-system board	2004	2003	2003	No	No

duction that revolutionized manufacturing throughout the world.[6] In recent years, it has garnered even greater respect by posting stellar financial results while so many other Japanese companies struggled, and Toyota executives, particularly Chairman Hiroshi Okuda, have publicly defended the Japanese model.

Toyota executives are remarkably unapologetic about their refusal to convert to a more liberal brand of capitalism. Okuda declares: "We have not changed our approach to labor relations. Other companies have resorted to layoffs and other measures, but we have a commitment to protecting the jobs of our employees so long as we have the means to do so. I see this as one of

6. Womack et al. 1990.

our greatest strengths."[7] Toyota managers not only insist on upholding the principle of "lifetime" employment but stress the importance of maintaining strong channels of communication with workers. This facilitates labor-management collaboration to reorganize production and maximize productivity. Even so, Toyota Motor Corporation has gradually trimmed its workforce from 73,000 in 1992 to 67,000 in 2002 by reducing new hires and transferring workers to affiliates. Toyota managers continue to deploy temporary transfers (*shukkō*) to facilitate collaboration between Toyota and its most important suppliers. Toyota has moved toward performance-based pay more for white-collar workers than for blue-collar workers. "This reflects the difference between positions that require technical skill, which improves gradually year by year," explains Mitsuo Kinoshita, a managing director with responsibility for personnel issues, "and jobs that demand intuition and savvy, where it makes sense to offer larger differences in rewards." Toyota eliminated a strictly seniority-based wage for white-collar workers in 1999, but managers still believe in rewarding seniority. "We want workers to train and to cultivate their capabilities throughout their career," Kinoshita adds, "and we want the older workers to be motivated to help out the younger ones."[8] Toyota managers use nonregular (contract) workers to cope with fluctuations in demand, and they gradually increased the number of these workers to 9,478 by 2004.[9] Beginning in 2004, they took advantage of the revision to the Worker Dispatching Law to hire five hundred dispatch assembly-line workers on three-month contracts. The dispatch workers are generally paid less, have shorter contracts, and can be deployed to the assembly lines more quickly than other categories of nonregular workers.[10]

As noted in the previous chapter, Toyota has not merely refrained from loosening ties with favored suppliers but has recentralized control over core group companies. Toyota managers insist that their close relationship with suppliers is the key to the company's competitive edge, enabling it to lower costs, enhance quality, and spur innovation. They claim that they are very demanding of their suppliers but that they are also very loyal. "The suppliers tell us that we are 'tough but warm' (*kibishii kedo atatakai*)," boasts one manager, "while our competitors are 'soft but cold' (*yasashii kedo tsumetai*)."[11]

7. Okuda interview, June 18, 2003.
8. Interview, Toyota City, January 18, 2002.
9. Company data.
10. *Nikkei Weekly* (April 12, 2004), 21.
11. Interview with Hidehiko Tajima, General Manager, Global Purchasing Planning Division, Global Purchasing Center, Toyota Motor Corporation, Toyota City, January 18, 2002.

Toyota is so large and financially sound that it can fund its own investments, either directly through retained earnings or via the capital markets on favorable terms. Yet many Toyota group companies still rely heavily on bank lending, so the head company strives to maintain good working relations with its primary banks. Toyota resisted any kind of board reform until 2003, when it reduced the number of board members from 58 to 27 and established 39 new nonboard posts of executive manager.[12] Okuda remains adamant, however, that Toyota has no need for outside directors. "At Toyota we feel that outside directors could not possibly understand our business. If we brought them in, they would just get in the way." I press him on this point: "But don't you feel pressure from foreign shareholders to change your ways?" He hesitates for only a moment. "Not so far," he shrugs.[13]

NISSAN: NO FRENCH REVOLUTION

Only Nissan has been more influential than Toyota in the public debate over the virtues and vices of the Japanese economic model, yet its story seems to offer a diametrically opposed lesson: only radical change imposed from outside can rid Japanese firms of their outmoded ways. Nissan president Carlos Ghosn transformed from Japan's public enemy no. 1 to a national hero in the space of two years. When he first announced his dramatic "Revival Plan," popular commentators demonized him as a merciless cost cutter and shamelessly deployed his name as a metaphor for heartlessness, both as an adjective (*gōn rashii*—"Ghosn-esque," meaning ruthless) and a verb (*gōn suru*—"to Ghosn," meaning to restructure drastically). After orchestrating a remarkable rebound in the company's financial performance, Ghosn was embraced by the media and the public as a brilliant corporate leader. He even produced his own bestseller, cleverly entitled *Runessansu* (a wordplay on Renault combined with "renaissance").[14] Yet even Nissan under Ghosn deployed some distinctively Japanese elements in its turnaround plan.

Nissan managers were acutely aware of their troubles before Ghosn's arrival and made substantial efforts to reduce costs, for example, by gradually cutting the workforce via attrition. They caused a major uproar when they decided to close the Zama plant in 1993. The LDP labor minister, Masakuni Murakami, condemned the plan; the Socialist Party launched a full-fledged investigation; and Zama City refused to authorize the sale of the property.[15] In May 1998, company leaders announced a "Global Business Reform Plan" to reduce the number of car models from 50 to about 35, cut the number of

---

12. *Nikkei Weekly* (June 30, 2003), 2.
13. Interview, June 18, 2003.
14. Ghosn 2001. Also see Ghosn and Riès 2005.
15. Madsen 2004.

manufacturing "platforms" (the basic floor plans that form the core of a car's body) from 25 to 14, consolidate domestic sales networks from four to two, lower inventories, sell non-core assets, and freeze new overseas operations.[16] The government provided a long-term loan of ¥100 billion through the Japan Development Bank in August, and a syndicate of commercial banks— led by main banks Fuji and IBJ—offered a credit line of ¥500 billion in October.[17]

Meanwhile, managers worked with the government to find an outside investor. By March 1999, interest-bearing liabilities led to a financial crisis, and Fuji and IBJ decided not to come to the rescue. Insiders suspect that the banks had concluded that Nissan would need a financially powerful partner in the auto business even if the banks were to forgive some debt.[18] Surprisingly, Nissan found its savior in Renault, a company in solid financial shape but with its own history of troubles and without a strong international reputation. Renault installed Ghosn, a Brazilian-born strategist who had played a critical role in Renault's own turnaround, to run the new Nissan. Renault invested ¥643 billion, and Ghosn raised ¥530 billion by selling fixed assets and another ¥265 billion by selling shareholdings.[19] He cleverly booked a ¥684 billion loss in fiscal 1999 so that Nissan could restart at ground zero and post a ¥331 billion profit in 2000.[20] Ghosn differed from his Japanese predecessors in that he had a comprehensive plan for change, and he was not bound by local social ties or cultural norms. "The previous leaders faced the same choices and made similar calculations," reports a close adviser to top executives, "but when push came to shove, they could not pull the trigger. They were too bound by the web of human relationships (shigarami)."[21]

Ghosn departed most clearly from his predecessors, as noted in the previous chapter, in his approach to restructuring the Nissan group. Nissan shifted to a much more strictly cost-based approach to procurement. It reduced the overall number of suppliers from 1,145 in 2000 to 595 in 2002, but these numbers overstate the actual level of change: the company simplified the supply chain by having second- and third-tier suppliers sell parts to first-tier suppliers rather than directly to Nissan.[22] Nissan even encouraged its closest partners to compete for business from other auto assemblers. It pressed Jatco,

16. Cott and Piper 2000, 4–5.
17. Cott and Piper 2000, 6.
18. *Ekonomisuto* (June 3, 2003), 36–37.
19. Company data.
20. *Ekonomisuto* (September 2, 2002), 86–87.
21. Interview with Kazuhiko Satō, Manager, Secretariat, Nissan Motor Co., Ltd., January 15, 2002.
22. Interview with Seiji Uehara, Senior Manager, Purchasing Administration Department, Nissan Motor Co., June 20, 2003.

the former transmission division that was spun off in 1999, for example, to raise volume and lower unit cost, even if it meant allowing competitors to benefit from Nissan-developed technology. What's in this for Nissan? "Nissan still has a close relationship with Jatco," explains a former Nissan manager who transferred to Jatco, "so that gives it an advantage in terms of information flow. It is better positioned to make long-term plans based on the technology we are developing today."[23]

To reduce capacity, Ghosn and his comrades decided to close one of the flagship production facilities, the Murayama plant. The workers were outraged, but ultimately the union made its peace with the new management. Despite his reputation, Ghosn was extremely sensitive to the union's position. He realized that he would have to work closely with the union, and union leaders recognized that they had little choice but to work with Ghosn, given the company's dire financial situation. The union had two conditions for cooperation: preservation of employment (no layoffs) and thorough labor-management discussions on all restructuring measures.[24] In practice, Nissan had more overcapacity in facilities than in workers, and it had considerable ongoing demand for line workers in particular. The company transferred most of the Maruyama plant workers to other plants, left a few at the plant site for a transitional period, and offered a generous early retirement program to those who preferred to retire rather than move to a new location. The Revival Plan set a target of reducing the Nissan group workforce from 144,000 in 1999 to 129,000 by 2003. Nissan managers achieved (and surpassed) this goal primarily via natural attrition, although they also used personnel transfers and early retirement.

Nissan worked directly with its primary banks in implementing the Revival Plan and received financial support from the government-owned Japan Development Bank as well. Nissan nonetheless shifted to a more price-based approach to financing, employing a global cash management system to obtain capital at the lowest possible cost.[25] Nissan and Renault also worked together to maximize the benefits from their new alliance. They focused especially on reducing procurement costs through joint purchasing, but they also formed "cross-company teams" to collaborate on research, exchange manufacturing expertise, consolidate platforms, share factories overseas, and streamline distribution.[26]

23. Interview with Toshimasa Doi, Senior Vice President, Product Development Division, Product Planning Administrative Department, Jatco, Ltd., April 3, 2002.

24. Interview with Kōichirō Nishihara, President, Federation of All Nissan and General Workers' Unions (Nissan Rōren), and Vice President, Japan Automobile Workers' Unions, March 28, 2002.

25. *Nihon Keizai Shimbun* (April 29, 2004), 11, and *Nikkei Weekly* (August 9, 2004), 3.

26. Yoshino and Fagan 2003.

Over the longer term, Nissan managers face the challenge of maintaining quality standards, expanding production, and continuing to innovate—and there are signs that restructuring may have taken a toll. Nissan cut total research and development expenditures to less than half those of Toyota and 70 percent of Honda from 1999 to 2003, but it closed the gap to 60 percent of Toyota and 87 percent of Honda in 2004.[27] Nissan had to stop production at four assembly plants in 2004 owing to a shortage of steel, partly because it had reduced the number of its Japanese steel suppliers from five to two.[28] "We are concerned about our future ability to collaborate with suppliers," notes Vice Chairman Takeshi Isayama. "If you just procure what is cheapest, then what do you do about the cost of developing the next technology? If the suppliers do not have the money to develop or to invest in R&D, then can they really keep up?"[29]

In 2002, Nissan declared the revival complete and announced a three-year plan, called Nissan 180, to increase worldwide sales by one million vehicles, maintain an 8 percent operating margin, and bring interest-bearing debts for its auto divisions to zero.[30] Then, in 2005, it announced yet another three-year plan: Nissan Value-Up. It would maintain the top operating profit margin among global automakers, achieve a 20 percent return on invested capital, and boost production to 4.2 million units by the end of fiscal year 2007 (a 24 percent increase in three years). The plan centers on a partial reversal of the Revival Plan: at a November 2004 meeting with suppliers, Ghosn proclaimed that Nissan would strengthen *keiretsu* ties to enhance its ability to innovate and expand. Nissan and Jatco have substantially reinforced their ties, with close coordination on strategy as well as exchanges of directors.[31]

NEC: SELLING THE FAMILY SILVER

NEC remains firmly under Japanese management, yet it has broken from typical Japanese practices far more than Toyota. NEC experienced much greater financial challenges than Toyota, but NEC managers are also less self-confident about their own management practices and more adventurous with novel approaches. NEC gradually implemented cost-cutting measures throughout the 1990s, including modest reductions in workforce and some sales of divisions and subsidiaries. It experienced a disastrous financial performance (a ¥151 billion loss) in fiscal 1999, however, and announced a major

27. *Nihon Keizai Shimbun* (April 30, 2004), 9.
28. *Economist* (December 4, 2004), 63–64.
29. Interview, January 15, 2002.
30. *Oriental Economist* (January 2003), 10–11.
31. E-mail correspondence, June 14, 2005.

restructuring plan to refocus on core businesses, reduce fixed costs, restructure finances, and strengthen corporate governance. It would reduce capital expenditures by 20 percent and management expenses and R&D by 10 percent each. Top executives were explicit about achieving specific financial targets, including boosting the share price and maintaining a single "A" credit rating, and they were promptly rewarded by a stock price gain from ¥1,054 to ¥1,170 in two days. They set out to reduce their worldwide workforce by 15,000 in three years, with 9,000 (7 percent of total domestic) coming from domestic operations and 6,000 (21 percent of total overseas) from overseas. In fact, they achieved a reduction of 14,000 in only two years. They reduced 5,000 by natural attrition, 3,500 by sales of divisions, 1,500 by early retirement programs, 500 via transfers, 3,000 by closure of plants abroad, and 500 by other means (primarily by not extending contracts of nonregular workers).[32] They even sold the corporate headquarters in Tokyo, to the horror of the company's "old boys," although NEC continued to occupy the building as long-term lessee.

NEC reorganized itself into three divisional "companies" to target different customer groups within the information technology market: NEC Solutions, focusing on the household and corporate consumer market; NEC Networks, targeted at network operators; and NEC Electron Devices, aimed at equipment vendors. It also reorganized its board, reducing directors from 37 to 19, and introduced a corporate officer system. It developed a stock option plan for directors and corporate officers (about 150 of the top executives), plus stock price–linked bonuses for about 1,800 managers. In July 2000, it announced that it was disbanding its supplier association, which it had created in 1957 and consolidated in 1985. It shifted to greater reliance on overseas parts and increased electronic procurement.

It closed NEC Home Electronics and Packard Bell NEC and sold production facilities in the United States, the United Kingdom, and Brazil to electronic manufacturing service companies. It sold shares in Ando Electronic to Yokokawa Electric and transferred laser printer facilities to Fuji Xerox. When selling production facilities within Japan, company managers negotiated with the buyer to maintain workers at the facility and to offer workers comparable wages and benefits. In the case of the sale of NEC Medical Systems in 1999, for example, they transferred 310 workers to the buyer company, shifted 20 to new positions within the NEC group, and offered early retirement to 160.

32. These figures (from company materials) differ slightly from the changes in total employment reported in Tables 8 and 9 because some cuts were partially offset by increases in other regions, especially abroad.

NEC merged its memory chip (DRAM) business with Hitachi in 1999, forming Elpida Memory, Inc., to share costs and invest in new technology. The government provided tax and regulatory relief under the Industrial Revital- ization Law (Chapter 4). METI's Industrial Revitalization Division proudly reports this merger, plus the broader consolidation of the semiconductor industry, as a model for industrial reorganization.[33] Elpida suffered annual losses of more than ¥25 billion for three straight years, fiscal 2001–3, but it became profitable in early 2004 and went public in November 2004. Mean- while, it committed ¥500 billion to a new production facility in Hiroshima Prefecture.[34]

NEC managers began to focus more energy on investor relations. They judged, for example, that reporting results as clearly as possible and separat- ing results for each divisional "company" would appeal to analysts. They set corporate value as an explicit goal, defining it as a combination of shareholder value, client value, and employee value, and they ranked shareholder value at the top of the three. In the short run, these efforts paid off, as NEC returned to profitability in fiscal 2000 and the share price surged from just over ¥1,000 at its low in February 1999 to a high of ¥3,450 in July 2000. Meanwhile, NEC stuck with its main bank—Mitsui Sumitomo—a loyal buyer of NEC computers.

NEC introduced an innovative system to cultivate the company's own internal labor market, actively promoting a more market-based approach to personnel transfers both within NEC itself and among some group compa- nies. The personnel division encouraged managers to post openings and employees to post their qualifications and their preferences for future job assignments on the firm's internal network. This system gave managers and employees greater freedom to arrange their own job matches and increased mobility across operational divisions within the company. By 2004, about four hundred matches were being made per year, although the managers initiated the action in the vast majority of cases.[35] The company redefined its commit- ment to lifetime employment to one of "lifetime career support." In practice, this meant that the company would do its best to arrange transfers inside the NEC group but would also serve as a sort of employment agency to help employees find jobs elsewhere. In articulating its new personnel philoso- phy, the firm announced a new motto: "the shining individual" (*kagayaku kojin*).

33. METI documents.
34. *Nikkei Weekly* (May 2, 2005), 21.
35. Interview with Kenta Fujino, Assistant Manager, Human Resources Division, NEC Corporation, July 20, 2004.

In 2002, NEC introduced a surprisingly ruthless new employment system for white-collar managers in which evaluations would include negative as well as positive recommendations and managers would be asked to identify the bottom 10 percent of their workers for possible demotion. Those in the bottom 10 percent would be given a "rechallenge" program for one year that would include career counseling, along with such options as demotion, transfer within the NEC group, and employment outside the company. Those remaining within the company would work with counselors to develop an action plan for improvement. In practice, the company never implemented the program as originally conceived. It ended up designating less than 1 percent of the managers for the rechallenge program, reserving it for only the most extreme cases of poor performance. "The program just did not fit with Japanese custom," one personnel manager concedes.[36] Instead, the company tried to handle demotions and nonpromotions as inconspicuously as possible, simply transferring the nonperformers to new sections.

NEC's financial condition deteriorated once again with the bursting of the IT bubble, and the company embarked on an even more dramatic reform plan in 2001. It reported a ¥312 billion loss in fiscal 2002, and its share price dropped from ¥3,430 to a low of below ¥500 in October 2002. Managers expanded their program for cutting fixed costs via rationalization of production lines, sales and mergers of facilities, wage restraint, reductions of workforce, and cuts in investments in plant and equipment. In April 2001, they targeted a 30 percent reduction in materials costs over two years. They introduced a comprehensive e-procurement system and reduced the overall number of suppliers but at the same time reinforced ties to suppliers with critical technology. They instituted a more systematic and codified procedure for evaluating parts, including a "supplier score card." As in the Toyota case, NEC managers sought to use their collaboration with suppliers to reduce real production costs rather than simply to demand lower prices. They further rationalized the semiconductor business, spinning off the electronic devices division as NEC Electronics in November 2002. They sold factories in Miyagi and Yamanashi to Celestica and one in Ibaraki to Solectron, laser printer operations to Fuji Xerox, automotive electronics to Honda, printed circuit boards to Toppan Printing, and a plasma display subsidiary to Pioneer.[37] And they accelerated the shift of production offshore, especially to China. Meanwhile, NEC announced in 2004 that it would form a new joint venture with

36. Fujino interview, July 20, 2004.
37. *Nikkei Weekly* (February 9, 2004), 14. METI reportedly intervened to ensure that NEC sold the plasma display subsidiary to a domestic firm to keep the technology in Japan (*Economist*, April 10, 2004, 57).

Hitachi to integrate the two companies' network router businesses. President Kōji Nishigaki encountered public criticism of his cost-cutting measures from legendary chairman Tadahiro Sekimoto, who accused Nishigaki of wantonly selling off the group Sekimoto himself had so painstakingly built. Nishigaki dismissed Sekimoto as adviser in December 2002, and Nishigaki himself resigned in March 2003.[38]

The new president, Akinobu Kanasugi, launched his own revival plan. He set a target of doubling profits and increasing shareholder capital. He disbanded the internal company system and replaced it with a more lateral structure with nine operational divisions designed to promote synergy across computers and communications. And he introduced a "key performance index" (KPI) to link business unit performance with the company's overall financial goals.[39] In 2005, NEC became one of the first electronics companies to announce its own takeover defense scheme. It would double the number of issuable shares to make it more difficult for a hostile bidder to gain a controlling share, and it would cut the maximum allowable number of directors from forty to twenty to make it harder for a bidder to seize control of the board.[40]

SONY: PERPETUAL REORGANIZATION

Sony has a reputation as a non-establishment company: it does not belong to an industrial group; unlike Toyota and NEC, it does not have a full-fledged supplier group; and it does not enjoy close ties to the bureaucracy. It has never adhered to the classic Japanese model, and it has been a forerunner in moving further away from the model. Although it does not have a foreign owner, it is still a much more international company than NEC in the sense that it has an unusually high percentage of foreign shareholders (40 percent) and a very high level of foreign production (over 50 percent) and sales (over 70 percent). Yet even Sony has remained sensitive to Japanese norms, especially in labor relations.

Sony continued to be profitable through much of the 1990s, so it did not turn to major restructuring until it experienced substantial losses in the second half of fiscal 1999. Sony announced a target of reducing its worldwide workforce of 173,000 by 10 percent by March 2003, primarily by selling off divisions and reducing staff overseas. Otherwise, Sony gradually shifted the composition of the workforce, reducing workers in manufacturing while recruiting for software, entertainment, and Internet-related positions. Sony

38. *Nikkei Weekly* (January 27, 2003), 8.
39. Interview with Tetsuya Nakamura, General Manager, Corporate Planning Division, NEC Corporation, July 20, 2004.
40. *Nikkei Net* (March 5, 2005).

has tried to transfer workers outside the Sony group but has had difficulty arranging transfers because of the weakness of its corporate network. Managers have sought to increase midcareer hires, but they complain that the market for these recruits remains small.[41] Sony employs a fairly aggressive performance-based pay system for managers, with stock options for those in the top ranks and a share-price-based component in bonuses. Pay differentials are considerably larger than in most Japanese companies: as high as ¥5 million a year for a section chief or ¥6 million for a division chief.[42] Personnel managers have experimented with five-year contracts for some engineers. They encounter problems with contract renewals, however, because the law requires that renewed contract workers become permanent employees. "Some companies end up doing tricks to get around the rules: terminating workers for a month and then re-hiring them," laments one manager. "This is not a normal situation."[43]

Sony has been a national frontrunner in corporate board reform, reducing its board from thirty-eight to ten in 1998, and adding two new outside board members for a total of four. One manager stressed that Sony needs outside board members because it relies so heavily on equity markets for financing. "We need people on our board who can take the view of investors and the financial community," he explained.[44] Yet even Sony executives make it clear that they have no intention of giving the outside directors a central role in guiding the firm.[45]

Sony reorganizes so often that employees complain about having to order new name cards on a regular basis. The personnel managers note that frequent reorganization complicates employee evaluations because the employees are constantly shifting into newly defined business units.[46] Sony has taken advantage of commercial code reforms to use share swaps to turn affiliates into wholly owned subsidiaries.[47]

Sony has never had as integrated a supply network as NEC, let alone Toyota, so reforming the supply chain implies a less dramatic shift. Sony reduced its

---

41. Interview with Hideaki Naoe, General Manager, Industrial Relations and Planning, Employee Relations, Corporate Human Resources, Sony Corporation, January 25, 2002.

42. Interview with Kei Sakaguchi, General Manager, Corporate Communications, Sony Corporation, July 21, 2004.

43. Naoe interview, January 25, 2002.

44. Interview with Yoshinori Hashitani, General Manager, Board Secretariat, and General Manager, CEO Strategy Office, Sony Corporation, April 5, 2002.

45. Chairman and CEO Nobuyuki Idei put it this way: "Companies should be run by their full-time executives and employees. Outside directors are in a position just to judge and oversee what we executives decide" (*Nikkei Weekly*, March 21, 2005, 14).

46. Naoe interview, January 25, 2002.

47. *Japan Times* (March 8, 2002).

number of suppliers from 4,700 to 2,400 and the number of parts used from 800,000 to 400,000 from 2002 to 2004. Yet even Sony managers see their collaboration with core suppliers as a competitive edge. "We work very closely with our Japanese suppliers to develop the lightest, smallest, and thinnest products," declares Teruaki Aoki, a corporate executive vice president. He continues: "The personal relationship between our top managers and their top managers is critical. This is less true abroad, more in Japan. The relationship is based on a commitment, but not a written commitment. From our side, a high volume of orders shows our commitment. And from their side, high quality, reasonable price, and stable supply shows their commitment." Sony managers review these relationships every year, but they do not simply sever ties if a supplier ceases to perform. "We do not suddenly decide one day that we do not need them," Aoki explains. "That could force them into bankruptcy. Rather, we explain the situation, and we make sure that they accept the result. We began this process in 2000, and it has taken a long time to gain the suppliers' acceptance."[48]

The "Sony shock" struck in the spring of 2003, as disappointing earnings reports triggered a 25 percent drop in the company's share price. Sony announced a three-year restructuring plan, dubbed "Transformation 60," under which it would reduce its 160,000 global employees by 20,000, with 13,000 coming from overseas and 7,000 from domestic operations. Sony managers concede that they handle workforce reductions differently at home than overseas: domestically, they freeze new hires and transfer workers whereas overseas they simply lay them off.[49] Sony also planned to reduce its manufacturing, transport, and service branches by 30 percent and to reduce the number of components used for audiovisual equipment by 90 percent.[50] Sony president Nobuyuki Idei promised to raise operating profits above the 10 percent level by March 2007, but the company managed only 1.5 percent in the year ending March 2005.

Sony then performed a surprising management reshuffle that brought in a foreigner, Sir Howard Stringer, as chairman and CEO in June 2005. Stringer had successfully led Sony Corporation of America, playing a key role in reviving Sony's entertainment business. Sony also restructured the board, increasing the number of outside directors to eight out of a total of twelve. Stringer announced a turnaround plan in September 2005 that would shed ten thousand jobs, sell off unprofitable business lines, and promote coordination across divisions. Investors were disappointed with the plan, however, and the

48. Interview with Teruaki Aoki, Corporate Executive Vice President, Sony Corporation, July 21, 2004.

49. Sakaguchi interview, July 21, 2004.

50. *Asahi Shimbun* (October 29, 2003), 17.

company share price dropped 5 percent immediately after the announcement. Stringer argued that Japanese norms and social relations had prevented him from going further. "I went as far as I could go and still preserve the relationship with people that I have to work with and who have to drive the change in this company," he explained in a press interview. "Japanese society is more humanitarian than American society."[51]

MIZUHO: A GIANT REGROUPS

Japanese restructuring in the financial sector has taken the form of consolidation, as noted in the previous chapter, and the result has been the emergence of mega-banks that have reorganized the horizontal *keiretsu* and redefined the main bank system. In April 2002, three of Japan's largest banks—Fuji, Daiichi Kangyo (DKB), and the Industrial Bank of Japan (IBJ)—merged to form Mizuho, the world's largest financial group. Mizuho took advantage of the lifting of the holding company ban and the reforms of the commercial code permitting share swaps to reorganize as a holding company comprising three core financial institutions: Mizuho Bank, Mizuho Corporate Bank, and Mizuho Securities. Fuji, DKB, and IBJ, like all of Japan's major banks, had suffered from massive nonperforming loans and low (and sometimes negative) returns throughout the 1990s. They scaled back their workforce gradually during this decade: Fuji by 13 percent 1990–99, DKB by 17 percent, and IBJ by 2 percent.[52] For the masterminds of the deal, including the presidents of the three merging banks plus the financial authorities, Mizuho was meant to be a model case for the rehabilitation of the Japanese financial sector. Mizuho created a mechanism for reducing capacity by closing Fuji or DKB branches in close proximity to each other; it complemented Fuji and DKB's strength in retail with IBJ's expertise in investment banking; and it achieved a scale that would allow huge investments in IT. Commentators were less sanguine, arguing that the new entity had little going for it but size. As if to validate the doomsayers, Mizuho got off to a disastrous start as its computer system failed immediately. Depositors were unable to withdraw money from the company's automatic teller machines and received mistaken transaction information. The three banks had remained loyal to their respective software vendors, and the three vendors had tremendous difficulties coordinating their efforts to forge the new IT system.[53]

In 2000, Fuji president Tōru Hashimoto stressed that Mizuho would become Japan's first real universal banking group. "As companies move to direct

---

51. *Financial Times* (September 24, 2005), 13.
52. *Kaisha nenkan* [Company Annual], various issues (unconsolidated basis).
53. *Economist* (April 19, 2003), 56.

finance, they need a backup facility, whether it be in the money markets or commercial paper, so we can provide a commitment line for them," he explained. "We can link this to bond underwriting as a way to maintain stable relations, even as these clients move away from traditional borrowing." Hashimoto stressed, however, that banks would have to take a hard line on rescuing firms in distress. "We have to base bailout decisions on a rational assessment of costs and benefits. We used to do anything we could to help out our clients, but we just cannot do that anymore," he insisted.[54]

Mizuho planned to reduce permanent employees from 32,000 in March 2001 to 25,000 in March 2006. It would achieve this goal through natural attrition plus transfers for about 600 to 700 employees a year, with 60 percent going to subsidiaries and 40 percent to business partners. It would reduce domestic offices from 588 to 460 and overseas offices from 82 to 53, and it would cut board directors from 51 to 36. At the same time, it would increase its 14,000 nonregular employees, substantially shifting the ratio between permanent and nonregular employees. The permanent employees subdivide into 20,000 core workers, mostly male, and 12,000 "special workers," mostly female. The turnover among the latter is especially high. Nonregular workers, also mostly female, account for more than half the workforce at the branches. They handle most of the clerical functions, the more routine sales work, some telemarketing, and the processing of home loans. Meanwhile, Mizuho restructured the personnel system to facilitate reductions in wages and related costs. It shifted from a job ability wage (*shokunōkyū*) to a job description wage (*shokumukyū*), which allows for more variation based on ability and performance.[55]

If it was not that difficult to reduce the workforce—a stock analyst might ask—then why didn't Mizuho move more quickly? Mizuho was saddled with such extraordinary levels of bad debt that its own bond ratings hit the bottom of the rankings. Mizuho managers recognized that their survival depended more on government policy and economic conditions than on their own efforts to slim down. Mizuho continued to make a profit, not including the burden of writing off bad debts. Its restructuring program contributed but would not return the firm to financial health without some help. In addition, the branches were not able to reduce personnel without integrating their computer systems. Nobuo Tanaka, the branch manager in Utsunomiya (Tochigi Prefecture), for example, reports that his branch brought together a Fuji and a DKB branch but that it continued to operate as two branches in one

54. Interview, August 1, 2000.
55. Interview with Nobuhiro Ishikawa, Manager, Personnel Planning Division, Mizuho Financial Group, January 16, 2002.

building, with the Fuji employees working on Fuji systems and the DKB employees working on DKB systems. It could only begin staff reductions when the branch finally integrated the computer systems in December 2004. Tanaka expected to reduce the workforce of 100 to 90 over one to two years, cutting only permanent employees by natural attrition and transfers.[56]

In 2003, Mizuho raised ¥1.08 trillion, roughly equal to its market capitalization, by issuing preferred shares to its main bank clients and other business partners. Dai-ichi Mutual contributed ¥45 billion, Yasuda Mutual ¥33 billion, and Sompo Japan Insurance ¥31.5 billion.[57] Nissan Motor, which had been a main bank client of Fuji and IBJ, was conspicuously absent from the list of contributors.[58] Mizuho relationship managers also began to take a harder line on maintaining reasonable lending spreads to improve profitability. "We do not just want to increase lending anymore," declared one manager, "because we have to make money."[59] By March 2005, thanks to pressure from the FSA and an upturn in the stock market, Mizuho had reduced its bad-loan ratio to 2.2 percent, well below the government target of 5 percent.[60] Mizuho then began turning its energy toward expanding in potential growth areas, setting up a new group to focus on corporate turnarounds and announcing a private banking subsidiary.[61]

SHINSEI: REBORN AS AN ALIEN

Shinsei Bank managers proclaim that they are simply trying to bring global best practice to Japanese banking. They maximize returns rather than volume, demand performance from their employees, price loans on the basis of risk, and cut off borrowers that are unable to pay their debts. That is what any good bank *should* do, they insist.[62] In Japan, however, Shinsei's brand of common sense so blatantly violates standard norms and practices that Shinsei has infuriated government officials, unnerved its own employees, and alienated many potential business partners. Shinsei, even more than Nissan, challenges the Japanese model at its core. Yet, like Nissan, Shinsei has won its share of admirers by proving that its approach can achieve results, even in Japan.

Shinsei emerged out of the ruins of a very traditional Japanese institution, the Long-Term Credit Bank (LTCB). LTCB was one of three long-term credit

---

56. Interview, Utsunomiya, July 22, 2004.
57. *Nikkei Weekly* (March 17, 2003), 2; *Ekonomisuto* (July 8, 2003), 28–33.
58. *Nikkei Weekly* (March 24, 2003), 7.
59. Interview with Takehiro Mikoda, General Manager, Corporate Banking Division No. 1, Mizuho Corporate Bank, June 13, 2003.
60. FSA data.
61. *Nikkei Weekly* (May 2, 2005), 8.
62. Interviews, 2002–4.

banks in the postwar era (along with IBJ and Nippon Credit Bank), which were given the exclusive privilege of issuing bank debentures in exchange for fulfilling the public-interest function of providing long-term credit to industry. As the financial sector evolved with regulatory changes, however, the long-term credit banks lost their original mission. LTCB executives realized this by the late 1980s and devised a comprehensive plan to reinvent LTCB as a more Western-style investment bank. As the bubble economy flourished in the late 1980s, however, the balance of power within the firm shifted from the internationally oriented investment bankers, who advocated reform, to the domestic lenders, who preferred business as usual. The latter group felt the bank was making too much money off the standard lending business to give it up, so top managers scratched the reform plan.[63] When the bubble burst, LTCB found itself with a huge portfolio of nonperforming loans and an outmoded business model. As its financial situation deteriorated in the late 1990s, LTCB announced a major restructuring program—abandoning overseas operations, selling off subsidiaries, closing branches, and reducing the workforce—but it was too late. LTCB had actually continued to increase its workforce up through the peak in 1993 (3,878 employees, on an unconsolidated basis) and then slowly cut back to 3,499 in 1997 (a 10 percent reduction over four years).[64] As plans for tie-ups with Swiss Bank Corporation and then Sumitomo Trust fell through, LTCB found itself at the mercy of the government.

The government injected ¥170 billion into LTCB in early 1998 and then nationalized the bank in October. It reviewed LTCB's assets and sold off those deemed "inappropriate" (clearly nonperforming) to the Resolution and Collection Corporation (RCC). Under temporary nationalization, LTCB withdrew completely from overseas operations, cut personnel-related expenses by 40 percent, and sold off nonessential assets such as company dormitories, golf club memberships, and works of art. In 1999, the government decided to sell the bank to the U.S. investment fund Ripplewood Holdings. In the course of negotiations, the government agreed to grant the new bank "cancellation rights," whereby it could sell back loans to the government for a period of three years if their value dropped more than 20 percent from the original net book value.[65] For its part, the bank would have certain obligations, including providing a specified amount of credit to small and medium-sized enterprises.

63. Interview with Kōji Hirao, former Deputy Chairman, Long-Term Credit Bank, and Chairman, Institute for Socioeconomic Infrastructure and Services, Inc., March 25, 2002.
64. *Kaisha nenkan*, various issues.
65. Fagan and Yoshino 2001, A4–8. Also see Tett 2003 for a detailed account of the Shinsei story.

The Japanese press and the public were astonished at this unprecedented pact, and the case fueled widespread paranoia about U.S. vulture funds storming in and buying Japanese assets on the cheap. Shinsei installed Masamoto Yashiro, a retired Citicorp executive, as its new CEO, and put together an international management team combining personnel from Ripplewood, Citicorp, and the old LTCB. "We are still fraught with divisions between the foreign managers and the Japanese ones," concedes one executive who began with LTCB. "But isn't Yashiro able to mediate between the two?" I inquire innocently. "No," he retorts. "He is one of *them!*"[66]

Whereas most Japanese bankers spend their time trying to hold on to their corporate clients, Yashiro wanted to weed them out:

> We think it is O.K. for corporate clients to leave us. We lost 40 percent of our customers, 40 percent of our employees, and 40 percent of our assets. So everything is 60 percent the size. The clients we inherited from before nationalization were not the best. We have to balance risk and return. If the return is only 1–3 percent, then you don't want the high-risk clients. For some of our clients, the question is not how to keep them but how to get rid of them.[67]

Shinsei developed a severe public relations problem by refusing to roll over credit to some of its most troubled borrowers. In June 2000, Shinsei pulled out of a debt-forgiveness scheme to rescue Sogo, a major department store chain, and thereby contributed to Sogo's subsequent failure. Yashiro was even summoned to the Diet to explain Shinsei's actions. Shinsei clashed directly with FSA officials, who ordered it to keep lending to certain clients. The FSA officials felt that since Shinsei had received public funds, it had an obligation to play a public-interest role, and that included keeping companies afloat. Yashiro saw it precisely the other way around: "We were not given this money to support bad borrowers."[68] Shinsei also struggled with the FSA over its pledge to provide loans to smaller companies. In December 2001, the FSA determined that Shinsei was not honoring its commitment and issued a "business improvement order" demanding that the bank meet its targets. Shinsei executives countered that they should not be forced to make uncollectable loans. FSA officials went so far as to direct Shinsei to make loans to four specific companies. Shinsei executives leaked this directive to the press, generating a considerable public furor.[69]

66. Interview, March 2002.
67. Yashiro interview, January 24, 2002.
68. Interview, January 24, 2002.
69. Madsen 2004.

Shinsei began with 2,300 employees, down from 3,800 at LTCB (on a consolidated basis) at the time of nationalization. Of the 2,300, 1,900 were from LTCB and 400 were new. Of the 400 new employees, 300 were midcareer Japanese and 100 were foreign experts, many of them Indians in the IT area. Shinsei did not have much trouble reducing the workforce because more than 1,000 had left voluntarily after nationalization, and more continued to leave after Ripplewood took over. Some LTCB executives used their connections to arrange transfers to other firms. One board member arranged a transfer of 40 to 50 employees to IBJ. Shinsei hired 63 new graduates in April 2001 and another 70 in April 2002.

Shinsei established a two-track system for promotion and compensation, divided between permanent staff, or "Ps", mostly Japanese from LTCB, and market staff, or "Ms," mostly foreigners and midcareer hires. The Ms had much higher average compensation but less security. The former LTCB employees had the option to become Ms, but almost all of them declined.[70] Shinsei enacted a particularly rigid performance-pay regime in which employees were evaluated on the basis of individual and product group performance. In theory, low performers were expected to transfer to other divisions or to leave the firm. "Our shareholders would like us to achieve percentage targets for how many of these employees we move out of the firm," reported one personnel manager, somewhat incredulously, "but we have not been able to hit these targets."[71] In 2003, however, several leaders among the former LTCB managers persuaded the top leadership to dispense with the two-track system and to moderate the wage differentials among employees. Meanwhile, Shinsei began to set targets for hiring and promoting more female managers. "This has posed some problems," concedes Deputy Chairman Thierry Porté, "more on the corporate side than on the retail side, and more on the traditional business side than the new business side. But this is not altruism: we think it will help us over the long term."[72]

The relationship managers—employees assigned to a particular corporate client—experienced the rockiest adjustment. "They are the ones who have the face-to-face relations with the corporate clients," explains one personnel manager. "They understand the clients' situation and they want a comfortable relationship, but they are told they are supposed to shift to a new [price-based] model. In addition, they just happen to be stuck in this role, while their colleagues in more profitable groups are earning more money under the new compensation system. So they feel this is not fair."[73] Shinsei sought to achieve

70. Fagan and Yoshino 2001, D13–14.
71. Interview, March 2002.
72. Interview, July 14, 2004. Porté became CEO in June 2005.
73. Interview, March 2002.

synergies across commercial and investment banking, but it confronted a fundamental conflict of cultures between the relationship managers, who valued the relationship with the client first and foremost, and the product specialists on the investment banking side, who wanted to promote certain products aggressively and make deals quickly. The relationship managers doubted whether the new products would meet their clients' needs, and the product specialists questioned whether the relationship managers really understood Shinsei's new strategy.[74] To help resolve these differences, Shinsei hired a consulting firm, which devised a scheme to get the relationship managers and the product specialists to work together more effectively: they would work in teams, and both sides would have to approve major business decisions.

Shinsei tried to develop a business model that would diverge from that of its Japanese competitors. Yashiro believed that it might be easier to break into retail banking than corporate finance because retail relies less on long-term business relationships. Shinsei would appeal to retail customers with innovative services and then focus on the most profitable niches in corporate finance. Shinsei executives hoped to turn other companies' financial misfortune into a profitable business niche. They felt that they had a comparative advantage in the corporate revival business, buying out small firms and then restructuring them. They were not encumbered with the obligational ties of their Japanese competitors, yet they had an advantage over foreign rivals because they knew how to handle Japanese personnel issues. "Goldman Sachs and Morgan Stanley cannot absorb excess workers. They cannot take one hundred people and place them," explains one executive, "but we can."[75] Shinsei's turnaround experts did not fire workers outright, but they reduced wages for lower-performing workers in the hope that they would quit. They also abandoned the seniority principle and cultivated young and energetic managers. Yet Shinsei faced a dilemma in deploying this strategy, for its tactics damaged its reputation. Many Japanese firms would not sell to Shinsei because they feared that it would not take good care of the workers. And the domestic banks involved in these deals fiercely opposed sales to Shinsei. Even so, Shinsei executives saw a window of opportunity while the major domestic banks were preoccupied with their own bad loans. "The big Japanese banks will get to this eventually," concedes one manager, "but then we will already be ahead."[76]

In February 2004, Shinsei successfully relisted at an initial price of ¥872 per share. Ripplewood earned ¥220 billion from sales of one-third of its stake,

74. Fagan and Yoshino 2001, D10–13.
75. Interview, March 2002.
76. Interview, March 2002.

a handsome return on its initial investment of ¥121 billion. Some critics hailed the Shinsei case as a model for turning around a troubled bank while others decried the huge cost to taxpayers. The government had invested about ¥7.8 trillion in Shinsei, but because it retained preferred shares, the eventual cost was likely to be in the ¥4–5 trillion range.[77]

MITSUKOSHI: A TRADITION IN TROUBLE

Japan's elite department stores, including Mitsukoshi, have combined long-term employment and flexibility with a distinctive variant of the more typical two-tiered employment system. On the one hand, Mitsukoshi has a remarkably high percentage of permanent employees, given that the retail sector does not benefit from long-term employment in the same way as manufacturing. Retailers do not require the same level of labor-management collaboration to enhance productivity, and they benefit less from investment in company-specific skills. On the other hand, more than half the salespeople in the stores do not even work for Mitsukoshi but are dispatched directly by merchandise vendors. Mitsukoshi also has its own tier of nonregular workers, plus armies of part-time workers who help out at peak sales periods, such as the summer gift (chūgen) season. With hard times, however, Mitsukoshi sought to cash in on its labor flexibility, to enhance that flexibility by increasing the share of nonregular employees, and to cut costs by reorganizing operations, reducing capacity, and negotiating with suppliers.

The Japanese department store is a distinctive genre, combining sales with art exhibits, cultural activities, restaurants, a food floor or two, and sometimes even a miniature amusement park for children. Mitsukoshi, like most retailers, ran into financial difficulties with the softening of consumer demand after 1990, but Mitsukoshi had the added burden of a disastrous investment in a golf course. The company was slow to respond to its problems, gradually chiseling away at costs by reducing new hires, closing overseas operations, and selling off a few peripheral businesses. In 1999, Mitsukoshi announced a broader restructuring plan, but it still failed to impress the analysts.[78] The company offered an early retirement program, finding 1,151 employees who accepted the terms. It cut new hires from 250 college graduates per year to 50. It increased the share of temporary workers from 13 percent in 1990 to 35 percent in 2004. It turned permanent employees into nonregular ones by rehiring staff on retirement. The company paid out the pension but then rehired selected employees under a new, nonregular, "senior staff" category. As it increased the proportion of nonregular employees, it also upgraded their

77. *Nikkei Weekly* (January 26, 2004), 9; (February 16, 2004), 28.
78. *Far Eastern Economic Review* (March 4, 1999), 58.

benefits under pressure from the unions and the government. Yet it still saved money by reducing the share of permanent employees. It also shifted to a system in which permanent employees were designated by geographical region. Those in areas with a lower cost of living could obtain a guarantee that they would not be rotated out of their region, but they were then locked into a lower wage structure.

Mitsukoshi moved toward a more performance-based wage system in 1999, using sales volume statistics to evaluate salespeople and supervisor and peer evaluations for administrative employees. It adopted an even more performance-oriented system in November 2003, dividing managers into two tracks: a management line and a specialist line. The top 21 sales specialists in the company, who were designated "meister," could earn more than a store manager. The next 1,073 comprised the "pro specialist" (*puro sennin shoku*) category, which also enjoyed high potential for performance bonuses. Even so, the performance premiums remain modest in comparison with U.S. department stores, where sales commissions can account for 80 percent of income.

Mitsukoshi sought to reduce suppliers from 6,200 at the peak to 4,600 and possibly fewer. It hoped to reduce costs by translating higher-volume purchases into leverage with suppliers and by cutting out wholesalers for standard products bought in large quantities, such as beer. It collaborated with its suppliers to develop new products and to streamline supply and delivery. It worked directly with the suppliers in some cases and through the industry association in others.

Mitsukoshi gradually loosened relations with other Mitsui group companies. At the same time, Mitsukoshi actively sought out new alliances to lower costs and develop new business. It temporarily found a new ally in its archrival Takashimaya. The two worked together in delivery, information systems, and procurement of standard office supplies for several years until Takashimaya opted out of the collaboration as part of its own restructuring scheme.[79]

Mitsukoshi still relies heavily on its main bank, Sumitomo Mitsui. "You need a main bank when you are having trouble," stresses Tsunekazu Ōba of Corporate Planning. "We always go to our main bank first. Sometimes the bank will ask us to buy shares in another group company that is having trouble, and we will help out. This is just a matter of preserving relationships."[80] Mitsukoshi reorganized its board, shifting from 25 members from all

79. Interview with Hiroshi Agawa, Project Leader, Planning and Coordination, Mitsukoshi, July 14, 2004.

80. Interview with Tsunekazu Ōba, Director, Corporate Planning Division, Headquarters Management Team, Mitsukoshi, January 24, 2002.

over the country to only 10 concentrated mostly in the Tokyo area. Meanwhile, Mitsukoshi managers put much more time and energy into investor relations. "IR [investor relations] has become the new buzzword. We have to explain our strategy, short-term and long-term, to the financial analysts and the rating agencies," reports one executive. "But that does not mean we have adopted U.S.-style short-term management."[81]

In September 2003, Mitsukoshi absorbed four regional subsidiaries, primarily to reduce consolidated losses by offsetting the subsidiaries' debt with unrealized profits. Accounting reforms, especially the impending introduction of impairment accounting (Chapter 4), were a critical factor driving this reorganization. "In the past, we could smooth out earnings with latent profits [by selling real estate and other assets]," explains one manager, "but the accounting change forced us to clean up our finances."[82] Along with the reorganization, Mitsukoshi sought to reduce procurement costs by increasing volume, streamlining the payment of suppliers, and enhancing its sales system.[83] In February 2004, it announced that it would reorganize functional divisions within the company. Headquarters would restrict its functions to personnel and accounting, thereby reducing staff from 650 to 400, and sales management would shift to local stores.[84] In 2004, Mitsukoshi transformed its Tokyo Shinjuku store into an emporium, leasing retail space to specialty stores, and decided to close stores in Yokohama, Osaka, and Kurashiki.[85] It designed an early retirement program for 800 employees from these stores, but 1,000 employees applied for the program.[86]

SEIYU: EMBRACING THE WAL-MART WAY

Seiyu, a humble supermarket chain, stunned the world of Japanese retail in March 2002 by announcing an alliance with U.S. super-retailer Wal-Mart. Seiyu managers then willingly, almost gleefully, embarked on a cultural conversion to the Wal-Mart way. Seiyu had begun to encounter difficulties in the early 1990s but took action only gradually, selling off some subsidiaries and a few stores between 1991 and 1997. Like Mitsukoshi and unlike the auto and electronics firms, Seiyu relies more on flexibility in deploying its workforce and less on long-term employee loyalty. Unlike Mitsukoshi, however, Seiyu's comparative advantage hinges on low prices, so Seiyu has been even more

---

81. Interview with Kazunari Nagamatsu, Project Leader, New Proposals, Corporate Planning Division, Mitsukoshi, July 14, 2004.

82. Agawa interview, Mitsukoshi, July 14, 2004.

83. *Nikkei Weekly* (September 15, 2003), 20.

84. *Nikkei Kinyū Shimbun* (December 17, 2003), 5; *Nikkei Ryūtsū Shimbun* (February 24, 2004), 5.

85. *Nikkei Weekly* (December 27, 2004), 13.

86. *Nikkei Net* (February 28, 2005).

zealous in controlling costs. Seiyu offered an early retirement program targeted for 1,000 employees in 1995, but 1,500 volunteered. In practice, the firm selected the prospective volunteers based on work evaluations (poor performance) and status (high pay). In 1997, the company faced a financial crisis stemming from losses at its nonbank subsidiary, and this spurred more dramatic action. It closed 41 stores from 1997 through 2002 and reduced permanent employees from 10,000 to 7,000. It achieved the reductions via natural attrition quite easily, because about 500 employees quit or retired each year. It cut bonuses 25 percent for union members and 30 percent for managers in 1997, then 20 percent for union members and 25 percent for managers in 1998, resulting in a 5–6 percent annual decrease in wages. It experimented with performance-pay systems, but managers report that supervisors tended to clump their evaluations in the "B" range so that actual wages did not vary much. It increased nonregular workers from 56 percent of the workforce in 1995 to 65 percent in 2000, 75 percent in 2003, and 79 percent in 2005, toward a midrange goal of 85 percent.[87] Seiyu managers recognized that they would have to upgrade the status of these workers over time since the nonregular workers would take over core positions, including department manager, shift manager, and even store manager.

Seiyu spun off Hokkaido and Kyushu Seiyu into new companies in fall 2000 and spring 2001. The employees formally quit one company and joined the other. This measure enabled the company to lower average wage rates for these employees to match the lower living costs relative to Tokyo or Osaka. Seiyu then began working on a scheme to separate employees into store and area employees. Store employees would receive lower wages, but they would stay in a given geographical location.

Seiyu reduced its debt to ¥600 billion from ¥1,200 billion at the peak. The banks kept lending to it through the crisis. The main bank's share of this lending increased over this period, as some of the regional banks and credit associations did not keep pace.

Seiyu began a much bolder transformation, however, after announcing its alliance with Wal-Mart. Wal-Mart took advantage of reforms in corporate law to schedule a series of options to increase its ownership stake from 6.1 percent initially to 66.7 percent by 2007. A Wal-Mart–Seiyu joint task force scrutinized options throughout 2002 and began implementing an "integration" program in January 2003. Seiyu drastically simplified its organization, merging 34 divisions into 11 and bringing in one female executive and two executives from subsidiaries as division chiefs. It began implementing a comprehensive program to educate Seiyu workers in Wal-Mart's philosophy. Wal-Mart sent

87. Company data; *Nikkei Weekly* (January 10, 2005), 20.

11 managers to Wal-Mart for extended stays, and another 40 to 50 on a more temporary basis. Seiyu held a three-day Wal-Mart-style convention at the Saitama Super Arena (north of Tokyo) in March. Seiyu salespeople wore jumpers color-coded by geographical region, and the company gave out prizes for star store managers, buyers, and even janitors. Then 430 Seiyu employees attended the Wal-Mart shareholder meeting in the United States. Seiyu's top managers and a few sales associates, about 2–3 percent of total employees, participated in special training in the Wal-Mart way. The managers then spread the word to the stores via internal communications, print media, and word of mouth. "This is all part of the cultural training," reports Watanabe. "The Seiyu employees' response has been outstanding. At Wal-Mart, they have a Wal-Mart cheer. It goes: 'Who is number one? . . . The customer! The customer!' So now our employees have decided to do their own Seiyu cheer every morning."[88]

Seiyu then proceeded with further reforms: cutting the workforce, reducing the ratio of managers (mostly permanent employees) to salespeople (mostly nonregular employees), otherwise increasing the overall share of nonregular workers, renegotiating supply chain relationships, consolidating subsidiaries, streamlining the corporate headquarters, and adopting a U.S.-style corporate board with outside directors.[89] In February 2004, Seiyu offered a voluntary retirement program to eliminate 1,500 jobs. It publicly warned that it might resort to dismissals if the target was not met. More than 1,600 applied for the program, of whom about 10 percent expressed interest in being rehired as nonregular workers.[90] It divided nonregular workers into three categories: ordinary workers, leaders, and managers. Those in the higher ranks might be eligible to join the same labor union as permanent employees and would receive the same performance-based component in their wages. And the top group, the managers, would be eligible for promotion to permanent employees.[91]

Seiyu reached agreement with about sixty of its main suppliers, accounting for about 40 percent of total purchases, to employ a new type of negotiation, with teams from sales, distribution, finance, and information systems from both the buyer and seller sides. Seiyu and Wal-Mart also began to deploy Wal-Mart's "retail link" system, which connects stores and suppliers via the Internet and provides the suppliers with detailed sales information. Seiyu consolidated the operations of six subsidiaries and affiliates, dividing opera-

88. Interview with Noriyuki Watanabe, Chairman, The Seiyu, Ltd., January 23, 2002.
89. Watanabe interview, June 11, 2003.
90. *Nikkei Sangyō Shimbun* (February 24, 2004), 31; *Nikkei Ryūtsū Shimbun* (March 30, 2004), 4.
91. Watanabe interview, July 22, 2004.

tions along regional lines, in order to streamline management, procurement, and sales.[92]

Seiyu discovered that introducing Wal-Mart's "Every Day Low Prices" did not boost sales in the short run and may even have compromised sales by eliminating traditional sales flyers and discounts. Seiyu then reintroduced some traditional sales strategies, including offering daily specials and providing goods at a wider range of price levels.[93] Seiyu managers remained committed to conversion to the Wal-Mart way over the long term, however, and they set a timetable for phasing out discounts and bringing in everyday low prices for good. Chief executive officer Masao Kiuchi resigned after the company posted a third straight year of losses in 2004 and continuing losses in the first half of 2005, and Watanabe—who had been president before Kiuchi—took the helm once again.

SOFTBANK: THE RISE OF THE "NETBATSU"

Japanese corporate practices are resilient in part because so few existing firms exit and so few new firms really challenge the incumbents. Nevertheless, Japan has some younger firms that have demonstrated novel approaches to growth and restructuring. Here we look at two of these companies, Softbank and Hikari Tsushin, to examine how they both conform to and violate traditional Japanese norms of corporate behavior.

Softbank has diverged from standard Japanese practice in how it hires and promotes its employees, finances its operations, organizes its corporate group, and adjusts to business downturns. Softbank has itself contributed to the evolution of the Japanese model by devising a new brand of venture financing, developing a new type of corporate group, sponsoring a stock exchange, and waging a price war to bring low-cost Internet access to Japan. Softbank raised hopes for a new Japanese business model with its initial success and then brought disappointment with subsequent failures. In the process, Softbank reinvented itself several times, survived a colossal boom-and-bust cycle, and confronted established power centers, including the Ministry of Finance and NTT. Softbank has experienced both phenomenal success (Yahoo) and failure (Webvan) in the marketplace, and it has both triumphed (broadband expansion) and faltered (Nasdaq Japan and Nippon Credit Bank) in its challenges to the establishment. As much as Softbank has rejected the Japanese model, however, it has incorporated elements of traditional practice as well. Its approach to corporate group management reveals elements of *zaibatsu* (prewar conglomerate) behavior, and its ruthless commitment to building

---

92. *Mainichi Shimbun* (March 25, 2004), 8.
93. *Nikkei Weekly* (February 21, 2005), 3.

market share in the broadband market is reminiscent of Japan's earlier business pioneers.

Masayoshi Son, a Japanese of Korean descent with a 1980 bachelor's degree from the University of California, Berkeley, founded Softbank in 1981 as a software distribution company. It quickly emerged as the market leader in the field and expanded into computer-related publishing and related businesses. It went public in 1994 and subsequently transformed into a major venture investor. It made key investments in U.S. start-ups in the Internet field, most notably Yahoo, with spectacular results. Son's strategy was to invest early in a wide range of ventures, to be more selective at the next stage and substantially increase its investment in the most promising ventures, and to get out early when things did not go well. Softbank funded initial investments from operating profits and bank loans but later used investment gains to fuel further investments.

In 1999, Softbank partnered with the National Association of Securities Dealers to launch Nasdaq Japan, an over-the-counter market designed to bring smaller ventures, including some of Son's own businesses, to the public market. In 2000, Softbank took a 48.9 percent stake in the failing Nippon Credit Bank (now Aozora Bank). Softbank, like Ripplewood in the Shinsei case, insisted that the government agree to buy back Nippon Credit loans that fell 20 percent or more in value within three years. Son's vision for the bank was to combine electronic banking with venture investments in information technology. However, his own chief financial officer, Yoshitaka Kitao, preferred to maintain it as a midmarket lender.[94]

Softbank began its expansion by creating wholly owned subsidiaries across a range of fields, but by the late 1990s it shifted to a portfolio investment strategy, accepting less control for smaller equity shares. In April 1999, it took advantage of legal reforms (see Chapter 4) to create a pure holding company to make it easier to reshuffle the organization. Son initially left only a minimal staff of eight in the holding company itself but decided to recentralize the finance, accounting, and legal functions into the holding company in September 2000 with an expanded staff of more than fifty.[95] "It really did not make sense to separate out finance, because that is where you control the cash flow," explains a Softbank group executive. "This impaired the governability of the enterprise."[96]

For all its innovative flair, Softbank built on earlier forms of corporate organization. Softbank's "netbatsu"—so named for its combination of an

94. *Economist* (March 18, 2000), 63–65.
95. *Nihon Keizai Shimbun* (September 30, 2000).
96. Interview with Yoshirō Kitahara, President and CEO, AtWork Corporation, January 21, 2002.

Internet focus with a *zaibatsu* structure—has a financial function at its core and actively promotes business links between member companies.[97] Softbank subsidiaries and affiliates also mimicked the practice of cross-shareholding by making substantial investments in other group firms.

At its peak, in 2000, Softbank's market valuation exceeded that of Toyota and Sony.[98] Then came the bursting of the Internet bubble, and Softbank shares dropped from a high of ¥198,000 in fiscal 2000 to a low of ¥1,542 in fiscal 2002.[99] Some foreign investors have been critical of Softbank for being all too Japanese in its opaque accounting and disclosure practices and its lack of concern for operating profits relative to capital gains.

Softbank's approach to restructuring differs markedly from the cases reviewed above. Son and his colleagues never cultivated a lifetime employment system and never believed in seniority-based promotions. They introduced a performance-based wage system in 1998 and began issuing stock options to all employees in 2003. Rather than a traditional personnel division, Softbank has a wholly owned subsidiary, AtWork, which performs most personnel functions for the group, including dispatching temporary workers to group companies as needed. Softbank relies heavily on midcareer hires, especially for new ventures. The average age of Softbank employees is thirty-two, and most have no expectation of staying with the company for life. Owing to high turnover, Softbank can reduce staff levels easily via attrition. When subsidiaries lay off workers, AtWork provides job consultation but makes no guarantees of results.[100] Personnel managers at Softbank subsidiary Yahoo Japan have introduced a quarterly evaluation system that they feel fits the fast-paced and competitive nature of the Internet service business. They ask employees to set about ten specific objectives, and then supervisors assess their achievement of these goals, assigning grades ranging from S (highest) to A, B, C, and D. The supervisors translate the grades into numerical values with a specially designed computer program and use them to calculate salaries and bonuses.[101]

Softbank responded to its financial woes by aggressively selling off its stake in various companies to pay off debts and fuel new investments. Son

97. Lynskey and Yonekura (2001) argue that Softbank also combines elements of vertical and distribution *keiretsu*.

98. Softbank (¥1.82 trillion) ranked third among all Japanese companies in market value in February 2000, behind NTT DoCoMo (¥3.76 trillion) and NTT (¥2.36 trillion) but ahead of Toyota (¥1.71 trillion) and Sony (¥1.24 trillion). Hikari Tsushin (¥650 billion) was ninth (Lynskey and Yonekura 2001).

99. Softbank shares split three-for-one in April 2000, so a single share actually sold for ¥5,400.

100. Kitahara interview, January 21, 2002.

101. *Nikkei Weekly* (May 17, 2004), 21.

did not want to borrow any more from banks, and the firm could not issue bonds because of its low market rating. Son devised a scheme to raise funds by securitizing the revenue stream from its broadband connections.[102] Softbank shifted from its "netbatsu" strategy to focus on advanced digital subscriber line (ADSL) broadband infrastructure. It took advantage of the government's policy of forcing NTT to lease unused lines and to reduce interconnection charges (Chapter 4) and relentlessly expanded its market share in broadband service at the expense of profits to preempt NTT and to raise demand in its other Internet-related businesses. "Son thrives on disorder (*konran ga ikigai*)," boasts Kōki Tabe, general manager for public relations.[103] Softbank invested about ¥37,000 to line up each new customer, including handing out modems for free at train stations. Meanwhile, it brought Japanese Internet access fees from among the highest in the world to the lowest, charging an average flat rate of ¥3,740 per month. It broke open Japan's telecommunications market and outstripped NTT in broadband by installing 2.36 million subscriber lines by March 2003, but it posted huge losses—¥89 billion in fiscal 2002, ¥100 billion in fiscal 2003, and ¥107 billion in fiscal 2004—because of investment costs combined with various portfolio losses. "This is not charity," insists Tabe, "but a carefully crafted business strategy. It takes a lot of money to sign up subscribers, but once we have them, then we can enhance services and increase profits. And we can benefit from the synergy with our other businesses, like online brokerage."[104] In 2004, however, Softbank managers began to reconsider their personnel strategy after employees leaked information about broadband service customers. They concluded that they had not done enough to cultivate employee loyalty to the company and decided to increase the share of permanent employees in the workforce from about 20 percent to 60 percent.[105]

Softbank announced its intention to sell off its stake in Aozora Bank in 2002. Son complained publicly that the Financial Services Agency was pressuring him to sell to a domestic institution. The FSA was eager not to repeat its experience with Ripplewood's investment in Shinsei, so it discouraged sales of banks to foreign investors. The government changed the rules after the Cerberus Group, a U.S. investment fund, bought a stake in Aozora, so that any buyer seeking to purchase more than a 20 percent of a Japanese bank would require government approval.[106] FSA officials stressed that Softbank

102. *New York Times* (May 10, 2003), B2.

103. Interview, July 21, 2004.

104. Interview with Kōki Tabe, General Manager, Public Relations, Softbank Corp., July 21, 2004.

105. *Nikkei Weekly* (August 16, 2004), 21.

106. *New York Times* (January 11, 2003), B2.

had a social responsibility to maintain a long-term investment in the bank. Softbank agreed to maintain at least a 14.99 percent share.[107] In the end, Softbank sold the bulk of its share to Cerberus, giving Cerberus a 61 percent stake overall. Softbank's venture finance side also unraveled in August 2002, as the U.S. Nasdaq Market pulled the plug on Nasdaq Japan.[108]

In May 2004, Softbank reached an agreement to buy out troubled telecommunications operator Japan Telecom. Son hoped that the acquisition would help Softbank to improve earnings by streamlining overlapping operations and marketing Softbank's broadband services and other new services to Japan Telecom subscribers. By 2005, Softbank shifted from expanding its broadband market share at all costs to increasing profitability as it prepared to enter the cellular telephone business. Softbank was the first company to apply for a cellular telephone service license in September 2005 after the government announced that it would allow two new entrants into the market. Softbank planned to introduce data services in selected areas by fall 2006 and telephone services in 2007, with an initial target of 10 million subscribers.[109] "Son has had a consistent strategy from the beginning: pursue opportunities in network-related businesses," reports Tabe. "He wanted to get famous in his twenties, make money in his thirties, take on a big challenge in his forties, overcome the challenge in his fifties, and designate a successor in his sixties. So far, he has implemented his vision to perfection."[110]

HIKARI TSUSHIN: FROM SUPERBOOM TO SUPERBUST

Only Hikari Tsushin has exceeded Softbank in the speed of its rise and the depth of its fall. Hikari Tsushin's founder, Yasumitsu Shigeta, envisioned the firm as the ultimate outsider. He hired young managers who stood out more for their initiative and assertiveness than for academic credentials, including some Chinese and other foreign nationals. Shigeta and his team dispensed with standard protocol, including formal attire, uniformed receptionists, and office ladies who pour tea for guests. They developed a business model that relied on speedy decisions, hard work, and generous rewards for performance, and not on long-term relationships with banks and other business partners. "We are unique," proclaims Kōji Shibayama, manager for investor and public relations. "We are the anti-system firm!"[111]

Shigeta dropped out of Nihon University after three months in 1985 and began selling telephones for a local retailer. In 1988, at age twenty-two, he

107. *Nikkei Weekly* (September 9, 2002), 13.
108. *Nikkei Weekly* (August 19, 2002), 15.
109. *Nikkei Weekly* (September 12, 2005), 13.
110. Tabe interview, July 21, 2004. Son was born in August 1957.
111. Interview, June 17, 2003.

founded Hikari Tsushin to market long-distance phone services for NTT's new competitors, especially DDI. He recognized that the 1985 privatization of NTT and liberalization of telecommunications was generating substantial new business opportunities. His timing was auspicious once again in 1994 when he shifted to selling mobile telephones and services, just before that business really took off. Hikari Tsushin charged the mobile telephone companies a fee for each new subscriber it signed up plus a percentage of the monthly service fee. It dominated the sales of non-NTT DoCoMo mobile telephones and built up a national network of more than two thousand retail outlets.[112]

Hikari Tsushin employees, who average twenty-seven to twenty-eight years of age, are paid on a strict performance basis. Salespeople are paid commissions based on sales volume, and productive ones could easily earn ¥10 million a year in the firm's heyday. The company even applies performance standards in administrative positions such as finance or accounting. Administrative workers set personal performance goals for the short term (three months) and long term (one year) and are evaluated on their ability to meet these targets. "We want employees to propose new projects," Shibayama explains. "This can be difficult in a routine job like accounting, but we want them to come up with something anyway. Otherwise they do not get a raise. This system can be pretty harsh, but it does motivate people."[113]

Hikari Tsushin's success attracted institutional shareholders eager to profit from Japan's IT revolution, and its share price rose from the ¥3,000 range in 1999 to ¥241,000 in February 2000. At its peak, Hikari Tsushin's market valuation made it the seventh largest company in the country and Shigeta the fourth wealthiest man in the world. More than one hundred Hikari Tsushin executives became millionaires via stock options.[114]

In April 2000, Shigeta announced that the company had lost ¥13 billion in the six months prior to February, instead of the ¥6 billion in profits that had been expected.[115] The firm's share price began a freefall of more than 98 percent to a low of ¥930 in fiscal 2002. U.S. shareholders of Crayfish, an American affiliate, filed a class action lawsuit for ¥5 billion against Hikari Tsushin for failure to disclose critical information.[116] Meanwhile, the company's venture capital subsidiary, Hikari Tsushin Capital, had been betting wildly on venture investments. When the Internet bubble burst, these investments collapsed. As Hikari Tsushin's reputation soared, the venture compa-

112. *Forbes* (December 13, 1999), 69–74.
113. Shibayama interview, June 17, 2003.
114. "The options were not healthy incentives," laments one Hikari Tsushin executive, who asked not to be identified, "but a kind of poison that changed our lives forever." Interview, January 2002.
115. *Financial Times* (July 12, 2000), 19.
116. *The Guardian* (November 25, 2000), 30.

nies themselves declined further investment.[117] "The Japanese establishment just pulled the plug on the company," charges Shibayama.[118] The press bludgeoned the company and its founder. *Bungei Shunjū* published a chilling profile, accusing Shigeta of feeding live rabbits to a pet python, among other things, and suggesting that company salespeople engaged in extreme hard-sell tactics and misreported their sales figures.[119] Meanwhile, the firm's lenders demanded early repayment, even though Hikari Tsushin was abiding by its payment schedule. "The situation was very Japanese," recalls Shibayama. "The banks had no legal basis for this, but they would just show up every day and harass us anyway."[120]

In April 2000, Shigeta announced a drastic restructuring program, closing half the retail outlets and selling off subsidiaries and investments. "Shigeta is rather dry and stoic," Shibayama notes, "so that is how he approached reform." The company did not lay off workers in the parent company but sold off subsidiaries and affiliates without attempting to save jobs. It used undesirable transfers and drastic pay cuts to force employees in the home office to quit. Shibayama describes the process: "It was all pretty brash. We transferred about two hundred people to group companies. We did not interview them one by one, or ask them where they would like to go. We just assigned them, pretty much randomly. Along the way, 30 to 40 percent quit. We had predicted this, so it worked out pretty rationally in a way."[121] The company reduced its Japanese permanent workforce (on a consolidated basis) from 3,107 at the peak in 2001 to 2,140 in 2002.[122] It also reallocated workers to profitable sections, cutting the ratio of administrative employees to salespeople from about 3 in 10 to 1 in 10. Even after these initial cuts, Hikari Tsushin's turnover remained extraordinarily high, with more than 1,000 employees leaving and 1,500 signing on in a typical year.[123]

Meanwhile, Shigeta used some of his own personal wealth to reduce the company's debt, and the company sold off venture investments and listed stock. These measures helped to reduce interest-bearing liabilities from ¥230 billion in April 2000 to ¥37 billion in March 2003. Hikari Tsushin went from ¥18.3 billion in operating losses (consolidated) in fiscal 2000 to ¥5.5 billion profits in 2002.[124]

117. *Financial Times* (July 12, 2000), 19.
118. Shibayama interview, June 17, 2003.
119. *Bungei Shunjū* (March 2000).
120. Shibayama interview, June 17, 2003.
121. Shibayama interview, June 17, 2003.
122. Company data. The even sharper reduction in Table 8 is due to the sale of a business overseas.
123. *Nikkei Bijinesu* (September 1, 2003), 46–51.
124. Company documents.

Ironically, Hikari Tsushin—which had so thoroughly rejected the traditional model of Japanese finance—then found itself looking for bank loans. The more established banks were wary of such an unconventional company, so Hikari Tsushin executives began with some of the newer banks, such as Aozora and eBank. "In the past we thought direct finance was best and banks were the second choice," conceded Shibayama in 2003. "That's great when things are good. But when things go badly, a main bank can really help. So in the future, we would like to cultivate a sub-main bank, a bit more like a traditional Japanese company."[125] A year later, Shibayama reported that Hikari Tsushin had found its main bank in none other than Mizuho. Moreover, the two companies devised a new type of main bank relationship in which Mizuho introduces corporate customers to Hikari Tsushin and charges a fee for the service that reflects the actual amount of sales generated by the introduction. Hikari Tsushin had been successful in selling to small businesses, but it had been having trouble breaking into the well-established corporate networks characteristic of larger firms, so Mizuho helped it to penetrate these networks. "The bank is not just a financial adviser but a business partner," Shibayama explains. "Because we pay a fee, that makes us equal partners. If we didn't pay a fee, then we would be obligated to heed their requests and to accept their influence. This way everything is clear, and that makes things easier."[126]

Patterns of Variation

CORPORATE PERFORMANCE

As noted at the beginning of this chapter, we would expect corporate performance to influence the degree of restructuring. Everything else equal, companies in more trouble—those with substantial negative returns and/or sharply decreasing sales—should restructure more. This follows the logic of the first circle of rationality presented in Chapter 1, a narrow financial calculus of costs and benefits. Not surprisingly, we find substantial evidence to confirm this relationship in both the case studies and the statistical analysis. Differences in financial performance help to explain, for example, why Nissan has restructured more than Toyota, or NEC more than Sony, or Hikari Tsushin more than Softbank. But it cannot explain, for example, why Mitsukoshi—which has performed even worse than Seiyu—has restructured less. And it cannot explain why Mizuho and its predecessors were so slow to restructure despite poor results and huge exposure to nonperforming loans over an extended period.

125. Shibayama interview, June 17, 2003.
126. Shibayama interview, July 20, 2004.

Moreover, we have found that variations in industrial sector and levels of foreign ownership also affect restructuring. The hypotheses about industrial sector build on the logic of the second circle of rationality, a broader cost-benefit calculus that considers how restructuring affects a firm's comparative institutional advantage. Since the foundations of institutional advantage vary from one sector to another, we would expect variations in patterns of restructuring across sectors along the lines of the hypotheses presented at the beginning of this chapter. The hypotheses about foreign ownership build on the third circle of rationality, a calculus that broadens to consider social ties and social norms. If a foreign manager acts differently from a Japanese manager in the same situation, then it is likely that something more than a simple assessment of costs and benefits accounts for the difference. The foreign manager either is less sensitive to local norms or feels less bound by local social ties, or both.

FOREIGN OWNERSHIP

Aside from corporate performance, foreign ownership has the clearest and most powerful impact on restructuring. Foreign-owned companies focus more on maximizing returns and less on preserving long-term relations with workers, banks, suppliers, and other business partners. They are more likely to base business decisions on price than on relationships and to cut off business partners than negotiate with them. We can view this effect most clearly by comparing Nissan, Shinsei, and Seiyu across time, before and after a foreign partner assumed managerial control. Such a comparison allows us to control for other factors and to isolate how the shift to foreign management affected business practices. The companies' objective circumstances did not change, yet their behavior fundamentally transformed. In each case, Japanese managers had been fully aware of the company's troubles and had enacted substantial reform programs. The new managers were less bound by personal relationships, corporate obligations, and social norms, however, so they departed from the companies' traditional business strategies much more boldly.

We can confirm this pattern by comparing pairs of companies within each sector, one under foreign ownership and one not. Nissan, Shinsei, and Seiyu under foreign management have restructured much more aggressively than Toyota, Mizuho, and Mitsukoshi. Turning to Sony and NEC, however, we do not find that Sony has restructured more. In part, as noted above, this reflects the fact that Sony has performed somewhat better than NEC financially. In addition, Sony differs from Nissan, Shinsei, and Seiyu in that it has not come under foreign managerial control, although it does have a higher level of foreign portfolio investment and a higher level of international exposure.

This suggests that foreign managerial control is a more powerful predictor of more aggressive restructuring than high foreign ownership alone. In more subtle ways, nonetheless, Sony has gone further than NEC with those measures most likely to appeal to foreign portfolio investors: buying back shares, issuing stock options, restructuring its board, appointing outside directors, and creating a U.S.-style committee-based board of directors.

The regression results (below) confirm that high foreign ownership correlates with more aggressive downsizing as defined by reductions in workforce. Studies have also demonstrated that foreign ownership correlates with better corporate governance practices as defined by the investment community, including the use of stock options, share buybacks, higher standards of disclosure, independent directors, and U.S.-style corporate board structures. The Policy Research Institute, for example, reports that firms with higher levels of foreign ownership are more likely to enact corporate governance reforms, especially with respect to investor protection and information disclosure.[127] Gilson and Milhaupt find that companies with high levels of foreign ownership have been more likely to adopt U.S.-style boards.[128] In essence, Japanese firms with higher levels of foreign ownership act more like foreign firms. We cannot be sure of the direction of causality, but it most likely runs both ways: Japanese firms with higher foreign investment restructure and reform corporate governance more actively, and Japanese firms that adopt these practices are rewarded by higher levels of foreign investment.

CROSS-SECTORAL COMPARISONS

Competitive versus Protected Sectors and Manufacturing versus Services. We began with two plausible theses pointing in the opposite direction: the "two Japans" thesis predicts greater restructuring in exposed/competitive sectors (autos and electronics) than in protected/uncompetitive sectors (banking and retail) whereas the sectoral VOC thesis suggests that service firms will restructure more than manufacturing firms. The regression results (below) support the sectoral VOC thesis. The case studies allow us to differentiate more carefully between service sectors and types of restructuring and to develop a more nuanced, if less generalizable, picture of these differences. The case studies indicate that retailers have restructured their labor relations more boldly than manufacturers, but manufacturers have restructured more boldly than banks.[129] Comparing the two retail cases with the four manufacturing cases, we find that the retailers downsized more abruptly, shifted from per-

127. Ministry of Finance, Policy Research Institute 2003a, 90–103.
128. Gilson and Milhaupt 2005, 27–30.
129. This is roughly analogous to what Budros (1997 and 1999) finds for downsizing in the United States.

manent to nonregular employees more rapidly, sold off divisions more aggressively, and reorganized more thoroughly. Mitsukoshi reduced its workforce by 15 percent in 2000 and by 18 percent in 2001, and Seiyu cut its force by 18 percent in 1996 and 13 percent in 2001. They both resorted to voluntary retirement programs that verged on dismissals. The four manufacturers have not cut workers by more than 9 percent, except for Nissan (17 percent) in the first year of its Revival Plan (see Table 9). The retailers started with a higher level of nonregular employees than the manufacturers and moved rapidly to increase that proportion. The manufacturers used nonregular employees quite differently, cutting them (by not renewing contracts) when they needed to reduce their workforce. Following the logic of a sectoral VOC model, retailers rely less on close collaborative relations with workers to enhance productivity and more on flexibility in deploying human resources. Thus they offered long-term employment guarantees to a smaller proportion of their workforce to begin with, and they have responded to hard times by reducing this proportion further.

Survey data from the Ministry of Health, Labor, and Welfare from the previous chapter confirms these patterns at the aggregate level. Manufacturers of transport equipment (14.0 percent) and electronic machinery (8.6 percent) were more likely to allow nonregular workers' contracts to expire; but retailers (6.8 percent) were just as likely as electronic machinery manufacturers (6.8 percent) and more likely than transport equipment manufacturers (4.1 percent) to resort to outright layoffs (see Table 2). Meanwhile, retailers increased part-time workers from 27.9 percent of the workforce in 1990 to 48.4 percent in 2000, and financial institutions increased their share from 5.4 to 8.4 percent, while manufacturers of electronic machinery and transport equipment decreased their share (12.6 to 11.0 percent and 5.6 to 3.3 percent, respectively).[130] A Japan Institute of Labor survey also reports that retailers have been more aggressive in adopting performance-based pay systems (52.2 percent) than consumer products manufacturers (24.2 percent), machinery manufacturers (25.3 percent), and financial institutions (23.8 percent).[131]

Banking versus Retail. The Mizuho case plus the aggregate evidence on bank restructuring pose a substantial puzzle because the banks seem to diverge from the pattern of lower performance fueling more restructuring. The banks confronted an unprecedented crisis, yet they were extremely cau-

---

130. MHLW, "Survey on Employment Trends," various years. Japan Institute of Labor (2002: 14, 19, 97) reports similar trends. And for the top ten supermarket chains, the share of part-time employees has risen from 70 percent in 2001 to 77 percent in 2005 (*Nikkei Net*, May 21, 2005).

131. Japan Institute of Labor 2002, 68.

tious with reforms, including downsizing personnel, closing offices, and restructuring their loan portfolios. The crisis may have been so severe, and its resolution so reliant on government action, that the banks had little incentive to accelerate restructuring without being forced by the government to do so. One FSA regulator conceded that he was concerned about just such a moral hazard.[132] The fact that the banks finally accelerated restructuring efforts after the FSA cracked down beginning in 2003 further supports this interpretation.

Autos versus Electronics. In line with the sectoral VOC thesis, we find that NEC and Sony, with a more modular production model, restructured their supply chains more dramatically than Toyota, with a more integrated production model. They probably even reformed their supply networks more than Nissan, although that is a tougher judgment to make. We also find that the electronics firms have been carefully differentiating the subsegments of their business. Sony managers, for example, recognize the very different logic of the home entertainment and audiovisual equipment businesses, yet they find that their approach to suppliers, workers, and financiers is not sufficiently differentiated across these product areas. Accordingly, they are trying to vary their supply chain practices to reflect the specific product involved.[133]

New IT Companies versus more Established Companies. The Softbank and Hikari Tsushin cases demonstrate that new companies in the IT sector have departed radically from standard Japanese corporate practices, and that this shift affects restructuring as well. Even so, both companies exhibit some features of a distinctively Japanese approach to reform. More critically, the fact that so few new companies have succeeded—and that these two model success stories have themselves faltered—demonstrates just how difficult it will be for new firms to transform the broader Japanese system. Japan's market institutions are more likely to evolve through incremental reforms by existing firms than via the emergence of new ones. As noted in the first chapter, it is likely that existing institutions will leave a particularly heavy imprint on the trajectory of institutional change.

Beyond these patterns, of course, we find substantial variation among companies due to idiosyncratic factors. Older, more established firms, with closer ties to existing corporate networks, are more cautious in restructuring. They have more to lose from straining these ties, they have more to gain by making use of these ties during hard times, and they may have a more conservative mindset.[134] Mitsukoshi's conservative corporate culture may have

132. Interview, June 2003.
133. Interviews, 2002, 2004.
134. Ahmadjian and Robinson 2001.

made it more hesitant with reform than one might have expected given its business results, for example, whereas NEC's more innovative flair may have made it more prone toward experimentation in corporate strategy. These generalizations do not always hold, however, as traditional firms sometimes reinvent themselves and firms with a greater reputation for dynamism sometimes stick with traditional practices.

Expanding the Sample

We can examine some of the same hypotheses from a different angle with data from a much larger number of companies. To analyze the larger sample, we must simplify both the independent variables (the level of foreign ownership and the industrial sector) and the dependent variable (the extent of restructuring). Nevertheless, by combining the case studies with this quantitative analysis, we obtain a more complete understanding of how these factors affect patterns of corporate restructuring in Japan.

Ahmadjian and Robinson look at how foreign ownership affected downsizing during the 1990–97 period. They measure downsizing as reductions in labor force or tangible fixed assets of greater than 5 (or 10) percent in one year. They find that foreign ownership was the most important factor determining the degree of downsizing when controlling for firm performance. They also report that smaller, younger, and lower-reputation firms were more likely to downsize. They note that these effects diminish from 1990 to 1997, and they conclude that firms may have become less reluctant to downsize over time. That is, firms may have broken through social constraints via a "safety in numbers" effect.[135] It is also possible, however, that firms that resisted or delayed downsizing in the early 1990s simply gave in as the economic crisis continued. Ahmadjian and Robbins extend this analysis to the 1991–2000 period. They find that foreign ownership significantly increased the likelihood of downsizing, but they note that this effect is weaker for companies with strong ties to banks and corporate groups.[136]

We follow Ahmadjian and her collaborators in constructing our model, with a few differences.[137] We use the Development Bank of Japan (DBJ) database, with a sample of 2,632 nonfinancial firms listed on major stock exchanges, examining the 1990–2002 period. In line with the case studies, we look at industrial sector as an additional factor that might influence restructuring outcomes.[138] We define downsizing as a reduction of labor force of greater

135. Ahmadjian and Robinson 2001.

136. Ahmadjian and Robbins 2004.

137. Yasuyuki Motoyama and Iris Hui conducted the statistical analysis presented in this section.

138. Ahmadjian and Robinson 2001 and Ahmadjian and Robbins 2004 test industrial-sector dummies but do not report their results.

than or equal to 5 percent, and then we reproduce the analysis for reductions of greater than or equal to 10 percent.[139] These measures do not distinguish among different types of labor force reductions—such as attrition, layoffs, or sales of operational divisions—but they capture substantial changes in one clear manifestation of downsizing. We define foreign ownership as the proportion of total shares held by non-Japanese investors. This means that we cannot separate foreign portfolio investment from foreign managerial control as we did in the case studies. Foreign managerial control is relatively rare, however, so portfolio investment is the dominant factor in the larger sample. Institutional investors from the United States and Britain account for the bulk of this investment.[140]

Although the distinctions between manufacturing and services, on the one hand, and competitive and protected sectors, on the other, overlapped in the case studies (that is, all the manufacturing firms were in competitive sectors, and all the service firms were in protected sectors), we can separate these factors in the larger sample.[141] We look at three of the sectors examined in more detail in the case studies: transportation machinery (including automobiles), electrical machinery (including electronics), and distribution (including retail). We expect that firm performance will be a powerful determinant of downsizing, so we control for performance to focus on how foreign ownership and industrial sector affect downsizing. We use two different variables to control for firm performance: return on assets (ROA) and annual change in sales.[142]

139. We have a larger sample for firms reducing workforce by 5 percent in a given year (20.5 percent of the total sample) than for 10 percent (8.4 percent of the total). For the total sample, we found that reductions of 5–10 percent and 10 percent or more rose steadily in the 1990s to a peak in 2000 before beginning to decline.

140. Ahmadjian and Robbins 2004. Consistent with the national data showing an increase in foreign ownership (see Table 5), we find that the percentage of companies in our sample with greater than 10 percent foreign ownership rose steadily from 5.9 percent in 1990 to 19.9 percent in 2000.

141. We use the DBJ database's categories to identify manufacturing sectors. We define competitive sectors as those manufacturing sectors with an industry average of exports greater than 10 percent of total output. We use the DBJ classification for services, which excludes distribution, real estate, utilities, and finance. The manufacturing sectors with an industry average of exports greater than 10 percent of total output are machinery, electrical machinery, transportation machinery, and precision instruments and machinery. The manufacturing sectors with an industry average of exports greater than 6 percent of total output but less than 10 percent are chemicals, rubber, ceramics, steel, nonferrous metals, and other manufacturing. We also ran tests for manufacturing sectors with an industry average of exports greater than 6 percent of total output, with equivalent results.

142. We control for firm size with the log of sales. We also add a continuous variable for year, from 1990 to 2002, to control for year effect. We use panel data with observations for 2,632 firms listed between 1990 and 2002. Since ordinary least squares (OLS) estimates assume that observations are independently distributed across time, OLS standard errors

TABLE II. *How Foreign Ownership and Industrial Sector Affect Labor Force Reductions of 5 Percent or More*

	Model 1		Model 2		Model 3	
	Coefficient	Standard error	Coefficient	Standard error	Coefficient	Standard error
Firm variables						
Foreign stock	0.0013	0.0004***	0.0013	0.0004***	0.0012	0.0004***
ROA	−2.3981	0.0587***	−2.4162	0.0588***	−2.3961	0.0584***
Sales change	−0.3248	0.0151***	−0.3229	0.0150***	−0.3234	0.0150***
Log (sales)	−0.0196	0.0023***	−0.0191	0.0023***	−0.0187	0.0023***
Year variable	0.0226	0.0007***	0.0226	0.0007***	0.0227	0.0007***
Industrial dummies						
Manufacturing	−0.0324	0.0067***				
Services	−0.0098	0.0140	−0.0024	0.0134		
Exporting			−0.0518	0.0072***		
Electric machinery					−0.0128	0.0111
Transport machinery					−0.0478	0.0138***
Distribution					0.0288	0.0082***
Constant	−44.4581	1.3234***	−44.4430	1.3212***	−44.6287	1.3207***
Wald chi-square	4535.30***		4569.82***		4540.62***	
No. of groups	2,590		2,590		2,590	

Note:***significance level at 99 percent.

As expected, we find that companies that are not performing well were more likely to downsize at a level greater than 5 percent (Table 11). More interestingly, we find that companies with higher foreign ownership were *more* likely to downsize while manufacturers and exporters were *less* likely to downsize. We had similar results for the exporters defined by either of our two measures: an industry average of exports greater than 10 percent of total output, or greater than 6 percent of output. Distribution firms were more likely to downsize, and transportation machinery firms were less likely to downsize. The results for services and electrical machinery were negative

---

ignore the serial correlation in the error term. This can produce biased estimates of the variance of the parameters of interest. Therefore, we employ the XTREG function in STATA to estimate our models. The XTREG function estimates the random effects models using the general least squares (GLS) estimator. Some firms disappeared from the list during the time period, primarily owing to mergers. In order to check for biases due to the censoring of firms, we repeated the analysis with the smaller sample of 1,795 firms with all thirteen years of records. The results are comparable with the results obtained using all 2,632 firms, so we present only the latter here.

(less likely to downsize) but insignificant. This is consistent with the case studies, where we found retailers reducing their workforce more aggressively than automobile manufacturers, with the electronics firms in between. When testing for workforce reductions of more than 10 percent, we had comparable results.[143]

Combining the statistical evidence with the case study results, we find consistent evidence that companies with higher levels of foreign ownership restructure more aggressively, especially with respect to workforce reductions. We also find support for the sectoral VOC thesis that service sectors such as retail, which rely less on long-term investment in company-specific skills and close management-labor collaboration to improve productivity, should be more proactive with employment adjustment, including reducing the workforce and increasing the share of nonregular workers. This finding also challenges the conventional wisdom that Japan's competitive manufacturers have been boldly restructuring while the protected sectors (including services, construction, and utilities) have not. Since we controlled for firm performance in the data analysis, the stronger overall performance of the manufacturing and export sectors cannot account for this difference.

143. The only exception was that the results for electrical machinery were positive but still insignificant.

7 JAPAN'S NEW MODEL

The evidence from Chapters 3–6 evokes two seemingly contradictory images, both of which capture an important part of the reality of Japan's institutional evolution. In the first view, Japanese government officials and corporate executives have seized on reform as a sort of fashion. They have jumped to conclusions on the basis of deteriorating macroeconomic performance, searched for solutions without carefully matching them to problems, and borrowed practices from the U.S. economic model without ascertaining whether these practices actually worked in the United States. In the second perspective, Japanese leaders have engaged in a more selective process of evaluating the specific features of the Japanese model and then making adjustments to reduce the costs and enhance the benefits of these institutions. If we can resolve the apparent contradiction between these two images of the reform process—reform fashion versus reform calculus—we will have gone a long way toward revealing the logic of institutional change in Japan.

The Japanese people experienced a collective trauma with the breakdown of the Japanese economy. As the heady 1980s turned to the depressing 1990s, Japan's leaders searched for diagnoses and prescriptions. Many concluded that the Japanese model had failed and the U.S. model had triumphed, and they responded with attempts to emulate features of the U.S. model. The Japanese media shifted its tone from self-congratulatory to self-critical, and public attitudes turned from arrogant to insecure.

Japan's embrace of the U.S. model is particularly ironic because Americans had jumped to parallel conclusions about the superiority of the Japanese model only a decade earlier.[1] The irony does not end there, however, for just as the Americans did not appropriate the Japanese model in the 1980s despite enormous debate and much experimentation, the Japanese have not converted to the U.S. model since the 1990s despite even greater self-reflection and more fervent reform activity. In Chapter 2, I proposed a simple

---

1. See Grimes 2002 on how shifts in macroeconomic performance have affected U.S.-Japan relations.

explanation for this outcome: Japan has not adopted the U.S. liberal market model because the Japanese did not want to adopt it. Then I developed a more sophisticated version of the argument, demonstrating how Japanese actors' preferences about policy reform and corporate restructuring account for the specific substance of change. Japanese actors have been profoundly ambivalent about the U.S. model, and this has produced not a vague compromise between Japanese and U.S. practices but rather the distinctive patterns of policy reform and corporate restructuring presented in Chapters 3–6.

The dynamic of emulating the U.S. model—in rhetoric if not always in substance—has permeated the reform process. U.S. government officials such as Robert Rubin and opinion leaders such as Paul Krugman have strongly influenced policy debates. U.S. firms based in Japan have actively participated in the policy process. Japanese government officials and opinion leaders with American credentials—such as Finance Minister Heizō Takenaka and economist Iwao Nakatani—have risen in stature. Policymakers have been especially vulnerable to arguments that Japanese practices are out of line with "global standards," which they equate with U.S. standards. Foreign investment bankers and consultants have recast attitudes about corporate restructuring. And notable foreign executives, such as Carlos Ghosn at Nissan, or Japanese with foreign experience, such as Masahiro Yashiro at Shinsei, have brought new management models to Japan.

Despite the apparent rush to appropriate the U.S. model, however, we have found that government officials and corporate executives engaged in fairly sophisticated assessments when considering specific reforms. They weighed the relative costs and benefits of existing institutions when designing reforms, and these calculations conditioned the substance of reform. In the policy case studies, for example, we found that officials crafted corporate governance reforms to allow corporations to adopt U.S.-style governance models but not to force them to do so. They shifted incrementally toward U.S. practice in antitrust policy and enforcement, yet they also facilitated distinctively Japanese corporate adjustments by removing the ban on pure holding companies. In the company case studies, likewise, we found that corporations operated within all three of our circles of rationality (from Chapter 1) as they decided, for example, how to restructure their relationships with their main banks. They considered their specific financing needs (narrow cost-benefit analysis), they assessed how they might benefit from strong main bank ties in the future (comparative institutional advantage), and they measured the depth of their obligation to the main bank (social norms). The basic model introduced in Chapter 1 assumes precisely this sort of cost-benefit calculus, and we found that the model fared quite well in explaining the differences between

Japanese, U.S., and German patterns of reform and the variations across issue areas and industrial sectors within Japan.

If we look carefully at corporate restructuring, we find evidence of a trend from broad social acceptance of certain practices across a wide range of sectors, implying a more reflexive adherence to social norms, to a more differentiated and selective continuation of these practices by certain companies in certain sectors, implying a more conscious calculation of costs and benefits. For example, whereas most large firms adopted some form of long-term employment in the pre-bubble era, they have reassessed these practices since 1990. Those firms whose managers concluded that they continue to benefit from these practices, such as Toyota and other manufacturers, maintained or reinforced them. Those firms whose managers felt that they lose more than they gain from these practices, like Seiyu and other service companies, have phased them out.

How can we make sense of these two contradictory logics? To a certain extent, they reflect a tension within Japan itself. Japan has both embraced and rejected U.S. capitalism, and the specific combination of these impulses has shaped the content of reforms. At another level, however, these logics reflect distinct phases of adjustment. In the first phase, Japanese leaders recognized a need for reform, and they identified the United States as a model. In the next phase, they were more discriminating as they determined what measures to adopt. They had considerable leeway to define the U.S. model on their own terms.[2] In fact, some leaders may have even misinterpreted the U.S. model to suit their own purposes. This book has demonstrated that we must look at both these facets of Japan's reform in order to understand the unfolding substance of change.

The Costs and Benefits of Reform

Thus far I have focused on describing and explaining Japan's pattern of change, not on evaluating it. Yet the two goals are linked, as noted in Chapter 2. We cannot be sure how current reforms will affect future economic performance, but we know that past performance has strongly influenced current reforms. The shift from economic boom in the 1980s to bust in the 1990s fueled major reforms, at both the policy and the corporate levels. Actors' perceptions of the costs and benefits of reforms—right or wrong—have powerfully shaped the trajectory of reform.

Here we briefly review the available evidence on the costs and benefits of some of the reforms the Japanese government and Japanese industry have

2. See Zeitlin and Herrigel 2000 for historical case studies of the selective and creative adaptation of the U.S. model by Europe and Japan in the postwar period.

adopted. This survey gives us not only some hints about the impact of these changes but further insight on the process of reform. For if Japan has adopted reforms without good reason, it suggests that these reforms have been driven by fashion as much as by rational calculus.

Even a cursory look at the literature on the costs and benefits of policy reform and corporate restructuring generates a rather startling conclusion: Japanese policymakers and corporate executives enacted many reforms in the absence of clear evidence that these reforms actually do any good. We found in Chapters 5 and 6, for example, that Japanese firms engaged in considerable downsizing (workforce reductions), although they went to great length to realize these cuts without layoffs. In doing so, they explicitly or implicitly followed the example of U.S. firms that had been downsizing since the late 1970s. Many investment bankers, financial journalists, and casual observers find it self-evident that corporations benefit from downsizing because it reduces fixed costs and thereby increases profits. Layoffs have a substantial downside, however, including the short-term expense of compensating workers and the longer-term costs of eroding productive capacity, undermining employee morale, and impairing future recruitment. Most research on downsizing in the United States finds that it has no positive effect on corporate financial performance—as defined by profits, productivity, or stock price—and has a negative impact on organizational performance, especially employee morale.[3] The authoritative work of William Baumol et al. reveals that downsizing does not improve productivity, it lowers stock prices, and it raises profits (but only by depressing wages).[4] Others have found that downsizing does not increase profits and perhaps even decreases profits in subsequent periods.[5]

Since there is no clear connection between downsizing and corporate performance in the United States, scholars have naturally asked, Why have so many U.S. firms been doing it? Art Budros argues that downsizing is not economically rational but *socially* rational. By this he means that it adheres to a powerful social rule or "myth" that specifies acceptable practices without demonstrating empirically that these practices are efficient. Managers downsize in pursuit of non-economic rewards such as favorable reputations rather than economic rewards such as better financial performance.[6] William McKinley et al. take a more cognitive approach, stressing that managers have come

3. Budros 1997 and 1999 and McKinley et al. 2000 survey representative studies. Analysts have begun to raise similar questions about the related phenomenon of outsourcing (*New York Times*, June 6, 2004, 9).
4. Baumol et al. 2003.
5. McKinley et al. 2000, 230.
6. Budros 1997 and 1999.

to take for granted the proposition that downsizing is effective. They suggest that the ideology of shareholder value has contributed to this presumption, making it harder for managers to conceive of alternatives to downsizing.[7] Thus U.S. firms have not been biased against downsizing out of concern about dislocating workers but have been biased *toward* it because of social norms that attach value to it and/or preconceptions about its efficacy. This research implies that U.S. firms have been too quick to downsize: they have overestimated the benefits and underestimated the costs. If that is so, then Japanese firms that have been reluctant to downsize may have been acting more rationally than their U.S. counterparts.

Just because U.S. firms downsize too much, however, does not necessarily mean that the same applies to Japanese firms. Many commentators have argued that the Japanese economy was plagued with enormous overcapacity in the 1990s, so firms really needed to downsize. The substantial increase in corporate profitability without major increases in output in the early 2000s supports this view.[8] Thus, ironically, Japanese managers enhanced corporate performance by borrowing a U.S. practice that was not as successful for the U.S. corporations that pioneered it. Nevertheless, there is also evidence that those Japanese companies that have adhered more closely to the long-term employment model have fared better than those that did not. Among Japan's most successful companies, for example, those with the longest job tenure had the highest profits, an indication that investment in training and retaining employees was critical to their success.[9]

The evidence is similarly mixed or ambiguous with respect to many other features of the U.S. model that Japan has tried to emulate: stock options, mergers and acquisitions, outside directors, and the shareholder model of corporate governance itself. In theory, stock options are supposed to align managers' interests more closely with those of shareholders by giving managers a personal incentive to maximize the share price, yet there is no clear evidence that stock options improve corporate performance.[10] After the Enron scandal of 2002, stock options lost much of their luster and commentators

7. McKinley et al. 2000.

8. Others have argued that although downsizing may be rational for individual firms in Japan, it exacerbates the country's macroeconomic problems by increasing consumer anxiety and dampening demand (Katz 2003).

9. *Nikkei Net* (February 5, 2004). This study is merely suggestive, however, since it covers only a small sample of companies. Also see Brown et al. 1997, especially 191–207, for a discussion of the respective strengths and weaknesses of the U.S. and Japanese employment systems.

10. Blasi et al. 2003, cited in *New York Times* (November 10, 2002), 3/1, find that firms that award the biggest share of stock options to the top five executives had the lowest returns to shareholders.

began to stress their downside: they reward managers for good performance but do not punish them for bad performance; they encourage fraudulent practices to manipulate share prices; they shift returns from shareholders to top managers; and they increase inequalities in compensation.[11] Some analysts contend that stock options actually serve as camouflage, allowing top managers to increase their compensation without making this apparent to ordinary workers, minority shareholders, and the general public.[12] U.S. companies substantially reduced their reliance on stock options after 2002, with options dropping from 52 to 36 percent of compensation for U.S. chief executives in a single year. Corporate boards found that stock options were not maximizing shareholder value; moreover, executives tended to assess the options' value as less than the cost the company incurred to provide them.[13]

The U.S. experience suggests that mergers and acquisitions are as likely to destroy value as to create it. According to a Boston Consulting Group study of larger U.S. mergers from 1995 to 2001, mergers did not add value for the shareholders of the acquiring company in 61 percent of the cases.[14] Sara Moeller et al. find that mergers imposed huge losses for shareholders during the 1998–2001 period, although other investigations suggest that they provided modest benefits in earlier periods.[15] Merging can bring economies of scale, but expansion brings its own problems. With added layers of management, top managers have more trouble keeping up with developments at the operational level, and workers feel less connection between their effort and corporate performance. Individual business units become more likely to pursue their own interests over those of the corporation as a whole. Small and medium-sized firms often outperform their larger rivals, in industries from banking to retail.[16]

There is also no clear link between outside directors and better corporate performance in the United States. Sanjai Bhagat and Bernard Black find that firms with more independent boards do not perform any better than other firms. They also note that low-profitability firms have a tendency to increase the independence of their boards but that it does not help their performance.

11. See Bebchuk 2004.

12. *New York Times* (August 23, 2002), A17.

13. *Economist* (April 17, 2004), 63.

14. *Honolulu Advertiser* (February 22, 2004), F9.

15. Moeller et al. 2005. Robert Bruner (2005, 13–54), in a review of the academic literature on the costs and benefits of mergers and acquisitions, finds multiple examples within each of the following categories: studies reporting positive returns to target firm shareholders, studies reporting negative returns to buyer firm shareholders, and studies reporting positive returns to buyer firm shareholders.

16. *New Yorker* (May 27, 2002), 50.

They conclude that the large and sustained rise in the share of outside directors on U.S. corporate boards since the 1970s cannot be explained simply as a response to economic pressures to choose more efficient governance structures but more likely reflects changes in conventional wisdom and possibly legal pressures as well.[17] The initial results in Japan have been mixed as well. Among those Japanese companies that appointed outside directors, those whose stocks outperformed the industry average roughly matched those whose stock prices underperformed the average. Many companies have found that outside directors do not improve corporate governance, and some outside directors have resigned after very brief periods of service.[18]

Comparing the Japanese economic model as a whole with the U.S. model, we noted in Chapter 1 that the conventional wisdom has shifted along with the macroeconomic performance of the two countries, from a presumption of Japanese superiority to a presumption of U.S. superiority. If there is any rough consensus in the scholarly literature, it is that the Japanese and U.S. models both have their strengths and weaknesses.[19] Richard Freeman finds that coordinated market economies tend to have greater income equality than liberal market systems and comparable productivity. He stresses that attempts to switch systems are costly, both economically and socially, so countries are probably better off sticking with their own strengths.[20] Likewise, scholars in the Varieties of Capitalism school view the two ideal types as points of equilibrium with strong complementarities; more coherent systems of either type are superior to hybrid systems that combine contradictory elements, such as a stable employment system with a capital market–based based financial system.[21] Yamamura's analysis (see Chapter 2) suggests that Japanese leaders should not be too eager to embrace U.S. institutions because Japan's institutional strengths may become more salient in the years to come.[22]

With respect to government policy reforms, the Japanese government has changed course more in response to ideological shifts than to clear evidence linking proposed reforms to better economic performance. On many issues, the evidence on the merits of the policy measures is even more ambiguous than that on corporate practices. Given the mixed evidence on stock options,

17. Bhagat and Black 2002.

18. *Nikkei Weekly* (August 5, 2002), 12.

19. Mary O'Sullivan (2000) suggests that the shareholder model may be inferior to a stakeholder model in promoting innovation.

20. Freeman 2000.

21. Aoki 1994, Hall and Soskice 2001, Hall and Gingerich 2004.

22. Yamamura 2003. Vogel and Zysman (2002) differentiate the respective strengths and weaknesses of the two models by industrial sectors (such as manufacturing versus software) and functions (such as breakthrough innovation versus incremental improvement in production processes). Also see Kitschelt 1991.

outside directors, and mergers and acquisitions, the benefits of policy reforms that facilitate these measures are equally unclear. And where there has been relatively solid evidence available, the Japanese authorities have not used it particularly well. We observed in Chapter 2, for example, that the economic benefits from liberalization are greater and less ambiguous in some sectors, such as telecommunications, than in other sectors, such as energy. Yet the government has not given priority to regulatory reforms in those sectors in which the potential economic benefit is greatest. Likewise, where there is evidence that the sequence of reforms is critical, the government has not followed the preferable sequence. In finance, for example, scholars have found that governments that deregulate prior to strengthening prudential regulation—as in the United States before the savings and loan debacle—are especially prone to financial crises.[23] Yet Japan failed to heed this lesson. Thus the Japanese government's policy reforms have followed a political or sociological logic more than an economically rational one.

Japan's leaders devised the postwar policy profile not simply to maximize economic growth, of course, but to preserve social equity and stability as well. And though it is difficult—to say the least—to sort out the linkage between public policy and social well-being, Japan has outperformed the United States across a wide range of social indicators, including higher educational achievement, better public health standards, lower crime rates, and greater economic equity.[24] This raises the question whether some liberal reforms designed to strengthen Japan's economic performance may have compromised its social solidarity. For example, reductions in agricultural subsidies and public works spending, trade liberalization, and some regulatory reforms are likely to weaken Japan's de facto social safety net and exacerbate economic inequalities. Of course, that is why opponents fought these measures so fervently, with considerable success. Although we cannot prove cause and effect, we know that Japan has experienced increasing social strains in recent years, such as rising income inequality, decreasing educational standards, and higher crime rates.[25]

I do not mean to glorify Japan's traditional model or to decry all liberal market reforms. I am merely suggesting that Japanese leaders often enacted reforms in the absence of clear evidence of benefits. We should not be too nostalgic about a postwar Japanese model that discriminated against women, fostered industrial collusion, blocked out imports, impeded information

---

23. Mikitani and Posen 2000; Posen 2002.

24. See Wilensky 2002, especially 430–93, on the linkage of institutions, policies, and economic performance in rich democracies.

25. Toshiaki Tachibanaki (1998) offers one influential perspective on rising economic inequality in Japan.

disclosure, and excluded the broader public from much of the policy process. The Japanese system required reform, but Japanese government and industry have not matched the reforms to real needs particularly well.

On balance, our two images of reform offer slightly different bottom lines. The image of reform fashion suggests that the reform process was decoupled from a rational assessment of costs and benefits. Reform fever may have played a motivational role, but it also pointed Japan toward inappropriate models and pushed it to enact reforms in areas where they may not have been needed. The image of reform calculus implies that the Japanese approach to reform probably paid dividends overall. By taking a broader view of rationality that includes institutions, Japanese actors ended up with more appropriate reforms than if they had relied on a simpler calculus. Japanese government officials and corporate leaders have probably gone too far in emulating the U.S. model in their rhetoric and symbolic gestures, but they have achieved a more reasonable balance in the actual substance of their reforms. In the process, however, they have compromised some of the policies and practices that sustained social stability in the postwar era.

Continuity and Change

Let us now return to the question of how the Japanese model is changing—and how much it is changing—in light of the evidence presented in Chapters 3–6. How do we make sense of the combination of continuity and change? We can take a first step by distinguishing three levels of change: routine adjustments, patterned innovation, and fundamental breaks (see Table 12). In practice, it is tricky to differentiate these levels of change because routine adjustments can cumulate into substantial revisions over time, and substantial revisions can cumulate into radical breaks.[26]

ROUTINE ADJUSTMENTS

Japanese firms have built-in mechanisms of adjustment during an economic downturn, including negotiating for wage restraint, not renewing contracts of temporary workers, collaborating with workers and suppliers to cut production costs, and asking their banks to extend credit or bail them out. Exercising these options does not represent a change in the system. Japanese firms employed many of these strategies during the economic slowdown in the 1970s, but with the effect of modifying and reinforcing rather than transforming the core features of the Japanese model.[27]

26. See Streeck and Thelen 2005, especially 1–39.
27. Dore 2000.

TABLE 12. *If Japan Is Not Turning into a Liberal Market Economy (LME), Then How Is It Changing? Selective Examples*

LABOR

Current Adjustments	Future Possibilities
• Wage restraint	• Use holding company structure to differentiate tiers of workers
• Labor and management collaborate to raise productivity	• Enhance internal labor markets
• Nonrenewal of nonregular workers	Future Nonpossibilities
• Increase share of nonregular workers	• Preserve existing system
• Shift "lifetime" employment guarantee from company to corporate group	• Shift to LME model

FINANCE

Current Adjustments	Future Possibilities
• Renegotiate main bank ties	• Use holding companies to create "virtual" ventures
• Shift from lending to universal banking	• Use employee ownership/stock options to promote stable shareholding
• Sell off cross-held shares	Future Nonpossibilities
• Reform corporate boards	• Preserve existing system
• Introduce stock options	• Shift to LME model
• Restructure main bank relationships around reorganized corporate groups	

COMPETITION

Current Adjustments	Future Possibilities
• Reorganize supply networks: reinforce some ties, loosen others	• Use holding companies to reorganize corporate networks
• Internationalize supply networks	• Cultivate new forms of interfirm collaboration
• Replace government regulation with private-sector governance	• Design new forms of industrial policy
	Future Nonpossibilities
	• Preserve existing system
	• Shift to LME model

Some adjustments, however, have the potential to cumulate into substantial change over time. For example, selling off cross-held shares represents a standard mechanism of adjustment, yet it has real consequences for the level of mutual obligation between firms in the short term and could lead to an erosion of ties over the longer term. Likewise, if companies reduce permanent employees too much—even by voluntary retirement rather than layoffs—they alter employee expectations about the firm's commitment to lifetime employment. And if they shift the balance of permanent and nonregular employees too far, they undermine the benefits of the long-term employment system.

PARTIAL CONVERGENCE

The Japanese system has moved in the direction of a liberal market system by increasing competition and compromising stability in labor, financial, and product markets. Yet Japanese companies have borrowed foreign practices more in form than in substance, or they have experimented with them and modified them later on. Many large Japanese firms have introduced some form of merit-based pay, for example, but they have deployed it as camouflage for wage restraint and have kept pay disparities within a narrow range. Companies have announced radical downsizing programs but implemented more modest ones; they have issued stock options but restricted them to small amounts; or they have announced share buybacks but exercised few of them. They have appointed "outside" directors but selected them from affiliated firms, or they have simply not given these directors much real influence. Some companies have made dramatic changes, only to reverse them. Fujitsu and NEC introduced ruthless merit-based personnel systems, for example, but then pulled back when they did not get favorable results.

We have also found increasing diversity among Japanese corporations, with some embracing global practices while others resist. In finance, for example, the strongest multinationals have all but opted out of the main bank system, so if this group expands, the main bank system will be that much less salient in the economic system as a whole. Meanwhile, weaker large companies have reinforced relations with their main banks, and smaller companies have sought to cultivate their own main bank relationships. In labor relations, Toyota has staunchly adhered to the traditional long-term employment model while NEC has experimented with dramatic reforms.

These contrasts raise the question whether multiple models can coexist within Japan. The Varieties of Capitalism literature views national systems as relatively coherent models that apply more or less uniformly throughout a country.[28] In fact, however, as argued in Chapter 1, these models apply more to some sectors than to others within a given country. And there have always been firms that do not adhere to predominant norms, both foreign multinationals and nonmainstream domestic firms. When these nonstandard firms are successful, they can inspire more traditional firms to change their ways. In the future, Japan is likely to have more firms that behave outside estab-

28. Hall and Soskice 2001.

lished Japanese patterns, like some of those we encountered in Chapter 6 (Nissan, Shinsei, Softbank, Hikari Tsushin).

In some areas, the Japanese government has moved ahead of the private sector by making many of the reforms that could push Japan toward a liberal market model, yet corporations and consumers have not changed their practices accordingly. Companies have been relatively cautious, for example, in taking advantage of reforms that allow them to issue stock options, buy back shares, and set up committee-style corporate boards. Likewise, the government has implemented many of the most important regulatory changes to move Japan more toward a capital market–based financial system, yet Japanese savers have been slow to move assets out of banks into capital markets.

Despite all the talk of a shift toward a shareholder model, Japan still has few activist shareholders and many patient ones. Unless this situation changes, Japan will wind up with a truncated shareholder model in which much of the regulatory apparatus is in place and yet few shareholders try to voice their concerns. We may find that Japanese shareholders press for different things than their U.S. counterparts, focusing more on the overpayment of executives, for example, than on the overemployment of workers.

PATTERNED INNOVATION

Now let us look at patterned innovation, meaning institutional innovation shaped by existing institutions (Table 12). A period of institutional change is bound to incorporate some combination of routine adjustments, patterned innovations, and real breaks, yet I would contend that patterned innovations constitute the axial mode of adjustment in Japan since the 1990s. In periods of more moderate change, such as the 1970s, routine adjustments were the norm.[29] In periods of more radical change, such as the Meiji Restoration and World War II, there were more substantial breaks. In the current period, the economic crisis has been so severe, the loss of legitimacy so great, and the market pressure so intense that actors have been forced to go beyond routine adjustments. At the same time, there has been stability among the principal actors—the political parties, ministries, industry associations, and large corporations—so that adjustments have been powerfully patterned by existing institutions.

For example, Japanese companies have shifted the "lifetime" employment guarantee from the firm to the corporate group. In doing so, they not only downgraded the status of lifetime employment but also redefined the role of

29. Dore 2000.

corporate groups. Pressed by economic competition yet constrained by labor market institutions, Japanese firms devised an innovative solution that allowed them to cut labor costs without violating their commitment to stable employment. This solution built on existing institutions—corporate networks—but transformed them in the process. Japanese firms have also sought to enhance their internal labor markets. They have used information technology to make their internal labor markets work more like real markets and less like a centrally controlled rotation system. We found that NEC, for example, uses its online network to give its managers and employees much greater freedom to arrange their own job matches within the firm and the larger corporate group as well.[30]

Likewise, Japan's financial sector has fundamentally transformed from a segmented system to universal banking via holding company groups, yet the banks have still tried to leverage their traditional main bank ties in their new business lines. They have only partially succeeded, however, because underwriting debt, for example, does not require the kind of close working relationship involved in standard bank lending, and the organizational separation of banking and securities subsidiaries has complicated this strategy. The banks have also reconfigured Japan's main industrial groups—which used to be organized around a "one set" principle of one commercial bank and one major company per industrial sector—by merging with partners from other corporate groups. The bank mergers have fostered other corporate mergers across the same groups, creating recombined corporate groups.

Japanese government ministries have also converted to new roles. The major ministries, and especially MITI, have demonstrated a remarkable knack for reinventing themselves.[31] MITI officials helped to orchestrate the bureaucratic reorganization that gave them a new name (METI) and broader responsibilities, including the right to contribute to overall economic management by absorbing functions from the old Economic Planning Agency. MITI shifted goals from boosting exports to expanding investment abroad to promoting investment in Japan. Meanwhile, it moved from classic industrial policy to espousing deregulation, cultivating Japan's market infrastructure, and facilitating corporate restructuring. And it developed a new approach to industrial policy itself, one that seeks to upgrade certain technological capabilities rather than to sponsor specific sectors or firms, to promote joint ventures and strategic alliances rather than to organize cartels or consortia, to revitalize

---

30. Many other firms, including Toshiba, Denso, Asahi Kasei, and Hitachi, have explored methods of promoting free agency within the company to encourage mobility while retaining valued employees (*Nikkei Weekly*, January 20, 2003, 8, and November 10, 2003, 21).

31. Johnson 1989, 183–86; Elder 2003.

troubled companies with new financial techniques rather than recession cartels, and to spur innovation by triggering private investment rather than guiding it directly. Nevertheless, METI retains some of the essence of the old MITI: a commitment to promoting Japanese industry, a tradition of working closely with the private sector, and a fierce determination to preserve its own authority.

These examples illustrate the distinctive logic of patterned innovation. Corporate and government reforms go beyond routine adjustments to the point where they generate substantial institutional change, yet the trajectory of change is strongly shaped by existing institutions.

Japan's New Model

These routine adjustments and patterned innovations have combined to reshape the Japanese model. The current model does not represent a stable equilibrium, however, but rather is a matrix of institutions undergoing a continuous evolution. We shall speculate about future trends in the next section, but first let us take stock of the present situation. In Chapters 3 and 4, we identified a distinctively Japanese pattern of policy reform in which the government pursued incremental reforms; packaged delicate political compromises, with considerable compensation to the potential losers; and designed reforms to preserve the core institutions of the Japanese model in the face of new challenges and to build on the strengths of those institutions as much as possible. In Chapters 5 and 6, we identified a distinctively Japanese approach to corporate restructuring in which companies responded to pressures to cut costs by exercising voice rather than exit with their long-term business partners, including workers, banks, and suppliers. They strived to adjust as much as possible without undermining these cooperative relationships and to leverage the benefits of these relationships to overcome their problems. These policy reforms and corporate adjustments have combined to produce real change in labor relations, finance, corporate governance, and corporate groups.

In labor relations, the government has allowed firms to enhance the flexibility that was already embedded in the Japanese employment system. Specifically, it gave firms a greater ability to adjust working hours and to hire agency temps, and to lower labor costs via reorganization by spinning off divisions or forming pure holding companies. Companies have cashed in on this flexibility, preserving the long-term employment system for permanent employees while downgrading it and restricting it to a smaller proportion of the workforce. They have shifted the employment guarantee from the company itself to the wider corporate group and even beyond to unaffiliated firms.

In finance, the authorities confronted a major crisis, first colluding with the banks to hide the full extent of the problem and assisting them in riding through it, and later taking a harder line in pressing banks to write off or sell off nonperforming loans. The banks were slow to streamline operations, probably because they realized that their fate hinged more on government policy than on their own efforts to restructure. The government deregulated securities commissions, liberalized international transactions, and permitted financial institutions to cross business lines via holding companies. The major banks responded to this new environment by reorganizing themselves into mega-banks that would be too big to fail and reducing capacity via mergers. The relatively uniform main bank system of the postwar years has broken down into a much wider range of relationships, from traditional main bank relationships for loyal corporate clients, troubled large companies, and many smaller firms, to more distant transaction-based relationships for the most competitive multinationals and newer and more innovative firms. Meanwhile, the accounting reforms initiated under the rubric of the Big Bang have fundamentally altered corporate behavior by limiting their ability to hide losses or smooth out profits and forcing them to reorganize their operations.

In corporate governance, the government has given companies more options for structuring their boards and organizing their business units, yet companies have been slow to capitalize on these new possibilities. The companies have redesigned their corporate governance systems to appeal more to international investors without fundamentally altering the way they do business. Government reforms to facilitate reorganization, via spin-offs, for example, have also helped companies to restructure their relations with suppliers. Companies have spun off affiliates in some cases; in others, they have integrated them back into the corporate group. As a whole, these changes have made Japanese firms more oriented toward maximizing financial returns, less concerned with increasing market share, and more likely to focus on their core business.

The government's role in the economy has transformed as well. Government officials have lost legitimacy in the eyes of the Japanese people, they have lost confidence in their own ability to steer the economy, and they have become more ambivalent in their policy goals. In practice, they have combined liberalization with efforts to reassert control over industry and markets in new ways. As we discovered in Chapter 4, they have enacted pro-competitive regulatory reforms yet still tried to manage the terms of competition after reform; they have abandoned old-style industrial policy yet experimented with new variations; and they have enhanced foreign firms' ability to invest in Japan and yet backtracked in several instances. The government has not truly embraced the liberal model, but it has made substantial progress in areas critical for foreign corporations seeking access to the Japanese market. Although U.S. and Japanese capitalism will continue to differ, bilateral friction over differences in the two systems is not likely to return to 1985–95 levels.[32]

In sum, the remodeled Japan differs from the earlier version in at least three important ways. It is more *selective*: in the face of hard times, companies have become more discriminating in their partnerships. They have reevaluated their long-term relationships with workers, banks, and other firms, and they have loosened some and tightened others. They have shifted from a more reflexive acceptance of these long-term partnerships to a more rational assessment of their costs and benefits. It is more *differentiated*: companies have become more variable in their practices. There never was a uniform Japanese model that applied equally to all sectors and all companies, but the model has fragmented further. And it is more *open*: Japanese corporations have more foreign owners, managers, and business partners than ever before, and these foreign actors bring with them different practices and norms. Each of these trends has been driven not simply by companies freely choosing from a blank slate but through the interactive process of government reform and corporate adjustment described in detail in this book.

Future Prospects

Looking toward the future, we can expect the pattern of routine adjustment plus patterned innovation to continue. We cannot predict the precise form it will take, but we can engage in some informed speculation because we know that existing institutions close off certain options and favor others. The Japanese model constitutes a system of incentives and constraints (second circle of rationality) and norms and beliefs (third circle) that will shape future adjustments. Actors will innovate according to a logic that is consistent with the existing system. Firms may abandon specific mechanisms of collaboration with employees, banks, business partners, or the government, but they will look for new ones. They may renegotiate relationships within their business networks, but they will not lose their orientation toward networks. In other words, future adjustments will continue to follow a distinctively Japanese logic.

By lifting the ban on holding companies, for example, the Japanese government has opened up possibilities for further institutional change consistent with the logic of the existing Japanese model. Most countries have pure holding companies, but this option could solve Japan-specific problems in distinctive ways. As we saw in Chapter 4, Japanese industry pressed for lifting

32. Posen 2002, 221–32; Vogel 2002, 265–66.

the ban to increase its options for reorganization and restructuring. The Ministry of Posts and Telecommunications seized on this option as a creative compromise in the debate over breaking up Nippon Telegraph & Telephone. The Ministry of Finance adopted it as a mechanism for allowing cross-entry across different segments of the financial sector. In the future, the holding company could help companies to extend their practice of using interfirm links and diversification to manage labor costs without layoffs. They could develop multiple tiers of wages and benefits for permanent employees and reallocate workers across firms within the holding company structure. The holding company option could alleviate the problem of distinctive corporate cultures and ingrown resistance to mergers, which is especially acute in Japan. Firms may be more willing to merge with others if they can use a holding company structure to phase in the transition rather than join more abruptly.[33] Of course, companies that slow down the process of integration will also compromise the efficiency benefits from merging, but this may be a price they are willing to pay. Likewise, holding companies could make it easier to develop a functional substitute for venture capital by funneling investments into virtually autonomous subsidiaries with compensation structures designed to foster innovation. Corporations have already been experimenting with a variety of virtual ventures—corporate forms designed to maximize autonomy and flexibility while using capital from the home company—but the holding company structure could offer them a way to give these ventures more managerial autonomy and greater financial accountability.

Yet another possible adjustment that would be consistent with the logic of the Japanese model would be for Japanese firms to use employee ownership and stock options to stabilize ownership. Employee ownership thus far remains too small to influence ownership patterns, but it could become more significant in the future. Companies could compensate for reductions in cross-held shares within the corporate group by increasing shares held by employees. This would give them another way to reduce their vulnerability to pressure from outside shareholders within the changed financial climate. Some companies have even used stock options to encourage loyalty among part-time workers or to strengthen partnerships with suppliers.[34]

EVOLVING POLICY PREFERENCES

Returning to the model of macro-micro interaction (Figure 5), we can engage in some informed speculation about how corporate restructuring to

33. See Lincoln and Gerlach 2004, 318–21.
34. *Nikkei Weekly* (July 15, 2002), 9.

date may affect industry preferences about future policy reforms. In the past, as the Japanese government lowered trade barriers, those Japanese companies in competitive sectors became less wedded to protection and more open to further liberalization. At the same time, these companies became more sensitive to regulatory changes that might affect their ability to use private-sector partnerships to compete. As the government proceeded with financial reforms, Japanese industry gained more of a stake in further reforms that would strengthen capital markets, and institutional investors emerged that pressed for further liberalization. Likewise, now that the Japanese government has made some progress in promoting regulatory reform, strengthening antitrust policy, and reducing barriers to foreign direct investment, industry is less opposed to additional steps in this direction. In short, policy reforms make industry actors less wedded to the old institutional forms that gave them comparative institutional advantages in the past and more wedded to new ones that provide benefits in the present.

Moreover, policy changes have facilitated an increase in foreign direct investment, which in turn alters Japan's domestic political dynamics. Although the stock of foreign direct investment in Japan remains low in comparative terms, it has increased substantially from to ¥3 trillion in 1998 to ¥9.6 trillion in 2003.[35] This investment brings in new foreign actors that become participants in the political process and creates alliances between these foreign firms and their Japanese partners. The increasing foreign presence will have major political and social ramifications: foreign managers will provide influential examples of different modes of management, foreign-owned companies will lobby the government for a more open market environment, and foreign portfolio investors will press companies to increase returns to shareholders. Foreign players will increasingly infiltrate industry associations, making these organizations less parochial. The foreign presence will also make it more difficult for Japanese authorities to use administrative guidance to manage market competition. The United States and other trading partners may feel less need to pressure the Japanese government on issues of market access as their private-sector surrogates become more entrenched within Japan.[36]

35. Organization for Economic Co-operation and Development 2005, 165. As of 2003, Japan's inward direct investment balance as a percentage of GDP was 2.1 percent, compared with 21.2 percent for Germany and 22.1 percent for the United States (Merrill Lynch, Global Securities Research and Economics Group 2005, 8).

36. Leonard Schoppa (1997) argues that the U.S. government is more effective in bilateral negotiations when it cultivates allies within Japan. This will be all the more true to the extent that U.S. companies, and their Japanese partners, are participants in the Japanese policy process.

JAPAN AFTER RECOVERY

It is particularly difficult to separate temporary adjustments from longer-term shifts because Japan has been adjusting to a prolonged downturn in economic performance. By identifying the driving forces behind these adjustments, however, we can make some educated guesses about how economic recovery will affect these trends. We found that economic stagnation weakened the company-worker relationship and strengthened the company-bank relationship, for example, so recovery should have the opposite effect. The economic slump has driven many of the changes in Japanese labor markets, including wage restraint, reductions in new hires, increases in the proportion of temporary and dispatch workers, and the downgrading of lifetime employment. A stronger economy plus demographic trends imply that Japan will shift from labor surplus to labor shortage within the next five years. One analyst estimates that the labor surplus will disappear by 2009 and a labor shortage will emerge after that.[37] As this occurs, Japanese employers are likely to reverse some recent trends, increasing wages, hiring more new graduates, raising retirement ages, and working harder to retain valued employees. Instead of simply reverting to old strategies for retaining workers, they will explore new mechanisms to achieve this goal. They may deploy employee stock ownership, for example, to cultivate loyalty. They probably will not give up the increased flexibility they achieved by increasing the proportion of temporary workers, but they will continue to upgrade the status of temporary workers by giving them greater responsibilities and higher status, wages, and benefits relative to permanent employees.

In finance, the economic crisis drove weaker firms back to their banks because they did not have credit ratings that would enable them to tap capital markets or because they needed a bailout. As they recover, however, firms are likely to revert to the pattern of the late 1980s, shifting to capital market financing and loosening but not eliminating their ties with their main banks. Over the medium term, therefore, we can expect to see a growing gap between gradual change with partial reinforcement of old patterns in labor markets and a more rapid evolution away from the postwar model in financial markets.

Economic stagnation has also driven companies to focus on share prices. As share prices recover, some of the pressure for change in corporate governance may ease. Those companies that have genuinely converted to the U.S. model will continue in that direction, but those that were merely paying lip service to appease foreign investors could easily revert to earlier practices.

37. Saitō 2003.

THE END OF THE JAPANESE MODEL?

What would constitute a fundamental break? In practice, as noted above, it is difficult to distinguish incremental change from a fundamental break because the former can easily cumulate into the latter. For present purposes, however, we have identified a preference for voice over exit mechanisms as a defining feature of the Japanese system, and in that sense the system has not fundamentally transformed. Japanese firms continue to favor voice mechanisms over exit with their workers, banks, and suppliers. We could identify a break in the labor relations system, for example, if Japanese firms were to shift from an internal labor market model, hiring fresh graduates and transferring them internally, to an external labor market model, hiring midcareer employees and actively poaching from other firms. We could declare a break in the financial system if Japanese firms were to develop a full-fledged market for corporate control in which investors could buy and sell firms on the open market. We could proclaim a break in the competition regime if the government gave up trying to protect and promote domestic firms and if the firms themselves ceased collaborating with competitors, with the result that firms could freely enter and exit sectoral markets (see Table 1).

The Japanese model is changing, but the transition is continuous rather than discontinuous. For practical purposes, it is impossible to identify a clear break. If we look at Japan's postwar history, for example, we can see that the model in 2005 fundamentally differs from the model in 1960. But we cannot identify a breaking point at which one model transformed into the other. Likewise, in the future we are not likely to see an end to the Japanese model but only its continuous redefinition.

REFERENCES

Adelberger, Karen E. 2000. "Semi-sovereign Leadership? The State's Role in German Biotechnology and Venture Capital Growth." *German Politics* 9:103–22.

Administrative Reform Committee. 1996. *Hikari kagayaku kuni o mezashite* (Toward a bright and shining nation). Tokyo: Gyōsei Kanri Kenkyū Sentaa.

Ahmadjian, Christina L., and James R. Lincoln. 2001. "*Keiretsu*, Governance, and Learning: Case Studies in Change from the Japanese Automotive Industry." *Organization Science* 12:683–701.

Ahmadjian, Christina L., and Gregory E. Robbins. 2004. "A Clash of Capitalisms: Foreign Shareholders and Corporate Restructuring in 1990s Japan." Manuscript.

Ahmadjian, Christina L., and Patricia Robinson. 2001. "Safety in Numbers: Downsizing and the Deinstitutionalization of Permanent Employment in Japan." *Administrative Science Quarterly* 46:622–54.

Allen, Everett T., et al. 2003. *Pension Planning: Pension, Profit Sharing, and Other Deferred Compensation Plans*. New York: McGraw-Hill Irwin.

Amyx, Jennifer. 2004. *Japan's Financial Crisis: Institutional Rigidity and Reluctant Change*. Princeton: Princeton University Press.

Aoki, Masahiko. 1988. *Information, Incentives, and Bargaining in the Japanese Economy*. Cambridge: Cambridge University Press.

———. 1994. "The Japanese Firm as a System of Attributes: A Survey and Research Agenda." In *The Japanese Firm: Sources of Competitive Strength*, edited by Aoki and Ronald Dore, 11–40. Oxford: Oxford University Press.

———. 2000. *Information, Corporate Governance, and Institutional Diversity: Competitiveness in Japan, the USA, and the Transitional Economies*. Oxford: Oxford University Press.

———. 2001. *Toward a Comparative Institutional Analysis*. Cambridge, Mass.: MIT Press.

Aoki, Masahiko, and Haruhiko Andō, eds. 2002. *Mojūruka: atarashii sangyō aakitekuchaa no honshitsu* [Modularity: The new industrial architecture]. Tokyo: Tōyō Keizai Shimpōsha.

Aoki, Masahiko, and Ronald Dore, eds. 1994. *The Japanese Firm: Sources of Competitive Strength*. Oxford: Oxford University Press.

Aoki, Masahiko, and Hugh T. Patrick, eds. 1994. *The Japanese Main Bank System: Its Relevance for Developing and Transforming Economies*. Oxford: Oxford University Press.

Ariga, Kenn, Giorgio Brunello, and Yasushi Ohkusa. 2000. *Internal Labour Markets in Japan*. Cambridge: Cambridge University Press.

Arikawa, Yasuhiro, and Hideaki Miyajima. 2005. "Relationship Banking in Post-Bubble Japan: Co-existence of Soft and Hard Budget Constraint." Research Institute on Economy, Trade, and Industry (RIETI) Discussion Paper.

Baumol, William J., Alan S. Blinder, and Edward N. Wolff. 2003. *Downsizing in America: Reality, Causes, and Consequences*. New York: Russell Sage Foundation.

Bebchuk, Lucian A. 2004. *Pay without Performance: The Unfulfilled Promise of Executive Compensation*. Cambridge, Mass.: Harvard University Press.

Bergsten, Fred C. 2004. "The Resurgent Japanese Economy and a Japan–United States Free Trade Agreement." Paper presented to the Foreign Correspondents' Club of Japan, Tokyo, May 12.

Bernanke, Ben S. 2003. "Some Thoughts on Monetary Policy in Japan." Remarks before the Japan Society of Monetary Economics, May 31.

Bhagat, Sanjai, and Bernard Black. 2002. "The Non-correlation between Board Independence and Long-Term Firm Performance." *Journal of Corporation Law* 27:231–73.

Blasi, Joseph R., Douglas L. Kruse, and Aaron Bernstein. 2003. *In the Company of Owners: The Truth about Stock Options (and Why Every Employee Should Have Them).* New York: Basic Books.

Borrus, Michael, Francois Bar, Patrick Cogez, Anne Brit Thoresen, Ibrahim Warde, and Aki Yoshikawa. 1985. "Telecommunications Development in Comparative Perspective: The New Telecommunications in Europe, Japan and the U.S." Berkeley Roundtable on the International Economy (BRIE) Working Paper 14.

Boyer, Robert, and Michel Juillard. 2000. "The Wage Labour Nexus Challenged: More the Consequence Than the Cause of the Crisis." In *Japanese Capitalism in Crisis: A Regulationist Interpretation,* edited by Boyer and Toshio Yamada, 119–37. London: Routledge.

Broda, Christian, and David Weinstein. 2005. "Happy News from the Dismal Science: Reassessing Japanese Fiscal Policy and Sustainability." Manuscript.

Brown, Clair, Yoshifumi Nakata, Michael Reich, and Lloyd Ulman. 1997. *Work and Pay in the United States and Japan.* New York: Oxford University Press.

Bruner, Robert F. 2005. *Deals from Hell: M&A Lessons That Rise above the Ashes.* Hoboken, N.J.: John Wiley.

Budros, Art. 1997. "The New Capitalism and Organizational Rationality: The Adoption of Downsizing Programs, 1979–1994." *Social Forces* 76:229–49.

———. 1999. "A Conceptual Framework for Analyzing Why Organizations Downsize." *Organization Science* 10:69–82.

Bullock, Robert W. 2000. "The Social Bases of the Developmental State: Agriculture and the Conservative Coalition in Postwar Japan." Manuscript.

Cabinet Office, Quality-of-Life Policy Bureau. 2002. "Heisei jūsannen shōhisha dantai kihon chōsa no kekka" [2001 Basic survey of consumer groups]. Tokyo: Cabinet Office.

Calder, Kent E. 1988. *Crisis and Compensation: Public Policy and Political Stability in Japan.* Princeton: Princeton University Press.

Callon, Scott. 1995. *Divided Sun: MITI and the Breakdown of Japanese High-Tech Industrial Policy, 1975–93.* Stanford: Stanford University Press.

Chaudhry, Kiren. 1993. "The Myths of the Market and the Common History of Late Developers." *Politics and Society* 21:245–74.

Chuma, Hiroyuki. 2002. "Employment Adjustment in Japanese Firms during the Current Crisis." *Industrial Relations* 41:653–82.

Cioffi, John W. 2002. "Restructuring 'Germany Inc.': The Politics of Company and Takeover Law Reform in Germany and the European Union." *Law & Policy* 24:355–402.

———. 2004. "The State of the Corporation: State Power, Politics, Policymaking, and Corporate Governance in the United States, Germany, and France." In *Transatlantic Policymaking in an Age of Austerity: Diversity and Drift,* edited by Martin A. Levin and Martin Shapiro, 253–97. Washington, D.C.: Georgetown University Press.

Coase, Ronald. 1952. "The Nature of the Firm." Reprinted in *Readings in Price Theory*, edited by George J. Stigler and Kenneth E. Boulding, 18–33. Chicago: American Economic Association.

Cohen, Jeffrey. 2000. *Politics and Economic Policy in the United States*. New York: Houghton Mifflin.

Cohen, Stephen, Bradford DeLong, and John Zysman. 2000. "Tools for Thought: What Is New and Important about the 'E-conomy.'" Berkeley Roundtable on the International Economy (BRIE) Working Paper 138.

Cohen, Stephen, and Andrew Schwartz. 1998. "Deeper into the Tunnel." In *The Tunnel at the End of the Light: Privatization, Business Networks, and Economic Transformation in Russia*, edited by Cohen, Schwartz, and John Zysman, 1–23. Berkeley: International and Area Studies, University of California, Berkeley.

Cole, Robert. Forthcoming. "Telecom Competition in World Markets: Understanding Japan's Decline." In *How Revolutionary Was the Revolution? National Responses, Market Transitions, and Global Technology in the Digital Era*, edited by Abraham Newman and John Zysman. Stanford: Stanford University Press.

Corporate Governance Forum. 2001. "Revised Corporate Governance Principles." Report of the Japan Corporate Governance Forum Committee, Tokyo.

Cott, Jeremy, and Thomas R. Piper. 2000. "Nissan Motor Company." Harvard Business School Case 200–067. Boston.

Crouch, Colin, and Wolfgang Streeck, eds. 1997. *Political Economy of Modern Capitalism*. London: Sage.

Curtis, Gerald L. 1988. *The Japanese Way of Politics*. New York: Columbia University Press.

——. 1999. *The Logic of Japanese Politics*. New York: Columbia University Press.

Deeg, Richard. 1993. "The State, Banks, and Economic Governance in Germany." *German Politics* 2:149–76.

Derthick, Martha, and Paul J. Quirk. 1985. *The Politics of Deregulation*. Washington, D.C.: Brookings.

Dewey Ballantine. 1995. "Privatizing Protection: Japanese Market Barriers in Consumer Photographic Film and Consumer Photographic Paper." Memorandum in Support of a Petition Filed Pursuant to Section 301 of the Trade Act of 1974, as Amended. Washington, D.C.

Dore, Ronald. 1986. *Flexible Rigidities: Industrial Policy and Structural Adjustment in the Japanese Economy, 1970–80*. Stanford: Stanford University Press.

——. 2000. *Stock Market Capitalism, Welfare Capitalism: Japan and Germany versus the Anglo-Saxons*. Oxford: Oxford University Press.

——. 2004. "Corporate Governance: Change in Organization, Change in Managerial Objectives, Change in Society." Manuscript.

Dosi, Giovanni, Laura D'Andrea Tyson, and John Zysman. 1989. "Trade, Technologies, and Development: A Framework for Discussing Japan." In *Politics and Productivity: The Real Story of Why Japan Works*, edited by Chalmers Johnson, Tyson, and Zysman, 3–38. Cambridge, Mass.: Ballinger.

Elder, Mark. 1998. "Why Buy High? The Political Economy of Protection for Intermediate Goods Industries in Japan." Ph.D. dissertation, Harvard University.

——. 2003. "METI and Industrial Policy in Japan: Change and Continuity." In *Japan's Managed Globalization*, edited by Ulrike Schaede and William Grimes, 159–90. Armonk, N.Y.: M. E. Sharpe.

Estevez-Abe, Margarita. 2004. "Political Logics of Welfare Capitalism: Party, Bureaucracy, and Business in Postwar Japan." Manuscript.

Fagan, Perry L., and Michael Y. Yoshino. 2001. "Shinsei Bank." Harvard Business School Case 302–036. Boston.

Fligstein, Neil. 2001. *The Architecture of Markets: An Economic Sociology of Twenty-First-Century Capitalist Societies.* Princeton: Princeton University Press.

Freeman, Richard B. 2000. "Single Peaked vs. Diversified Capitalism: The Relation between Economic Institutions and Outcomes." National Bureau of Economic Research Working Paper 7556.

Frieden, Jeffry. 1999. "Actors and Preferences in International Relations." In *Strategic Choice and International Relations,* edited by David Lake and Robert Powell, 39–76. Princeton: Princeton University Press.

Frieden, Jeffry, and Ronald Rogowski. 1996. "The Impact of the International Economy on National Policies: An Analytical Overview." In *Internationalization and Domestic Politics,* edited by Robert O. Keohane and Helen V. Milner, 25–47. Cambridge: Cambridge University Press.

Friedman, Benjamin M. 2000. "Japan Now and the United States Then: Lessons from the Parallels." In *Japan's Financial Crisis and Its Parallels to U.S. Experience,* edited by Ryōichi Mikitani, and Adam S. Posen, 37–56. Washington, D.C.: Institute for International Economics.

Fukao, Mitsuhiro. 2000. "Zero kinri ka no kinyū seisaku no yūkōsei: Riron to jisshō" [The effectiveness of monetary policy under zero interest rates: Theory and evidence]. In *Zero kinri to nihon keizai* [The zero interest rate policy and the Japanese economy], edited by Fukao and Hiroshi Yoshikawa, 1–32. Tokyo: Nihon Keizai Shimbunsha.

——. 2002. "1980 nendai kōhan no shisan kakaku baburu hassei to 90 nendai no fukyō no genin" [Causes of the late 1980s asset price bubble and the 1990s recession]. In *Heisei baburu no kenkyū* [Research on the Heisei bubble], vol. 1, edited by Michio Muramatsu and Masahiro Okuno, 87–126. Tokyo: Tōyō Keizai Shimpōsha.

Gao, Bai. 2000. "Globalization and Ideology: The Competing Images of the Contemporary Japanese Economic System in the 1990s." *International Sociology* 15:3, 435–53.

——. 2001. *Japan's Economic Dilemma: The Institutional Origins of Prosperity and Stagnation.* Cambridge: Cambridge University Press.

Garon, Sheldon. 1997. *Molding Japanese Minds: The State in Everyday Life.* Princeton: Princeton University Press.

Gaunder, Alisa. 2001. "Leadership Looming Large: The Process of Self-Regulation in Japan." Ph.D. dissertation, University of California, Berkeley.

George, Alexander L. 1979. "Case Studies and Theory Development: The Method of Structured, Focused Comparison." In *Diplomacy: New Approaches in History, Theory, and Policy,* edited by Paul G. Lauren, 43–68. New York: Free Press.

Gerlach, Michael L. 1992. *Alliance Capitalism: The Social Organization of Japanese Business.* Berkeley: University of California Press.

Ghosn, Carlos. 2001. *Runessansu* [Renaissance]. Tokyo: Daiyamondosha.

Ghosn, Carlos, and Philippe Riès. 2005. *Shift: Inside Nissan's Historic Revival.* New York: Currency.

Gilson, Ronald J., and Curtis J. Milhaupt. 2005. "Choice as Regulatory Reform: The Case of Japanese Corporate Governance." *American Journal of Comparative Law* 51.

Golden, Miriam, Michael Wallerstein, and Peter Lange. 1999. "Postwar Trade-Union Organization and Industrial Relations in Twelve Countries." In *Continuity and Change in Contemporary Capitalism*, edited by Herbert Kitschelt et al., 194–230. Cambridge: Cambridge University Press.

Granovetter, Mark. 1985. "Economic Action and Social Structure: The Problem of Embeddedness." *American Journal of Sociology* 91:481–510.

Grimes, William W. 2001. *Unmaking the Japanese Miracle: Macroeconomic Politics, 1985–2000*. Ithaca: Cornell University Press.

——. 2002. "Economic Performance." In *U.S.-Japan Relations in a Changing World*, edited by Steven K. Vogel, 35–62. Washington, D.C.: Brookings Institution Press.

Gronning, Terje. 1998. "Whither the Japanese Employment System? The Position of the Japan Employers' Federation." *Industrial Relations Journal* 29:295–303.

Gwartney, James D., and Robert A. Lawson. 2004. *Economic Freedom of the World, 2004 Annual Report*. Vancouver: Fraser Institute.

Hacker, Jacob S. 2005. "Policy Drift: The Hidden Politics of U.S. Welfare State Retrenchment." In *Beyond Continuity: Institutional Change in Advanced Political Economies*, edited by Wolfgang Streeck and Kathleen Thelen, 40–82. New York: Oxford University Press.

Hackethal, Andreas, Reinhard H. Schmidt, and Marcel Tyrell. 2003. "Corporate Governance in Germany: Transition to a Modern Capital-Market-Based System?" *Journal of Institutional and Theoretical Economics* 159:664–74.

Hall, Peter A., and Daniel W. Gingerich. 2004. "Varieties of Capitalism and Institutional Complementarities in the Macroeconomy: An Empirical Analysis." Max Planck Institute for the Study of Societies Discussion Paper.

Hall, Peter, and David Soskice, eds. 2001. *Varieties of Capitalism: The Institutional Foundations of Comparative Advantage*. Oxford: Oxford University Press.

Hampton, Celia. 1997. "Curb on German Bank Power." *Business Law Europe*, November 12, 8.

Harada, Yutaka. 1999. *Nihon no ushinawareta jūnen: Shippai no honshitsu, fukkatsu e no senryaku* [Japan's lost decade: The essence of failure, a strategy for revival]. Tokyo: Nihon Keizai Shimbunsha.

Hatch, Walter, and Kozo Yamamura. 1996. *Asia in Japan's Embrace: Building a Regional Production Alliance*. Cambridge: Cambridge University Press.

Hatoyama, Yukio. 1996. "Minshutō watakushi no seiken kōsō" [My program for a Democratic Party government]. *Bungei Shunjū*, November, 112–30.

Herrigel, Gary. 1996. *Industrial Constructions: The Sources of German Industrial Power*. Cambridge: Cambridge University Press.

Hirota, S., and Hideaki Miyajima. 2000. "Ginkō kainyū-gata gabanansu wa henka shitaka" [Has bank-based governance really changed?]. Manuscript.

Hirschman, Albert. 1970. *Exit, Voice, and Loyalty: Responses to Decline in Firms, Organizations, and States*. Cambridge, Mass.: Harvard University Press.

Hiwatari Nobuhiro. 1991. *Sengo nihon no shijō to seiji* [Markets and politics in postwar Japan]. Tokyo: Tokyo Daigaku Shuppankai.

Holzhausen, Arne. 2000. "Japanese Employment Practices in Transition: Promotion Policy and Compensation Schemes in the 1990s." *Social Science Japan Journal* 3:221–35.

Hoshi, Takeo, and Anil K. Kashyap. 2001. *Corporate Financing and Governance in Japan: The Road to the Future*. Cambridge, Mass.: MIT Press.

Ibata-Arens, Kathryn. 2004. "Japan's Quest for Entrepreneurialism: The Cluster Plan." Japan Policy Research Institute Working Paper 102.

Inagami, Takeshi. 2001. "From Industrial Relations to Investor Relations? Persistence and Change in Japanese Corporate Governance, Employment Practices, and Industrial Relations." *Social Science Japan Journal* 4:225–41.

——, ed. 2000. *Gendai nihon no kōporeeto gabanansu* [Corporate governance in contemporary Japan]. Tokyo: Tōyō Keizai Shimpōsha.

Inoguchi Takashi and Tomoaki Iwai. 1987. *"Zoku giin" no kenkyū* [A study of "zoku" Diet members]. Tokyo, Nihon Keizai.

Itami, Hiroyuki. 2000. *Nihon-gata kōporeeto gabanansu* [Japanese-style corporate governance]. Tokyo: Nihon Keizai Shimbunsha.

Itō, Hideshi, ed. 2002. *Nihon kigyō henkakki no sentaku* [The Japanese firm in transition]. Tokyo: Tōyō Keizai Shimpōsha.

Itō, Takatoshi. 1992. *Shōhisha jūshi no keizaigaku* [Economics with the emphasis on consumers]. Tokyo: Nihon Keizai Shimbunsha.

Ito, Takatoshi, and Hugh Patrick. 2005. "Solutions for the Japanese Economy: An Overview." Manuscript.

Jackson, Gregory. 2003. "Corporate Governance in Germany and Japan: Liberalization Pressures and Responses during the 1990s." In *The End of Diversity? Prospects for German and Japanese Capitalism*, edited by Kozo Yamamura and Wolfgang Streeck, 261–305. Ithaca: Cornell University Press.

——. 2005a. "Toward a Comparative Perspective on Corporate Governance and Labour Management: Enterprise Coalitions and National Trajectories." In *Corporate Governance and Labour Management in Comparison*, edited by Howard Gospel and Andrew Pendleton. Oxford: Oxford University Press.

——. 2005b. "Stakeholders under Pressure: Corporate Governance and Labor Management in Germany and Japan." *Corporate Governance: An International Review* 13:419–28.

Japan Chamber of Commerce and Industry. 2000. "Shōhō ni okeru kaisha hōsei no kaisei ni kansuru iken" [Opinion on the revision of the commercial code]. Tokyo.

——. 2001. "'Shōhōtō no ichibu o kaisei suru hōritsu yōkō chūkan shian' ni taisuru iken" [Opinion on the draft law for the partial revision of the commercial code]. Tokyo.

Japan Institute of Labor. 2000. "Gyōseki shugi jidai no jinji kanri to kyōiku kunren tōshi ni kansuru chōsa" [Survey on personnel management and investment in education and training in the performance-based era]. Tokyo.

——. 2002. "Jigyō saikōchiku to koyō ni kansuru chōsa" [Survey on corporate restructuring and employment]. Tokyo.

——. 2004a. "Kigyō no keiei senryaku to jinji shogū seido tō ni kansuru kenkyū no ronten seiri" [Research report on corporate strategy and personnel management systems]. JIL Research Report No. 7. Tokyo.

——. 2004b. "Rōdōsha no hataraku iyoku to koyō kanri no arikata ni kansuru chōsa kekka." [Results of the survey on worker motivation and employment management].

Johnson, Chalmers. 1982. *MITI and the Japanese Miracle*. Stanford: Stanford University Press.

——. 1989. "MITI, MPT, and the Telecom Wars: How Japan Makes Policy for High Technology." In *Politics and Productivity: How Japan's Development Strategy Works*, edited by Johnson, Laura D'Andrea Tyson, and John Zysman, 177–240. Cambridge, Mass.: Ballinger.

Kato, Junko. 1994. *The Problem of Bureaucratic Rationality: Tax Politics in Japan*. Princeton: Princeton University Press.

Kato, Takao. 2001. "The End of Lifetime Employment in Japan? Evidence from National Surveys and Field Research." *Journal of the Japanese and International Economies* 15:489–514.

Katz, Richard. 1998. *Japan, the System That Soured: The Rise and Fall of the Japanese Miracle*. Armonk, N.Y.: M. E. Sharpe.

———. 2003. *Japanese Phoenix: The Long Road to Economic Revival*. Armonk, N.Y.: M. E. Sharpe.

Katzenstein, Peter J. 1987. *Politics and Policy in West Germany: The Growth of the Semisovereign State*. Philadelphia: Temple University Press.

———. 2005. "Conclusion: Semisovereignty in United Germany." In *Governance in Contemporary Germany: The Semisovereign State Revisited*, edited by Simon Green and William E. Paterson, 283–306. New York: Cambridge University Press.

Kikkawa, Mototada. 1998. *Manee haisen* [The money war defeat]. Tokyo: Bungei Shunjū.

King, Desmond, and Stewart Wood. 1999. "The Political Economy of Neoliberalism: Britain and the United States in the 1980s." In *Continuity and Change in Contemporary Capitalism*, edited by Herbert Kitschelt et al., 371–97. Cambridge: Cambridge University Press.

Kinney, Clay. 2001. "All Change for Japanese Accounting." *The Treasurer*, February, 58–60.

Kitschelt, Herbert. 1991. "Industrial Governance Structures, Innovation Strategies, and the Case of Japan: Sectoral or Cross-National Comparative Analysis." *International Organization* 45:453–93.

———. 2003. "Competitive Party Democracy and Political-Economic Reform in Germany and Japan: Do Party Systems Make a Difference?" In *The End of Diversity? Prospects for German and Japanese Capitalism*, edited by Kozo Yamamura and Wolfgang Streeck, 334–63. Ithaca: Cornell University Press.

Kobayashi, Keiichirō. 2000. "Mondai sakiokuri ni yoru chōki keizai teitai" [The long-term stagnation born of procrastination]. In *Zero kinri to nihon keizai* [The zero interest rate policy and the Japanese economy], edited by Mitsuhiro Fukao and Hiroshi Yoshikawa, 187–232. Tokyo: Nihon Keizai Shimbunsha.

Kobayashi, Keiichirō, and Sōta Katō. 2001. *Nihon keizai no wana* [Japan's economic trap]. Tokyo: Nihon Keizai Shimbunsha.

Koike, Kazuo. 1988. *Understanding Industrial Relations in Japan*. London: Macmillan.

Krugman, Paul. 1999. "It's Baaack: Japan's Slump and the Return of the Liquidity Trap." *Brookings Papers on Economic Activity* 2:137–205.

Kume, Ikuo. 1998. *Disparaged Success: Labor Politics in Postwar Japan*. Ithaca: Cornell University Press.

Kushida, Kenji. Forthcoming. "Japan's Telecommunications Regime Shift: Understanding Japan's Potential Resurgence." In *How Revolutionary Was the Revolution? National Responses, Market Transitions, and Global Technology in the Digital Era*, edited by Abraham Newman and John Zysman. Stanford: Stanford University Press.

Kuttner, Kenneth N., and Adam S. Posen. 2001. "The Great Recession: Lessons for Macroeconomic Policy from Japan." *Brookings Papers on Economic Activity* 2:93–185.

Lazonick, William, and Mary O'Sullivan. 2000. "Maximizing Shareholder Value: A New Ideology for Corporate Governance." *Economy and Society* 29:13–35.

Lehne, Richard. 2001. *Government and Business: American Political Economy in Comparative Perspective*. New York: Seven Bridges Press.

Levy, Jonah, Mari Miura, and Gene Park. Forthcoming. "Exiting *Étatisme*? New Directions in State Policy in France and Japan." In *The State after Statism*, edited by Jonah Levy.

Lijphart, Arend. 1971. "Comparative Politics and the Comparative Method." *American Political Science Review* 65:682–93.

———. 1975. "The Comparable-Case Strategy in Comparative Research." *Comparative Political Studies* 8:158–77.

Lincoln, Edward. 1988. *Japan: Facing Economic Maturity*. Washington, D.C.: Brookings Institution Press.

———. 2001. *Arthritic Japan: The Slow Pace of Economic Reform*. Washington, D.C.: Brookings Institution Press.

———. 2003. "Making Some Sense of the Japanese Economy." Japan Policy Research Institute Working Paper 94.

Lincoln, James R., and Michael L. Gerlach. 2004. *Japan's Network Economy: A Structural Perspective on Industrial Change*. Cambridge: Cambridge University Press.

Lynskey, Michael, and Seiichiro Yonekura. 2001. "Softbank: An Internet Keiretsu and Its Leveraging of Information Asymmetries." *European Management Journal* 19:1–15.

Mabuchi, Masaru. 1994. *Ōkurashō tōsei no seiji keizaigaku* [The political economy of MOF control]. Tokyo: Chūō Kōronsha.

Maclachlan, Patricia. 2002. *Consumer Politics in Postwar Japan: The Institutional Boundaries of Citizen Activism*. New York: Columbia University Press.

———. 2004. "Post Office Politics in Modern Japan: The Postmasters, Iron Triangles, and the Limits of Reform." *Journal of Japanese Studies* 30:281–313.

Madsen, Robert A. 2004. "A Reckoning Postponed." Manuscript.

Makin, John H. 2001. "Japan's Lost Decade: Lessons for America." *AEI Economic Outlook*, February.

Manow, Philip. 2001. "Comparative Institutional Advantages of Welfare State Regimes and New Coalitions in Welfare State Reforms." In *The New Politics of the Welfare State*, edited by Paul Pierson, 146–64. Oxford: Oxford University Press.

McKinley, William, Jun Zhao, and Kathleen Garrett Rust. 2000. "A Sociocognitive Interpretation of Organizational Downsizing." *Academy of Management Review* 25:227–43.

McKinnon, Ronald, and Kenichi Ohno. 1997. *Dollar and Yen: Resolving Economic Conflict between the United States and Japan*. Cambridge, Mass.: MIT Press.

McKinsey Global Institute. 2000. "Why the Japanese Economy Is Not Growing: Micro Barriers to Productivity Growth." Washington, D.C.

Merrill Lynch, Global Securities Research and Economics Group. 2005. "Japan Strategy: Corporate Law Modernization and Hostile Takeover Defense Measures." Tokyo.

Mikitani, Ryōichi, and Adam S. Posen, eds. 2000. *Japan's Financial Crisis and Its Parallels to U.S. Experience*. Washington, D.C.: Institute for International Economics.

Miles, Marc A., Edwin J. Feulner, and Mary Anastasia O'Grady. 2005. *Index of Economic Freedom, 2005*. New York: Heritage Foundation/Wall Street Journal.

Ministry of Economy, Trade, and Industry. 2004. *Shin sangyō kōzō senryaku* [Toward a new industrial structure]. Tokyo: Keizai Sangyō Chōsakai.

Ministry of Finance, Policy Research Institute. 2003a. "Nihon kigyō no tayōka to kigyō tōchi" [Japanese corporate diversification and corporate governance]. Tokyo.

———. 2003b. "Shinten suru kōporeeto gabanansu" [Corporate governance in transition]. Tokyo.

Miura, Mari. 2002. "Welfare through Work: The Politics of Labor Market Reforms in Japan." Ph.D. dissertation, University of California, Berkeley.

Miyajima, Hideaki. 1998. "The Impact of Deregulation on Corporate Governance and Finance." In *Is Japan Really Changing Its Ways? Regulatory Reform and the Japanese Economy*, edited by Lonny E. Carlile and Mark C. Tilton, 33–75. Washington, D.C.: Brookings Institution Press.

Moeller, Sara, Frederik Schlingemann, and René Stulz. 2005. "Wealth Destruction on a Massive Scale? A Study of Acquiring-Firm Returns in the Merger Wave of the Late 1990s." *Journal of Finance* 60:757–82.

Mulgan, Aurelia George. 2002. *Japan's Failed Revolution: Koizumi and the Politics of Economic Reform*. Canberra: Asia Pacific Press.

Muramatsu, Michio, ed. 1990. *Shakai keizai no henka to gyōsei sutairu no henyō ni kansuru chōsa kenkyū hōkokusho* [A report of research on socioeconomic change and the transformation of policy style]. Tokyo: Management and Coordination Agency.

Muramatsu, Michio, and Masahiro Okuno, eds. 2002. *Heisei baburu no kenkyū* [Research on the Heisei bubble], vol. 1. Tokyo: Tōyō Keizai Shimpōsha.

Muramatsu, Michio, and Noriyuki Yanagikawa. 2002. *Sengo nihon ni okeru seisaku jissetsu: seitō to kanryō* [The true story of policy in postwar Japan: Parties and bureaucracy]. In *Heisei baburu no kenkyu* [Research on the Heisei bubble], vol. 2, edited by Michio Muramatsu and Masahiro Okuno, 87–126. Tokyo: Tōyō Keizai Shimpōsha.

Nakamura, Yoshio, Kenichirō Yokoo, and Yoshihisa Masaki. 2004. *2004 nenban saishin kaisei kaisha hō Q&A* [2004 Latest revisions to corporate law Q&A]. Tokyo: Zeimu Keiri Kyōkai.

Nakatani, Iwao. 1996. *Nihon keizai no rekishi-teki tenkan* [The Japanese economy's historic transition]. Tokyo: Tōyō Keizai Shimpōsha.

Nakatani, Iwao, and Hiroko Ōta. 1994. *Keizai kaikaku no bijon* [A vision for economic reform]. Tokyo: Tōyō Keizai Shimpōsha.

Nihon Keieisha Dantai Renmei. 1998. "Nihon kigyō no kōporeeto gabanansu kaikaku no hōkō" [Japanese industry's reform of corporate governance]. Tokyo.

Nippon Keidanren. 2004. "2003 kaki tōki 'shōyo ichijikin chōsa kekka' ni tsuite" [2003 Survey on summer and winter bonuses]. Tokyo.

Nishikawa, Motoyoshi. 2001. "Korekara no kaishahō kaisei no kadai to kongo no shōten" [The revision of the commercial code: Current topics and future issues]. *Keidanren*, November, 31–33.

NLI Research Institute. 2004. *Kabushiki mochiai jōkyō chōsa 2003* [Cross-shareholding survey 2003]. Tokyo: NLI Research Institute.

Noguchi, Yukio. 1995. *1940-nen taisei* [The 1940 system]. Tokyo: Tōyō Keizai Shimpōsha.

Nomura Securities, IB Consulting Division. 2004. *"Tekitaiteki M&A" bōei manyuaru* [Hostile takeover defense manual]. Tokyo: Chūō Keizaisha.

North, Douglass C. 1981. *Structure and Change in Economic History*. New York: W. W. Norton.

———. 1990. *Institutions, Institutional Change, and Economic Performance*. Cambridge: Cambridge University Press.

Okimoto, Daniel. 1989. *Between MITI and the Market: Japanese Industrial Policy for High Technology*. Stanford: Stanford University Press.

O'Neill, Richard. 2005. "Re-examining Electricity Restructuring." Paper presented at the Conference on the Politics and Economics of the Market, Brandeis University, February 4–5.

Organization for Economic Co-operation and Development. 1999. *Regulatory Reform in Japan*. Paris: OECD.

———. 2005. *OECD Economic Surveys: Japan*. Paris: OECD.

Ostrom, Douglas. 1999. "Tokyo's Changing Role in Financial Markets: Taking a Step Backward?" *JEI Report* 43A, November 12.

O'Sullivan, Mary A. 2000. *Contests for Corporate Control: Corporate Governance and Economic Performance in the United States and Germany*. Cambridge: Cambridge University Press.

Ozawa, Ichiro. 1993. *Nihon kaizō keikaku* [Blueprint for a new Japan]. Tokyo, Kōdansha.

Park, Gene. 2004. "The Political-Economic Dimension of Pensions: The Case of Japan." *Governance* 17:549–72.

———. 2005. "The Origins of the Fiscal Investment and Loan Program: Solving the Dilemma of Industrialization and Redistribution." Manuscript.

Patrick, Hugh. 2004. "Evolving Corporate Governance in Japan." Center on Japanese Economy and Business, Columbia University, Working Paper 220.

Pempel, T. J. 1998. *Regime Shift: Comparative Dynamics of the Japanese Political Economy*. Ithaca: Cornell University Press.

———. Forthcoming. "A Decade of Political Torpor: When Political Logic Trumps Economic Rationality." In *Beyond Japan: East Asian Regionalism*, edited by Peter J. Katzenstein and Takashi Shiraishi. Ithaca, N.Y.: Cornell University Press.

Pempel, T. J., and Keiichi Tsunekawa. 1979. "Corporatism without Labor? The Japanese Anomaly." In *Trends toward Corporatist Intermediation*, edited by Philippe C. Schmitter and Gerhard Lehmbruch, 231–70. London: Sage.

Pierson, Paul. 2000. "Increasing Returns, Path Dependence, and the Study of Politics." *American Political Science Review* 94:251–68.

Pierson, Paul, and R. Kent Weaver. 1993. "Imposing Losses in Pension Policy." In *Do Institutions Matter? Government Capabilities in the United States and Abroad*, edited by Weaver and Bert A. Rockman, 110–50. Washington, D.C.: Brookings Institution Press.

Polanyi, Karl. 1944. *The Great Transformation: The Political and Economic Origins of Our Time*. Boston: Beacon Press.

Porter, Michael E., Hirotaka Takeuchi, and Mariko Sakakibara. 2000. *Can Japan Compete?* Cambridge, Mass.: Perseus.

Posen, Adam. 1998. *Restoring Japan's Economic Growth*. Washington, D.C.: Institute for International Economics.

———. 2002. "Finance." In *U.S.-Japan Relations in a Changing World*, edited by Steven K. Vogel, 198–238. Washington, D.C.: Brookings Institution Press.

———. 2004. "What Went Right in Japan?" Institute for International Economics Policy Brief.

Powell, Walter W., and Paul J. Dimaggio, eds. 1991. *The New Institutionalism in Organizational Analysis*. Chicago: University of Chicago Press.

Prime Minister's Office. 1988. *Nihonjin no shokuseikatsu to shokuryō mondai* [Japanese eating habits and food supply]. Tokyo: PMO.

———. 2000. "Nōsanbutsu bōeki ni kansuru seron chōsa" [Public opinion survey on agricultural trade]. Tokyo: PMO.

Rich, Andrew. 2005. "Reaching Competition despite Deregulation: The Case of Telecommunications Reform." Paper presented at the Conference on the Politics and Economics of the Market, Brandeis University, February 4–5.

Roberts, Lucy, and John Turner. 1997. "Enterprise and the State: Interactions in the Provision of Employees' Retirement Income in the United States." In *Enterprise and the Welfare State*, edited by Martin Rein and Eskil Wadensjo, 352–77. Lyme: Edward Elgar.

Roe, Mark. 1994. *Strong Managers, Weak Owners: The Political Roots of American Corporate Finance*. Princeton: Princeton University Press.

Rtischev, Dimitry, and Cole, Robert. 2003. "Social and Structural Barriers to the IT Revolution in High Tech Industry." In *Roadblocks on the Information Highway: The IT Revolution in Japanese Education*, edited by Jane Bachnik, 127–53. New York: Lexington Books.

Saitō, Tarō. 2003. "Semarikuru rōdōryoku fusoku jidai" [The impending era of labor shortage]. Nissay Research Report, Tokyo.

Sakakibara, Eisuke. 2002. *Atarashii kokka o tsukuru tame* [Institutional Reform for a New Japan]. Tokyo: Chūō Kōron Shinsha.

Sako, Mari, and Hiroki Sato, eds. 1997. *Japanese Labour and Management in Transition: Diversity, Flexibility, and Participation*. London: Routledge.

Salisbury, Dallas. 1994. "The Costs and Benefits of Pension Tax Expenditures." In *Pension Funding and Taxation: Implications for Tomorrow*, edited by Salisbury and Nora Jones. Washington, D.C.: Employee Benefit Research Institute.

Samuels, Richard J. 1987. *The Business of the Japanese State: Energy Markets in Comparative and Historical Perspective*. Ithaca: Cornell University Press.

——. 2003. *Machiavelli's Children: Leaders and Their Legacies in Italy and Japan*. Ithaca: Cornell University Press.

Satō, Seizaburō and Tetsuhisa Matsuzaki. 1986. *Jimintō seiken* [The LDP government]. Tokyo: Chūō Kōronsha.

Satō, Hikaru. 1998. "Daitenhō haishi ga motarasu mono" [What the abolition of the large-scale retail store law will bring]. *Ronsō*, March, 180–87.

Schaede, Ulrike. 1990. "Black Monday in New York, Blue Tuesday in Tokyo: The October 1987 Crash in Japan." Manuscript.

——. 2000. *Cooperative Capitalism: Self-Regulation, Trade Associations, and the Antimonopoly Law in Japan*. Oxford: Oxford University Press.

Schlesinger, Jacob M. 1997. *Shadow Shoguns: The Rise and Fall of Japan's Postwar Political Machine*. New York: Simon & Schuster.

Schmidt, Manfred G. 2003. *Political Institutions in the Federal Republic of Germany*. Oxford: Oxford University Press.

Schmidt, Vivien. 2000. "Still Three Models of Capitalism? The Dynamics of Economic Adjustment in Britain, Germany, and France." Manuscript.

Schoppa, Leonard J. 1997. *Bargaining with Japan: What American Pressure Can and Cannot Do*. New York: Columbia University Press.

Schwartz, Frank. 1998. *Advice and Consent: The Politics of Consultation in Japan*. New York: Cambridge University Press.

Shinn, James. 1999. "Corporate Governance Reform and Trade Friction." Paper presented at the Study Group on U.S.-Japan Economic Relations, Council on Foreign Relations, March, Washington, D.C.

Shishido, Zenichi. Forthcoming. "The Turnaround of 1997: Changes in Corporate Law and Governance." In *Corporate Governance in Japan: Organizational Diversity and*

Institutional Change, edited by Masahiko Aoki, Gregory Jackson, and Hideaki Miyajima. Oxford: Oxford University Press.

Shōhisha Dantai Rengōkai. 1987. *Shōdanren sanjūnen no ayumi* [A thirty-year history of Shōdanren]. Tokyo: Zenkoku Shōhisha Dantai Renrakukai.

Soskice, David. 1999. "Divergent Production Regimes: Coordinated and Uncoordinated Market Economies in the 1980s and 1990s." In *Continuity and Change in Contemporary Capitalism*, edited by Herbert Kitschelt et al., 101–34. Cambridge: Cambridge University Press.

Stigler, George. 1971. "The Theory of Economic Regulation." *Bell Journal of Economics and Management Science* 2:3–21.

Story, Jonathan. 1996. "*Finanzplatz Deutschland*: National or European Response to Internationalization?" *German Politics* 5:371–94.

Streeck, Wolfgang, and Kathleen Thelen, eds. 2005. *Beyond Continuity: Institutional Change in Advanced Political Economies*. New York: Oxford University Press.

Svensson, Lars E. O. 1999. "How Should Monetary Policy Be Conducted in an Era of Price Stability?" Paper presented at the 1999 Symposium on New Challenges for Monetary Policy, Federal Reserve Bank of Kansas City.

Swank, Duane, and Cathie Jo Martin. 2001. "Employers and the Welfare State: The Political Economic Organization of Firms and Social Policy in Contemporary Capitalist Democracies." *Comparative Political Studies* 34:889–923.

Tachibanaki, Toshiaki. 1998. *Nihon no keizai kakusa* [Japan's economic inequality]. Tokyo: Iwanami Shoten.

Takeuchi, Naokazu. 1990. *Nihon no shōhisha wa naze okoranai ka* [Why don't Japanese consumers get mad?]. Tokyo: Sanichi Shobō.

Tanaka, Naoki. 1997. "Nikyokuka ga nihon keizai o michi no ryōiki ni yūdō suru" [Polarization leads the Japanese economy into uncharted territory]. *Ekonomisuto*, May 13, 60–63.

Teramoto, Yoshiya, ed. 1997. *Nihon kigyō no kōporeeto gabanansu.* [Japanese corporations' corporate governance]. Tokyo: Seisansei Shuppan.

Tett, Gillian. 2003. *Saving the Sun: A Wall Street Gamble to Rescue Japan from Its Trillion-Dollar Meltdown*. New York: HarperBusiness.

Thelen, Kathleen. 1999. "Why German Employers Cannot Bring Themselves to Dismantle the German Model." In *Unions, Employers, and Central Banks*, edited by Torben Iversen, Jonas Pontusson, and David Soskice, 138–69. Cambridge: Cambridge University Press.

Tilton, Mark. 1996. *Restrained Trade: Cartels in Japan's Basic Materials Industries*. Ithaca: Cornell University Press.

Toya, Tetsurō. 2003. *Kinyū bigguban no seijikeizaigaku* [The political economy of the Japanese financial Big Bang]. Tokyo: Tōyō Keizai Shimpōsha.

Uchihashi, Katsuto. 1995. *Kisei kanwa to iu akumu* [A nightmare called deregulation]. Tokyo: Bungei Shunjū.

Uriu, Robert M. 1996. *Troubled Industries: Confronting Economic Change in Japan*. Ithaca: Cornell University Press.

Useem, Michael. 1996. *Investor Capitalism: How Money Managers Are Changing the Face of Corporate America*. New York: Basic Books/HarperCollins.

Vitols, Sigurt. 2000. "The Reconstruction of German Corporate Governance: Reassessing the Role of Capital Market Pressures." Background paper for the First Annual Meeting of the Research Network on Corporate Governance, Berlin, June 23–24.

Vogel, David. 1989. *Fluctuating Fortunes: The Political Power of Business in America.* Berkeley: University of California Press.

———. 1992. "Consumer Protection and Protectionism in Japan." *Journal of Japanese Studies* 18:119–54.

Vogel, Steven K. 1994. "The Bureaucratic Approach to the Financial Revolution: Japan's Ministry of Finance and Financial System Reform." *Governance* 7:219–43.

———. 1996. *Freer Markets, More Rules: Regulatory Reform in Advanced Industrial Countries.* Ithaca: Cornell University Press.

———. 1999a. "When Interests Are Not Preferences: The Cautionary Tale of Japanese Consumers." *Comparative Politics* 31:187–207.

———. 1999b. "Can Japan Disengage? Winners and Losers in Japan's Political Economy, and the Ties That Bind Them." *Social Science Japan Journal* 2:3–21.

———. 2001. "The Crisis of German and Japanese Capitalism: Stalled on the Road to the Liberal Market Model?" *Comparative Political Studies* 34:1103–33.

———. 2003. "The Re-Organization of Organized Capitalism: How the German and Japanese Models Are Shaping Their Own Transformations." In *The End of Diversity? Prospects for German and Japanese Capitalism,* edited by Kozo Yamamura and Wolfgang Streeck, 306–33. Ithaca: Cornell University Press.

———, ed. 2002. *U.S.-Japan Relations in a Changing World.* Washington, D.C.: Brookings Institution Press.

Vogel, Steven K., and John Zysman. 2002. "Technology." In *U.S.-Japan Relations in a Changing World,* edited by Steven K. Vogel, 239–61. Washington, D.C.: Brookings Institution Press.

Watanabe, Shigeru. 1999. "After Quasi-LBO Discipline: A Historical Reflection on Japanese Corporate Governance." In *Japanese Management in the Low Growth Era: Between External Shocks and Internal Evolution,* edited by Daniel Dirks, Jean-François Huchet, and Thierry Ribault, 161–74. Berlin: Springer.

Webber, Douglas. 1992. "Kohl's *Wendepolitik* after a Decade." *German Politics* 1:149–80.

Weinstein, David E. 2001. "Historical, Structural, and Macroeconomic Perspectives on the Japanese Economic Crisis." In *Japan's New Economy: Continuity and Change in the Twenty-First Century,* edited by Magnus Blomström, Byron Gangnes, and Sumner La Croix, 29–47. Oxford: Oxford University Press.

Werner, Richard A. 1998. "Bank of Japan Window Guidance and the Creation of the Bubble." In *El Japón contemporáneo,* edited by Florentino Rodao and Antonia Lopez Santos. Salamanca: University of Salamanca Press.

———. 2003. *Princes of the Yen: Japan's Central Bankers and the Transformation of the Economy.* Armonk, N.Y.: M. E. Sharpe.

Westney, D. Eleanor. 1987. *Imitation and Innovation: The Transfer of Western Organizational Patterns to Meiji Japan.* Cambridge, Mass.: Harvard University Press.

Wilensky, Harold L. 2002. *Rich Democracies: Political Economy, Public Policy, and Performance.* Berkeley: University of California Press.

Williamson, Oliver. 1985. *The Economic Institutions of Capitalism.* New York: Free Press.

Wilson, James Q. 1994. "Don't Bemoan Gridlock—The Constitution Likes It." *Los Angeles Times,* November 20.

Womack, James P., Daniel T. Jones, and Daniel Roos. 1990. *The Machine That Changed the World.* New York: Rawson Associates.

Woodall, Brian. 1996. *Japan under Construction: Corruption, Politics, and Public Works.* Berkeley: University of California Press.

World Bank. 2002. *World Development Report, 2002: Building Institutions for Markets.* Oxford: Oxford University Press.

Yamakawa, Ryūichi. 1999. "The Silence of Stockholders: Japanese Labor Law from the Viewpoint of Corporate Governance." *Japanese Institute of Labor Bulletin* 38:6–12.

Yamamura, Kozo. 2003. "Germany and Japan in a New Phase of Capitalism: Confronting the Past and the Future." In *The End of Diversity? Prospects for German and Japanese Capitalism,* edited by Yamamura and Wolfgang Streeck, 115–46. Ithaca: Cornell University Press.

Yamamura, Kozo, and Wolfgang Streeck, eds. 2003. *The End of Diversity? Prospects for German and Japanese Capitalism.* Ithaca: Cornell University Press.

Yoshikawa, Hiroshi. 2000. "1990 nendai no nihon keizai to kinyū seisaku" [The Japanese economy and monetary policy in the 1990s]. In *Zero kinri to nihon keizai* [The zero interest rate policy and the Japanese economy], edited by Mitsuhiro Fukao and Yoshikawa, 267–96. Tokyo: Nihon Keizai Shimbunsha.

Yoshimatsu, Hidetaka. 2000. *Internationalization, Corporate Preferences, and Commercial Policy in Japan.* Houndmills, U.K.: Macmillan.

Yoshino, Michael Y., and Perry L. Fagan. 2003. "The Renault-Nissan Alliance." Harvard Business School Case 303–023. Boston.

Yoshitomi, Masaru. 1998. *Nihon keizai no shinjitsu* [The truth about Japan's economy]. Tokyo: Tōyō Keizai Shimpōsha.

Zeitlin, Jonathan, and Gary Herrigel, eds. 2000. *Americanization and Its Limits: Reworking U.S. Technology and Management in Post-war Europe and Japan.* Oxford: Oxford University Press.

Ziegler, J. Nicholas. 2000. "Corporate Governance and the Politics of Property Rights in Germany." *Politics and Society* 28:195–221.

Zielinski, Robert, and Nigel Holloway. 1991. *Unequal Equities: Power and Risk in Japan's Stock Market.* Tokyo: Kodansha International.

Zysman, John. 1983. *Governments, Markets, and Growth: Financial Systems and the Politics of Industrial Change.* Ithaca: Cornell University Press.

INDEX

accounting reform, 68, 88–91, 96, 113, 186, 219

Administrative Procedures Act (1994), 44

administrative reform, 44, 59

Administrative Reform Committee, 99. *See also* Deregulation Committee

agricultural liberalization, 54

Ahmadjian, Christina L., 115n, 141, 201

Aizawa, Hideyuki, 90

Amyx, Jennifer, 48

Andō, Haruhiko, 158n

Anti-Monopoly Law, 104

antitrust policy, 103–5
  and accounting reform, 89
  and bureaucracy, 61–62
  and consumers, 54
  and corporate restructuring, 177, 190
  and Japanese reform process, 220–21
  and tax reform, 89, 104, 105
  and U.S. policy reforms, 66, 67

Aoki, Masahiko, 7, 12, 31n, 158n

Aoki, Teruaki, 176

Arikawa, Yasuhiro, 127–28

Asō, Tarō, 90

asset impairment accounting, 90–91

BADC (Business Accounting Deliberation Council), 89–90

banking crisis, 25–27, 39, 48–50

banking regulation. *See* financial reform

Bank of Japan (BOJ)
  and economic crisis, 23–24, 25, 27, 28
  and monetary policy, 47–48
  and post-2003 recovery, 29

Bank of Tokyo-Mitsubishi, 133

bank relations
  and client categories, 130
  and complementarity, 7
  and corporate restructuring, 126–34
  and cross-shareholding, 130–32
  and financial reform, 126, 127, 133–34, 219
  Germany, 70, 152–53
  and horizontal *keiretsu*, 9, 129, 134
  and industrial policy reform, 87
  and institutional change model, 16
  and Japanese postwar model, 9
  and Japanese reform process, 219, 223

  and savings/investment excess, 32
  See also bank relations case studies

bank relations case studies
  Hikari Tsushin, 195, 196
  Mitsukoshi, 185–86
  Mizuho Financial Group, 179
  Nissan, 168, 169
  Seiyu, 187
  Toyota, 167

bankruptcy procedures, 86

Baumol, William, 208

Bernanke, Ben, 28

Bhagat, Sanjai, 210

Big Bang reforms, 84, 89, 113
  and bank relations, 126, 133, 219
  See also financial reform

Black, Bernard, 210

Black Monday (1987), 24

Blasi, Joseph R., 209n

Blöm, Norbert, 75

BOJ. *See* Bank of Japan

British political system, 41

Broda, Christian, 27n

Brown, Clair, 117

Bruner, Robert, 210

bubble economy, 1
  and bank relations, 126
  as cause of economic crisis, 23–25
  and corporate restructuring, 180
  and financial reform, 26, 48
  and fiscal policy, 47–48
  and savings/investment excess, 32, 33
  and structural problems, 38–39

Buddhism, 60

Budros, Art, 208

Bundesverband der Deutschen Industrie (BDI) (Federation of German Industries), 70–71

Bundesvereinigung der Deutschen Arbeitgeberverbände (BDA) (Confederation of German Employers' Associations), 71

bureaucracy
  and accounting reform, 89–90
  and corporate governance reform, 92
  and economic crisis, 35
  and financial reform, 49, 50
  and Japanese postwar model, 8

CORNELL STUDIES IN POLITICAL ECONOMY

A series edited by Peter J. Katzenstein

Rival Capitalists: International
Competitiveness in the United States,
Japan, and Western Europe
by Jeffrey A. Hart

Economic Nationalism in a Globalizing
World
edited by Eric Helleiner and Andreas
Pickel

Reasons of State: Oil Politics and the
Capacities of American Government
by G. John Ikenberry

The State and American Foreign Economic
Policy
edited by G. John Ikenberry, David A.
Lake, and Michael Mastanduno

The Nordic States and European Unity
by Christine Ingebritsen

The Paradox of Continental Production:
National Investment Policies in North
America
by Barbara Jenkins

The Government of Money: Monetarism in
Germany and the United States
by Peter A. Johnson

A World of Regions: Asia and Europe in the
American Imperium
by Peter J. Katzenstein

Corporatism and Change: Austria,
Switzerland, and the Politics of Industry
by Peter J. Katzenstein

Cultural Norms and National Security:
Police and Military in Postwar Japan
by Peter J. Katzenstein

Small States in World Markets: Industrial
Policy in Europe
by Peter J. Katzenstein

Industry and Politics in West Germany:
Toward the Third Republic
edited by Peter J. Katzenstein

Beyond Japan: The Dynamics of East Asian
Regionalism
edited by Peter J. Katzenstein and
Takashi Shiraishi

Monetary Orders: Ambiguous Economics,
Ubiquitous Politics
edited by Jonathan Kirshner

Norms in International Relations: The
Struggle against Apartheid
by Audie Jeanne Klotz

International Regimes
edited by Stephen D. Krasner

Disparaged Success: Labor Politics in
Postwar Japan
by Ikuo Kume

Business and Banking: Political Change and
Economic Integration in Western Europe
by Paulette Kurzer

Power, Protection, and Free Trade:
International Sources of U.S.
Commercial Strategy, 1887–1939
by David A. Lake

Money Rules: The New Politics of Finance in
Britain and Japan
by Henry Laurence

Why Syria Goes to War: Thirty Years of
Confrontation
by Fred H. Lawson

The Rules of Play: National Identity and the
Shaping of Japanese Leisure
by David Leheny

Remaking the Italian Economy
by Richard M. Locke

France after Hegemony: International
Change and Financial Reform
by Michael Loriaux

The Power of Institutions: Political
Architecture and Governance
by Andrew MacIntyre

Economic Containment: CoCom and the
Politics of East-West Trade
by Michael Mastanduno

Business and the State in Developing
Countries
edited by Sylvia Maxfield and Ben Ross
Schneider

The Currency of Ideas: Monetary Politics in the European Union
  by Kathleen R. McNamara

The Choice for Europe: Social Purpose and State Power from Messina to Maastricht
  by Andrew Moravcsik

At Home Abroad: Identity and Power in American Foreign Policy
  by Henry R. Nau

Collective Action in East Asia: How Ruling Parties Shape Industrial Policy
  by Gregory W. Noble

Mercantile States and the World Oil Cartel, 1900–1939
  by Gregory P. Nowell

Negotiating the World Economy
  by John S. Odell

Opening Financial Markets: Banking Politics on the Pacific Rim
  by Louis W. Pauly

Who Elected the Bankers? Surveillance and Control in the World Economy
  by Louis W. Pauly

Regime Shift: Comparative Dynamics of the Japanese Political Economy
  by T.J. Pempel

Remapping Asia: The Emergence of Regional Connectedness
  Edited by T.J. Pempel

Remapping East Asia: The Construction of a Region
  Edited by T.J. Pempel

The Politics of the Asian Economic Crisis
  edited by T.J. Pempel

The Limits of Social Democracy: Investment Politics in Sweden
  by Jonas Pontusson

The Fruits of Fascism: Postwar Prosperity in Historical Perspective
  by Simon Reich

The Business of the Japanese State: Energy Markets in Comparative and Historical Perspective
  by Richard J. Samuels

"Rich Nation, Strong Army": National Security and the Technological Transformation of Japan
  by Richard J. Samuels

Crisis and Choice in European Social Democracy
  by Fritz W. Scharpf, translated by Ruth Crowley and Fred Thompson

Europeanization of Central and Eastern Europe
  edited by Frank Schimmelfennig and Ulrich Sedelmeier

The Social Sources of Financial Power: Domestic Legitimacy and International Financial Orders
  by Leonard Seabrooke

Digital Dragon: High Technology Enterprises in China
  by Adam Segal

Winners and Losers: How Sectors Shape the Developmental Prospects of States
  by D. Michael Shafer

Ideas and Institutions: Developmentalism in Brazil and Argentina
  by Kathryn Sikkink

The New Masters of Capital: American Bond Rating Agencies and the Politics of Creditworthiness
  by Timothy J. Sinclair

The Cooperative Edge: The Internal Politics of International Cartels
  by Debora L. Spar

The Hidden Hand of American Hegemony: Petrodollar Recycling and International Markets
  by David E. Spiro

Ending Empire: Contested Sovereignty and Territorial Partition
  by Hendrik Spruyt

The Origins of Nonliberal Capitalism: Germany and Japan in Comparison
  edited by Wolfgang Streeck and Kozo Yamamura